ENVIRONMENTAL MANAGEMENT

A Core Text for O Level and IGCSE®

JOHN PALLISTER

SECOND EDITION

OXFORD
UNIVERSITY PRESS

OXFORD
UNIVERSITY PRESS

Oxford University Press is a department of the University of Oxford.
It furthers the University's objective of excellence in research, scholarship,
and education by publishing worldwide. Oxford is a registered trade mark of
Oxford University Press in the UK and in certain other countries

Published in Pakistan by
Oxford University Press
No.38, Sector 15, Korangi Industrial Area,
PO Box 8214, Karachi-74900, Pakistan

ISBN 978-0-19-940707-1

Third Impression 2019

Printed on 70gsm offset paper

Printed by The Times Press (Pvt.) Ltd, Karachi

Acknowledgements
Photographs: cover: courtesy Muhammad Rizwan; p. 1: © T photography /
Shutterstock; p. 3: Shutterstock; p. 12 (Figure 1.12): © Pedarilhosbr / Shutterstock;
p. 15: © William Cushman / Shutterstock; p. 18: © Dmitrijs Kaminskis / Shutterstock;
p. 20: © Gigira / Shutterstock; p. 22: © David Hughes / Shutterstock; p. 23: © David
Quixley / Shutterstock; p. 25: courtesy Batul Ali; p. 27: © ssuaphotos / Shutterstock;
p. 42: © Neil Mitchell / Shutterstock; p. 44: © cunaplus / Shutterstock; p. 57: Hotel
Victoria, Freiburg, Germany; p. 63: © pikktee / Shutterstock; p. 70: © Nobelus /
Shutterstock; p. 86: © JP Chretien / Shutterstock; p. 90: © Feng Yu / Shutterstock;
p. 138: © Miguel Azevedo e Castro / Shutterstock; p. 153: © JeremyRichards /
Shutterstock; p. 157: © Igor_S / Shutterstock; p. 161: © Dmytro Balkhovitin /
Shutterstock; p. 167: © yankane / Shutterstock; p. 187: © Sohel Parvez Haque /
Shutterstock; p. 193: © Eric Pasqualli / Shutterstock; p. 194: Oxfam; p. 222:
© Steven TDW White / Shutterstock; p. 223: © EcoPrint / Shutterstock; p. 224:
© Thomas La Mela / Shutterstock; p. 274 (Figure 9.38 (1)): © Pics-xl / Shutterstock
and (Figure 9.38 (2)): © Skyward Kick Productions / Shutterstock; p. 278: © Asianet-
Pakistan / Shutterstock; p. 280: © 88studio / Shutterstock; p. 281 (both pandas
(1)): © Lynn Whitt / Shutterstock and (both pandas (3)): © Hung Chung Chih /
Shutterstock; p. 284 (Figure 9.46 (1)): © Jlwarehouse / Shutterstock, (Figure 9.46
(2)): © costas anton dumitrescu / Shutterstock, and (Figure 9.46 (3)): © javarman /
Shutterstock; p. 285: © Anton Watman / Shutterstock
pp. 38 and 47: Wikimedia Commons; pp. 67 and 69: courtesy NASA

Introduction

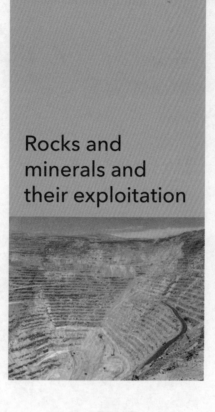

Rocks and minerals and their exploitation

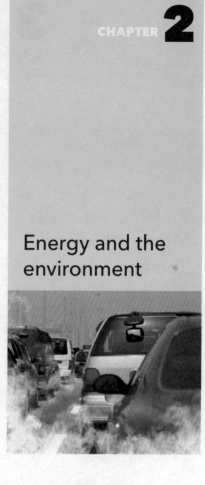

Energy and the environment

OBJECTIVES

In this chapter you will learn about:

- types of rocks and their formation
- extraction of rocks and minerals for human use
- impact of rock and mineral extraction
- strategies for landscape restoration
- strategies for sustainable use of rocks and minerals

OBJECTIVES

In this chapter you will learn about:

- fossil fuel formation
- energy resources and generation of electricity
- factors affecting energy demand
- conservation and management of energy sources
- impact and management of marine oil pollution

OXFORD
UNIVERSITY PRESS

CHAPTER **3**	CHAPTER **4**	CHAPTER **5**

Agriculture and the environment

Water and its management

Oceans and fisheries

71   **103**   **138**

OBJECTIVES

In this chapter you will learn about:

- soil composition
- what makes soils suitable for plant growth
- different types of agriculture
- techniques used to increase agricultural yields
- impact of agricultural practices
- soil erosion (causes, impacts, and management)
- strategies for sustainable agriculture

OBJECTIVES

In this chapter you will learn about:

- global water distribution
- the water cycle
- sources of water supply for people
- water usage, quality, and availability
- multipurpose dam projects
- sources of water pollution
- impact and management of water pollution
- managing water-related diseases

OBJECTIVES

In this chapter you will learn about:

- the resource potential of the oceans
- world fisheries and their exploitation
- exploitation of the oceans (overfishing) and its impact
- management of the harvesting of marine species

OXFORD
UNIVERSITY PRESS

CHAPTER **6**

Managing natural hazards

160

CHAPTER **7**

The atmosphere and human activities

196

CHAPTER **8**

Human population

224

OBJECTIVES

In this chapter you will learn about:

- five natural hazards and how they affect people
- tectonic hazards: earthquakes and volcanoes
- their causes, impacts, and management
- climatic hazards: tropical cyclones, flooding, and drought
- their causes, impacts, and management

OBJECTIVES

In this chapter you will learn about:

- the structure and composition of the atmosphere
- atmospheric pollution, its causes and impacts
- smog, acid rain, ozone layer depletion, and enhanced greenhouse effect
- causes, impacts, and strategies for their reduction
- strategies for managing atmospheric pollution

OBJECTIVES

In this chapter you will learn about:

- distribution and density of population
- growth of the human population
- population structure
- managing human population size

OXFORD
UNIVERSITY PRESS

CHAPTER **9**

Natural ecosystems and human activities

241

CHAPTER **10**

Techniques for investigation and examination

285

Index

296

OBJECTIVES

In this chapter you will learn about:

- natural ecosystems and how they operate
- natural ecosystems under threat
- causes and impacts of deforestation
- sustainable management of forests
- measuring and managing biodiversity

OBJECTIVES

In this chapter you will learn about:

- investigation skills
- methods for local investigations
- examination technique
- command words

OXFORD
UNIVERSITY PRESS

Introduction

Environmental Management, Second Edition, has been revised extensively to match the latest Cambridge O Level syllabus 5014 and the IGCSE® syllabus 0680 for Environmental Management (2019–2021). The content now matches the new sequence of chapters in the new syllabuses.

The approach taken is an international one. Examples (whether passing references or cases studies of varying length and depth) are drawn from all continents. Some environmental issues are of global importance and are well covered by this approach. These include climate change, deforestation and the loss of biodiversity, over-exploitation of natural resources (land and marine), land and water pollution, and continued world population growth. However, there are many environmental issues which are more significant at regional and local levels and demand more thorough investigation by students working individually or in groups.

Syllabus content and skills requirements are the same for both O Level and IGCSE® examinations. Paper 1 is the Theory paper. The majority of the questions are structured and require short answers, although some extended response questions based on related source materials are included. Paper 2 is titled 'Management in context'. It includes short-answer questions as well as data processing and analysis, and extended response based on source materials. They cover issues of environmental management. For better understanding of environmental issues and as preparation for the examination, students are encouraged to practise and develop their enquiry skills, especially in their home area. Study of local or regional examples of environmental issues is valuable as there is no better way of raising awareness of major global environmental issues among students than by study of the local environment. The core content of **Environmental Management** is supplemented and supported by new as well as updated statistics for each chapter, fresh illustrations relevant to the text, and new case studies, as mentioned above. The book's layout follows the syllabus content of nine chapters and concludes with a short chapter on skills and techniques that advises students on practice and preparation.

OXFORD
UNIVERSITY PRESS

The focus for Chapters 1 and 2 is the **lithosphere**, one of the Earth's four great natural systems. The theme is exploitation of natural resources, found at or just below the land surface—rocks, minerals, and energy resources, and the environmental impact. In Chapters 4 and 5 the focus shifts to a study of the **hydrosphere**, water on land and resources in the oceans, with a strong emphasis on management. The focus in Chapter 6 is on natural hazards, some tectonic and some climatic. Chapter 7 studies the **atmosphere**, a very important natural system. The **biosphere**, or living Earth of plants and animals, including humans, is the focus for Chapters 8 and 9. Included in the study of natural ecosystems are references to both the natural world and human population. Chapter 3, about agriculture and the environment, links in to all four great natural systems, and therefore all the other chapters.

This highlights the fact that it is impossible to study these nine chapters in isolation. They are presented separately in line with the syllabus layout. However, many environmental issues, notably water pollution and soil degradation, and the impact of human activities go across sphere and chapter boundaries. Cross-references given within the text should help to reinforce an awareness of the many inter-linkages within the natural world.

Through most of the chapters, a common arrangement of the content can be observed. The first part is typically about the natural resources that the Earth provides—everything that makes life on Earth possible. The next is about how people use these natural resources for survival and higher levels of economic development. The third part is concerned with impacts on the environment, i.e. how human activities influence and change natural systems. It is here that major global issues such as resource depletion and environmental pollution are discussed.

The final section of each chapter is dominated by strategies for sustainable management, to convey to students an awareness of human responsibilities to keep natural systems healthy for continued use by future generations. The focus is upon actions and strategies that will allow sustainable development of the Earth's resources now and in the future. The need to manage the four great natural systems is the core idea of environmental management. This needs to be accompanied by the search for alternative self-sustaining technologies, such as renewable energy supplies to replace fossil fuel use, on which the human world has depended for its economic development for hundreds of years.

The Earth is, and will continue to be, home to all life as we know it—till an alternative is discovered. Hence the focus of this subject is how humans today can do better than they have done in the past, and better than many are doing now, to preserve the welfare of the natural environment and all forms of life within it.

CHAPTER 1

Rocks and minerals and their exploitation

OBJECTIVES

In this chapter you will learn about

- types of rocks and their formation
- extraction of rocks and minerals for human use
- impact of rock and mineral extraction
- strategies for landscape restoration
- strategies for sustainable use of rocks and minerals

FIGURE 1.1   Chuquicamata, the world's biggest open-pit copper mine, Calama, Chile

INTRODUCTION

The Earth can be described as a 'ball of rock'. Figure 1.2 shows its structure. The hot core, hotter than 4000°C, is surrounded by the mantle. The mantle is a thick shell of molten rock. The outer part of the mantle is the source for the magma that reaches the Earth's surface during volcanic eruptions. Floating on the mantle is the crust, which forms the surface layer of rocks and minerals. This is the **lithosphere**. This is where people live and work.

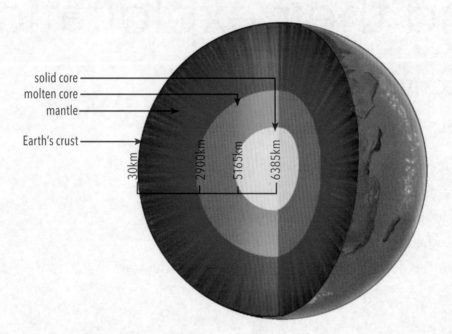

FIGURE 1.2   The structure of the Earth

Notice how thin the crust layer is. It is only 5km thick under the oceans and up to 100km thick below mountain ranges. Despite its shallow depth, this is the most important layer for people.

- It is made of a great variety of rocks, some of which provide people with useful products, including building stone, minerals and metals, and energy supplies.

- Most of the land has a surface covering of soil. Soil is formed from the breakdown of rocks; without soil, farming would be impossible.

Formation of rocks

When volcanoes erupt, the magma they release onto the surface as lava and ash cool to form new rock. Sediments already on the Earth's surface have been compressed and folded up by great earth movements to form chains of high fold mountains. The highest of these are the Himalayas, with Everest (8848 metres above sea level), the world's highest mountain.

OXFORD
UNIVERSITY PRESS

Over time, all rocks exposed on the surface are broken down into smaller pieces by weathering. There are different types of weathering (physical, chemical, and biological). The main type that breaks up rock in high mountain areas is freeze-thaw. Rocks are eroded by water, ice, and wind and carried away. Eventually, weathered and eroded rock fragments reach the sea, where they are deposited on the sea bed. Here they accumulate and are compacted again into rock. Millions of years later, during great mountain building periods, they will be upfolded to form new mountain ranges. This is the Earth's rock cycle.

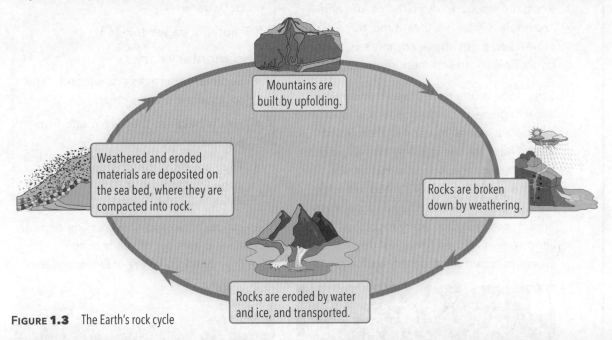

Mountains are built by upfolding.

Weathered and eroded materials are deposited on the sea bed, where they are compacted into rock.

Rocks are broken down by weathering.

Rocks are eroded by water and ice, and transported.

FIGURE 1.3   The Earth's rock cycle

Types of rocks

Although many different types of rocks make up the Earth's crust, they can be divided into just three groups, based on how they are formed.

A Igneous rocks

Igneous rocks are rocks 'formed by fire'. They are associated with volcanic activity as shown in Figure 1.4. Magma from the mantle reaches the surface during a volcanic eruption. When it cools and hardens, it forms igneous rocks. Granite and basalt are the two most common types. Granite is formed from magma forced into rocks during the formation of fold mountains along destructive plate boundaries. Basalt is formed from lava that pours out of volcanoes along constructive plate boundaries.

FIGURE 1.4   Volcanic eruption: the lava flowing out will form igneous rock.

B Sedimentary rocks

As the name suggests, these rocks are made of sediments. Sediments are small particles of rock broken off rocks which outcrop on the Earth's surface by weathering and erosion. Most of these particles eventually reach the sea bed, where they settle and accumulate in layers. Over time, the weight of new sediment above compresses the layers below into sedimentary rocks.

Sandstone is one type of sedimentary rock. When a piece of sandstone rock is examined carefully, it is seen to consist of grains of sand. These are the same as those you can find on any beach, but what is different is that the grains are concentrated in a rock instead of being loose. Clay and shale are other types of sedimentary rock; they form from the accumulation and compression of mud. Limestone is formed from the remains of plants and animals: masses of shells of sea creatures accumulate on the sea bed; when they die, they build up layers of limestone rock.

INFORMATION BOX

Igneous rocks

- Igneous rocks are new rocks in the Earth's crust.
- They are being formed along plate boundaries.

(Chapter 6, pages 162–163)

Sedimentary rocks

- Sedimentary rocks are 'second-hand' rocks in the Earth's crust.
- This is because they are made from old materials.
- They are most commonly found in large lowland areas.

Basalt cliffs in Iceland—notice how the lines of weakness (called joints) are vertical in these igneous rocks.

Limestone cliffs in England—notice how the lines of weakness (called bedding planes) are horizontal between the beds of rock.

FIGURE 1.5 Can you recognize the difference between igneous and sedimentary rocks?

C Metamorphic rocks

These are rocks which have been changed by heat and pressure in the Earth's crust.

Rocks in contact with new magma flows are changed by the heat. Rocks on plate boundaries are changed by the pressure and stress which accompanies great earth movements. For example, limestone is changed into marble and clay is turned into slate.

INFORMATION BOX

- Metamorphic rocks are old igneous and sedimentary rocks which have been changed.
- They are associated with old plateau blocks and ancient shields, such as the Deccan Plateau in India.

ACTIVITIES

1 Make a summary table for rock types, like the one below, but make it larger. Fill it in.

Rock types	Igneous	Sedimentary	Metamorphic
Definition			
Examples			
Formation			

2 (a) Name the four stages in the rock cycle.

(b) Explain why it is called a cycle.

Rock and mineral extraction

Rocks and minerals are cheap and easy to extract when they outcrop on or near the Earth's surface. All that needs to be done is to clear the vegetation and soil from the surface and start digging. The useful rock or mineral resource can then be extracted by **quarrying** or **opencast mining**.

INFORMATION BOX

- Quarrying is extracting rock and stone from the surface.
- Opencast mining is extracting minerals from the surface.
- Both leave a large hole (open pit) in the ground.
- Other names for surface mining are open-cut and strip mining.

The methods used are the same for both (Figure 1.6).

1 Clear the vegetation and remove the soil.

2 Break up and loosen the rock / mineral layer by using explosives.

3 Use diggers to remove the loose rock / mineral.

4 Load the rock / mineral onto trucks and take it away.

FIGURE 1.6 Stages in quarrying and opencast mining

Minerals are more expensive and more difficult to extract when they are located too deep for surface mining. The first stage in searching for minerals underground is to undertake a careful geological survey to discover the arrangement of rocks below the surface. From this survey, the depth, position, and amount of mineral resources can be estimated. The next stage is to sink a **deep mine** (Figure 1.7).

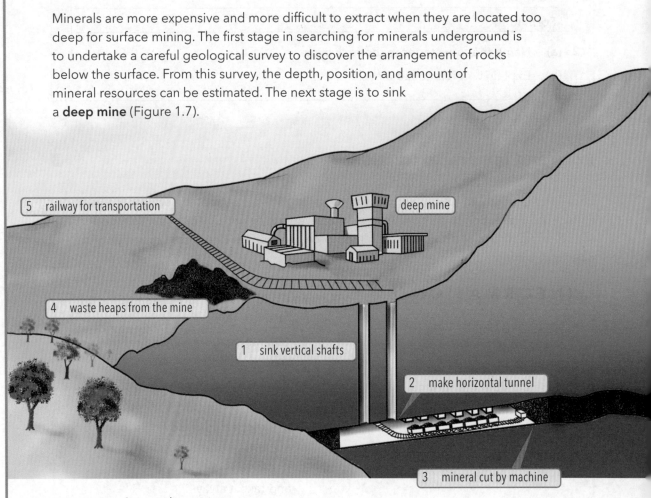

FIGURE 1.7 Stages in deep mining

Deep mining involves the following stages:.

1   sinking a vertical shaft down to the mineral bearing rock layer

2   making a horizontal tunnel following the mineral layer

3   extracting the minerals by digging done by miners or by machine

4   bringing the loose rock out of the mine to the surface and piling it up in waste heaps

5   transporting the minerals to market by railway or road

Of the two types of mining, deep mining is much more dangerous. The roof of the tunnel needs to be supported, but even in well-run mines with high safety standards, from time to time tunnel roofs collapse and miners are trapped, injured or killed. In some mines there are big problems with flooding; in others gas is present, which increases the danger of fire and explosion. When a disaster occurs, miners cannot escape as easily as they could if working on the surface, because their exit route may be blocked.

FIGURE 1.8   A modern, mechanized mine: notice the wide tunnel, strong roof supports, and the huge machine to cut out the rock and minerals.

INFORMATION BOX

The world's deepest mines

- These are in the gold fields of South Africa.

- Some are over 1000 metres deep.

- Miners work in great heat, over 45°C.

OXFORD
UNIVERSITY PRESS

ACTIVITIES

1 **(a)** Describe two ways in which deep mining is different from opencast mining.

   (b) Why do both types of mining lead to waste heaps on the surface?

2 Explain why opencast mining is **(a)** cheaper for the mining companies and **(b)** safer for the workers than deep mining.

3 Look at Figure 1.8.

   (a) Describe what it shows.

   (b) If this had been an old mine instead of a modern one, what differences would you have expected to see?

4 For your home area or country,

   (a) name any minerals mined;

   (b) state the mining methods used;

   (c) describe the problems for mining.

Factors that affect the decision to extract rocks and minerals ■

A mineral resource must be **viable** to be extracted. What does this mean? In simple terms, it has to be worthwhile for a company to mine the resource. In practical terms, what this means is that the mineral resource must be large enough, and of sufficient value, for mining it to be **economically viable**. If a mining company thinks it can make money from selling the rocks and minerals extracted, after covering all its mining costs, then it is likely to go ahead with extracting them.

Whether or not a mineral is viable has much to do with supply and demand.

- Supply refers to the amount of the resource that is known to exist; these are the known reserves that can be exploited when needed.

- Demand refers to the amount that people need; demand can go up and down, and can change quickly.

Looking at both of these factors helps to determine how much of a mineral deposit will be mined, and how quickly. When demand for a mineral increases, its world market price increases as well. It might then be economically viable for a company to mine small deposits in remote locations because they can make a profit. When the world market price falls again, mines like this are the first ones to be closed.

Several factors influence the viability of exploitation of rocks and minerals. These are summarized in Table 1.1.

TABLE 1.1   Chances of mineral exploitation

	Factor	Chances of a mineral being exploited (mined and used)	
		High chance	**Low chance**
1	Geology	▪ Simple geology e.g. thick layers in unbroken horizontal beds, at or near the surface ▪ Easy to use machines	▪ Difficult geology e.g. much folding and faulting of the mineral bearing rocks, especially those deep underground ▪ Impossible to use machines
2	Exploration and feasibility	▪ Easy place to look for minerals ▪ No sensitive local environmental issues	▪ Difficult to reach to look for minerals ▪ Environmental concerns and protected areas
3	Depletion rate (rate used up)	▪ Large deposits and plentiful reserves remain. Many good-quality deposits, easy to mine, are still present.	▪ Only small reserves are left. The best deposits have been used, leaving those that are more difficult and expensive to mine.
4	Location (Climate and Transport)	▪ Climate is easy to work in, with no extremes of weather such as great heat, intense cold, and heavy rain. ▪ Close to places where many people live and industries using minerals are already located, so there is likely to be a dense network of existing roads and railways.	▪ Extreme climates like those in hot deserts or cold polar lands, which make mining difficult and expensive ▪ In remote places far away from people and economic activities, new roads and railways will need to be built, adding to the costs of exploitation.
5	Supply and demand	▪ High demand, low supply ▪ High prices encourage more production. Even small mines in remote areas can be profitable.	▪ Demand low, supply high ▪ Low prices reduce output. Production is confined to large, well-located mines where costs of production are low.

Mineral deposits located far away from where people live are often exploited last. However, there are mines in some of the world's most remote places. The cold polar regions in Alaska and northern Canada, and Siberia in Russia are almost uninhabited, but are rich in minerals. Big deposits of minerals for which demand is high attract mining companies despite the high costs of building transport links and attracting workers. One example is drilling for oil in Alaska.

Demand for minerals fluctuates. It rises in times of industrial growth and falls during an economic recession. When cold winter weather hits Europe and North America, the demand for oil and gas for heating grows, which pushes up world prices. During warm winters the demand decreases. Surplus oil and gas means that prices fall again.

World market prices for all minerals fluctuate greatly. Figure 1.9 overleaf shows how the world price of gold has fluctuated during a forty-year period. When prices are high, even small mines that are expensive to work are kept open. If prices remain high, companies try to increase the supply by searching for new deposits and opening up new mines. However, when world prices are low, the smaller and less productive mines are closed as mine owners

OXFORD
UNIVERSITY PRESS

cut back on production and concentrate on their most profitable mines. South Africa is a leading producer and exporter of gold, but the amount of money it earns varies greatly from year to year. Low gold prices are not good news for the South African economy.

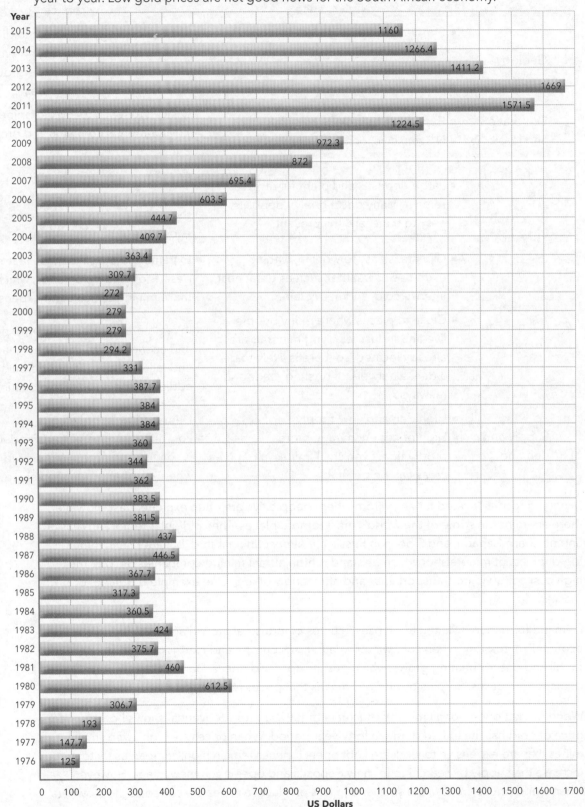

FIGURE 1.9 World price of gold (per troy ounce) in USD, 1976-2015

ACTIVITIES

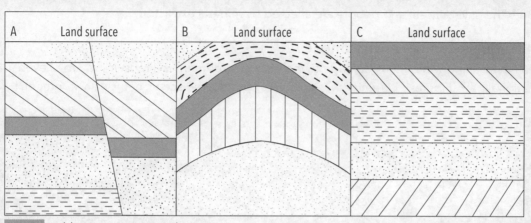

rock layer containing minerals

FIGURE 1.10 Three mineral deposits in different geological structures

1 Study Figure 1.10.

   (a) (i) Based on the geology only, give the letters of the mineral deposits most likely to be exploited first and last by a mining company.

   (ii) Explain your choices.

   (b) Suggest two reasons why the mining company might exploit these minerals in a different order from this.

2 Describe how and why the methods of mining used to extract the mineral deposits in A and C will be different.

3 Study the data in Table 1.2.

   (a) Draw a line graph to show world oil prices from 1996 to 2015.

   (b) State the positive and negative effects of changing oil prices for **(i)** producing countries and **(ii)** consuming countries.

TABLE **1.2** Average world price of crude oil (US$) 1996-2015							
1996	21	2001	25	2006	66	2011	95
1997	19	2002	25	2007	72	2012	94
1998	13	2003	31	2008	100	2013	98
1999	18	2004	41	2009	62	2014	93
2000	29	2005	57	2010	79	2015	49

Impact of rock and mineral extraction

Both the environment and people are affected by mineral extraction.

A Impacts on the environment

To have mining without any damage to the local environment is almost impossible, even in a national park (Figure 1.11) which was created to protect the scenic natural environment.

FIGURE 1.11   Smoke from the chimney of a potash mine in a national park–why is this not what you would expect to see in a national park?

FIGURE 1.12   Road through the Amazon rainforest in Brazil–what would the area have looked like before this road was built? Why has the risk of damage to the local environment been increased?

Both opencast and deep mining lead to surface waste heaps. At best these look unsightly and spoil the natural beauty of the area. Much worse, after periods of heavy rain, waste heaps can become unstable and flow downslope, destroying everything in their path and covering even larger areas of land. Mine waste can be highly toxic. Soil samples taken from the waste heaps next to the lead and zinc mine at Cerro de Pasco in Peru have revealed lead levels as high as 4500 parts per million (ppm) compared with an acceptable normal level of 70ppm. Leaks from oil wells and pipelines make the waters of the Niger Delta, (Nigeria's main oil-producing region) among the most polluted in the world.

New mines in remote areas need roads and railways for access and transport. Building of these can lead to forest clearance, resulting in loss of wildlife habitats and reductions in biodiversity. The Amazon Basin in Brazil and Peru is covered by the Earth's largest area of untouched tropical rainforest, but it is also mineral-rich (oil, iron-ore, gold, and others). A network of roads now cuts through what was previously jungle, in turn making it easier for illegal logging companies to clear more and more of the commercially valuable hardwood trees.

In many developing countries government controls are weak, while mining companies are big and powerful. Permission for mining is given even in sensitive environments within rainforests against the wishes and interests of local people. Even protected areas like national parks and nature reserves are not safe. Drilling rights for oil and gas were granted in the Kirthar National Park in Pakistan, disturbing the wildlife and affecting populations of ibex and deer.

The negative effects on the local environment are increased by the crushing and refining of mineral ores, which often takes place close to the mine. This is done to avoid the high costs of transporting a lot of useless rock that surrounds the useful minerals. Dust and fumes from chimneys during the crushing, refining, and smelting of mineral ores cause air pollution. Tall chimneys ruin the scenic view in national parks for many kilometres away (Figure 1.11).

Rivers and streams are polluted by water flowing through old mine workings. Some are so badly contaminated that they become 'dead' streams. Plants, fish, and other water creatures are killed by the high concentration of minerals and shortage of oxygen.

Opencast mining leaves bigger scars on the landscape than deep mining. As more of the mineral is mined, the surface pit is widened and deepened. Copper mining in the USA and Chile has produced some of the largest man-made holes on the Earth's surface at the Bingham mine and the Chuquicamata mine (Figure 1.1), respectively. Part of the explanation for this is that a small percentage (often just 1-3%) of the ore taken out of the ground is copper.

Although mining is vital for economic development, it is difficult to find any good impacts of mining on the environment. Companies aim to make as much profit as they can before the mineral deposits are exhausted. Mining is hard and dangerous work; miners are much more concerned about their safety and making a living than they are about protecting the environment.

FIGURE 1.13 Polluted stream from an old iron mining area–why is it this colour?

INFORMATION BOX

Chuquicamata—the world's largest opencast copper mine*

- It is located in the Atacama Desert of northern Chile.
- Everything about it is huge and it dominates the area.
- The open pit from which the ore is taken is about 5km long, 3km wide and 1 km deep.
- Giant trucks with wheels almost 4m high carry out 300 tonne loads on each trip.
- 60,000 tonnes of ore per year are processed next to the mine.
- 9000 people are employed here.

*Figure 1.1, page 1

DID YOU KNOW?

- Mining removes 28 billion tonnes of soil and rock per year.
- This is more than that removed by natural processes of erosion.

environmental management

Pollution

- In examination answers, the term 'pollution' is too vague.
- Never use the word pollution by itself.
- Be precise and state the type of pollution.
- State whether it is air, land or water pollution.

- Be even more precise and name examples:
  - ▲ land pollution from waste heaps
  - ▲ water pollution from mine workings
  - ▲ air pollution from crushing and smelting

ACTIVITIES

1 Identify examples of each of these impacts of mining on the environment: waste; land pollution; water pollution; air pollution; visual pollution; loss of habitat.

2 Explain why it is almost impossible to have mining without some environmental damage.

B Impacts on people – negative and positive

Although the impact of mining on the environment is definitely negative rather than positive, its impact on people can be good as well as bad.

Deep mining and its negative impact

The bad effects are mainly for miners. Usually they must work in narrow spaces, deep underground, in wet, dirty, and dusty conditions. Mining certainly cannot be described as one of the world's most pleasant jobs. The majority of miners suffer injuries at some time in their working lives because they are expected to work hard under difficult conditions.

Also, mining is unhealthy work. Not only is the air supply underground poor, but so too is the quality because of the large amount of dust. This causes breathing and chest problems. Life expectancy among miners is lower than for other workers living in the same area. Many die young from lung diseases such as silicosis, which is caused by workers inhaling quartz. It is enough to make you ask: why do men become miners?

Opencast mining and its negative impact

People living nearby are the ones most affected by noise, air, and visual pollution. Perhaps the greatest noise is when the rock is being blasted out with explosives, but there is also the continuous noise from the heavy machinery at work in the mine. The air is filled with dust and dirt, leading to poor air quality and risks to people's health. There is also noise and dust from trucks carrying the minerals away. As the opencast pit becomes larger, the size of the mining pit and waste heap increases, destroying the landscape even more. Wildlife is driven out of the area.

Impact

Mining and its positive impact

Mining can and does benefit both the economy of a country and its people. Exporting minerals is a very important source of foreign exchange income for many countries, both developing and developed. This income can then be used to buy goods from other countries. For some developing countries, including many in Africa (Figure 1.15), exporting minerals is their main source of income. Money earned can be used to fund development projects, modernize the infrastructure and improve their people's quality of life—by making new roads, supplying clean water, and building schools, clinics, and hospitals—provided that governments spend the money wisely.

Unfortunately, the high levels of political corruption found in many African countries limits the benefits. Benefits are most likely to be concentrated in the urban areas, especially the capital cities, instead of in the rural areas where the minerals exported are mined. For example, the bright new skyscraper office blocks and modern shopping malls make parts of the centre of Johannesburg look like a first world city. It grew in the middle of Witwatersrand, the rich Rand gold mines; it was gold which led to the city's growth and prosperity.

FIGURE 1.14 Business centre of Johannesburg, the most important city in Africa—it looks like a city in a developed country.

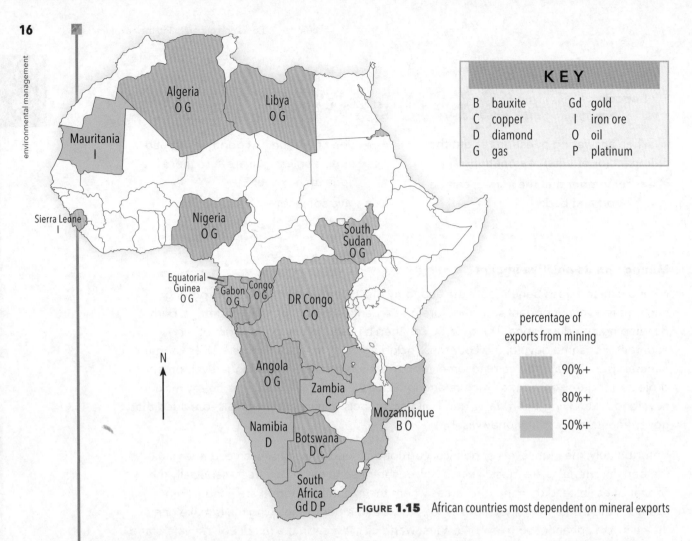

FIGURE 1.15 African countries most dependent on mineral exports

KEY

B	bauxite	Gd	gold
C	copper	I	iron ore
D	diamond	O	oil
G	gas	P	platinum

percentage of exports from mining

90%+

80%+

50%+

Mining does tend to be better paid than farming and other types of unskilled work. This is one of the reasons why there is no problem recruiting miners, despite it being hard and dangerous work. In Southern Africa, many families living in rural areas depend upon money sent back by their sons, who have gone to work in the gold, platinum, and copper mines, either in their own or in neighbouring countries.

Also, mining often takes place in areas where there are few other ways of making a living. Take the example of Chuquicamata from the previous pages. The Atacama Desert, where it is located, is the driest place on Earth: without mineral resources, 9000 people would not be able to live and work there. Mining creates small towns with strong communities of people, because everyone in the town is connected in some way with mining.

INFORMATION BOX

Infrastructure

Facilities and services are needed for economic development and higher living standards. They are often government-funded and provided, such as

- transport—roads, railways, airfields, ports;
- telecommunications;
- water supply, sewage works;
- schools, hospitals, and clinics.

ACTIVITIES

1 Identify examples of each of these impacts of mining on people:
noise; air pollution; employment opportunities; foreign exchange through export;
improvements in facilities and infrastructure.

2 Draw two spider diagrams like the ones below, but larger. Add as many advantages and
disadvantages of mining as you can.

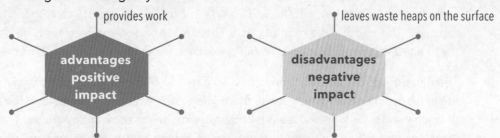

3 Study Figure 1.15. Describe two ways in which it shows that there is high economic
dependence on mineral exports among African countries.

4 Look at Figure 1.16.

FIGURE 1.16 Quarry in a national park: quarrying here is big business; about 5 million tonnes of limestone rock is extracted from this quarry every year.

(a) Draw a labelled sketch of the quarry.

(b) Describe what the area in the distance away from the quarry looks like.

(c) The quarry company is asking for permission to increase the size of the quarry.
Some of the local people are in favour, some are against.

　(i) Name one group of people likely to be in favour.

　(ii) Name one group of people likely to be against.

　(iii) Suggest reasons why local people have different views about a larger quarry.

Example: Cerro de Pasco—lead and zinc open pit mine in Peru

Cerro de Pasco is a mining town in the Andes of Peru. Lying at a height of 4380 metres above sea level, mining is the only reason for the town's existence. It is too high to grow crops. Silver, lead, and zinc have been mined here for over 400 years from a large open pit mine in the centre of town (Figure 1.17). The mine pit is more than 1500m long, 750m wide, and almost 500m deep. It is a very big hole to have in the middle of a built-up area. The streets of poor houses, their corrugated iron roofs black with mining dust, suddenly stop at the edge of the pit.

The mine produces 60,000 tonnes of lead and 150,000 tonnes of zinc a year. Reserves are plentiful, which is why the mining company keeps increasing the size of the mine. This is why houses near the edge of the pit show many cracks. The pit threatens to swallow up more of the town, and some of the old historic buildings in the city centre have already been lost.

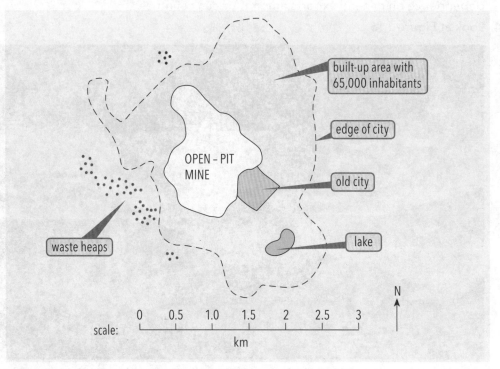

FIGURE 1.17 Location of the open pit mine inside the town of Cerro de Pasco

Large lead-based waste heaps cover the western edge of the town. Dust from these heaps blows everywhere. Earth samples taken next to these waste heaps show frighteningly high concentrations of lead (up to 65 times higher than acceptable norms for humans), arsenic (up to 26 times higher), and cadmium (up to 5 times higher). The lake shown on the map glows orange because of the mining run-off. Not surprisingly, none of the water in Cerro de Pasco is fit to drink. Instead, drinking water is brought in by trucks for which people pay 25 times more than water costs people in Lima.

Health tests have shown that over 90 per cent of children and 80 per cent of women of child-bearing age had high blood levels of toxic substances like lead. Most young children have blood lead levels between two and five times the level considered dangerous. Lung and heart diseases were found to be common in older residents.

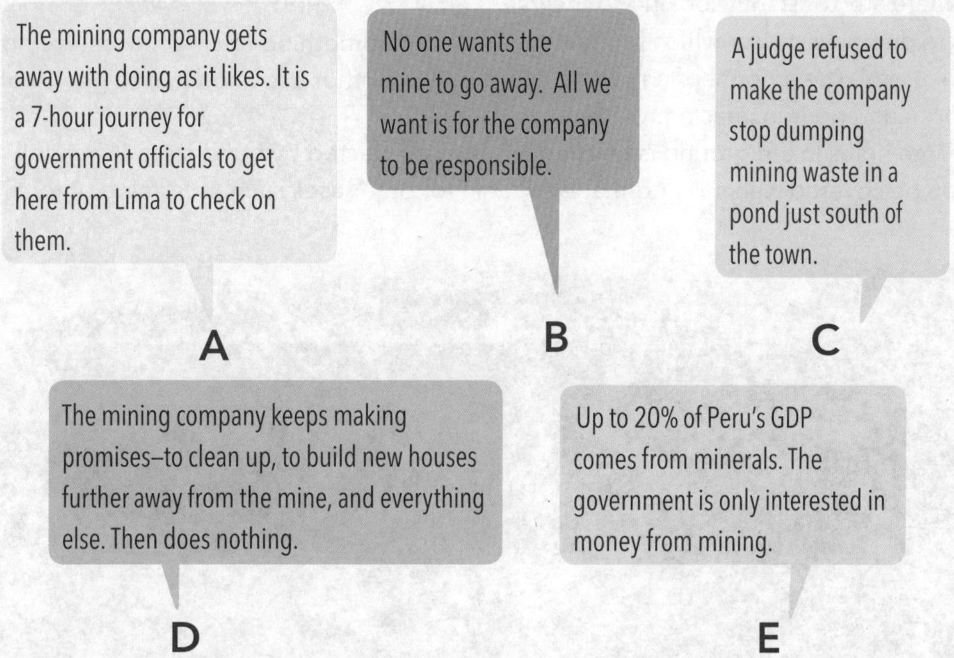

The mining company gets away with doing as it likes. It is a 7-hour journey for government officials to get here from Lima to check on them.

A

No one wants the mine to go away. All we want is for the company to be responsible.

B

A judge refused to make the company stop dumping mining waste in a pond just south of the town.

C

The mining company keeps making promises–to clean up, to build new houses further away from the mine, and everything else. Then does nothing.

D

Up to 20% of Peru's GDP comes from minerals. The government is only interested in money from mining.

E

FIGURE 1.18   Comments from people living in Cerro de Pasco about the mine and the mining company.

ACTIVITIES

1 **(a)**   State basic details about the Cerro de Pasco mine (such as location, size, minerals).

   (b)   What is unique about the location of this mine compared with most other mines?

2 Draw a large spider diagram. On it label the different ways in which the Cerro de Pasco mine has impacted the environment and the people.

3 **(a)**   Draw a line across the page from 0% on the left (environmentally friendly / sustainable) to 100% on the right (environmentally unfriendly / unsustainable). Mark the position on your line for the Cerro de Pasco mine.

   (b)   With the help of people's comments in Figure 1.18, explain why you marked this position on the line.

4 Research: search the Internet to find out dangers to human health from lead, especially for children.

Managing the impact of rock and mineral extraction

Old quarries and large holes left after mining work stopped some time ago are convenient places for the disposal of waste. This is **landfill**, a cheap and easy way to dispose of waste (Figure 1.19). City authorities everywhere are constantly looking for new places to dump waste, for which old quarries are very useful. The amount of city waste can be enormous, and is increasing. Waste tipped into holes in the ground is levelled off and compacted by bulldozers. When full, the land can be covered with soil and made suitable for other uses such as farming or forestry.

INFORMATION BOX

Waste definitions:

- 'all unwanted materials, including solids, liquids, and gases'
- 'something for which we have no further use and want to get rid of'

FIGURE 1.19   A garbage disposal site in Thailand

Disposal of waste in landfill sites needs careful management: otherwise it may contaminate the land and become a hazard to people living and working in the surrounding area.

- Land contamination: waste includes dangerous substances such as toxic metals, for example, lead and mercury.
- Water pollution: contaminated substances leak into the ground and are carried by filtration into ground water supplies and rivers.
- Health hazards: from rodents, flies, foul odours; from the presence of harmful substances, for example, asbestos and arsenic; from contaminated sources of drinking water.

Notice how similar these are to the problems from toxic waste heaps from mining, such as from the lead mining at Cerro de Pasco.

Landfill sites can be well managed. One way of doing this is to make alternating layers of compacted refuse and soil. Each day, after tipping refuse, the waste is compacted and covered with soil. The top covering of soil prevents many of the health issues. This is known as 'sanitary landfilling', but is practised in only a few places.

As soon as work stops in a quarry or surface mine, the last task of any responsible mining company is the safe disposal of all mining waste. The most environmentally friendly way of doing this is to enlist the help of nature. **Biomediation** involves the use of natural organisms to remove pollutants in soil or water, by enhancing the growth of pollution-eating microbes. Bacteria, fungi, and other micro-organisms are constantly at work breaking down organic matter in soil and in compost. Encourage more of them, and they will clean up the site naturally. This method does not work with toxic waste such as lead which needs to be physically removed from the site.

Non-toxic waste heaps can be levelled off or used to fill the hole left by mining or quarrying. The most vital part of any land restoration process is replacing the top soil that was removed before mining could begin. This should have been carefully stored. The task of restoring the landscape to look like it used to before mining began is most likely to happen where the mine or quarry was small, and where the company was forced to obey strict planning rules.

After the hole on the surface has been filled in, bulldozers can be used to level off and smooth out the surface. Stored top soil is spread back over the surface. Soil quality is vital to any successful programme of vegetation regeneration. Nutrients may need to be added. In the best examples, the land is made to look like the natural landscape by planting trees, bushes, and grasses, so that it looks similar to the surrounding land undisturbed by mining. This is known as **landscaping**. These plants should grow well provided that all the old top soil has been replaced.

Tree planting is often an important part of the restoration process. Trees bind the soil together. They shelter the ground surface from heavy rains which could easily wash away the loose surface in the first few years after the hole has been filled in. Trees can also be used as shelter belts against strong winds in areas where the land has been restored for farming use. In time, trees can become commercially profitable.

A different approach to restoration is to change the land use, either to benefit wildlife or to provide recreational opportunities for people. The holes left by quarrying and surface mining are natural places for rain water and surface run-off to accumulate to form lakes and marshes. These wetland sites are important for nature conservation because they provide a rich variety of habitats for birds and animals. Many are nature reserves.

In a few cases these natural water stores are used as reservoirs to supply drinking water. More commonly they are used for a wide range of recreation activities, such as sailing, diving, and fishing.

ACTIVITIES

1 (a) Give a definition of landfill.

(b) Make two lists, one of the advantages, and the other of the disadvantages of landfill.

(c) In your view, which is the greater: advantages or disadvantages of landfill? Explain your answer.

2 (a) Explain what is meant by landscaping old quarries and surface mines.

(b) Describe the methods used for landscaping an old quarry or mine.

Case study of management of an old mine: The Eden Project in Cornwall, England

When mining stopped in the 1980s, after about 150 years of removing china clay (used for making pots), it left a hole on the surface about 50 metres deep. What could be done with it? It was suitable for landfill, but the area is well away from big cities. Instead, a more imaginative use was suggested—build giant dome-like greenhouses and create biomes inside them. Make it a tourist attraction and bring work to an area suffering badly from job losses in mining. It opened in 2001 and attracts about a million visitors a year.

Biomes are large-scale ecosystems, named after the dominant vegetation cover. Inside the domes habitats from around the world have been recreated. The two principal ones are tropical rainforest and Mediterranean. The rainforest biome, for example, is kept at tropical temperature and moisture levels. Inside the domes, visitors used to living in the cool British climate, can walk past fruiting banana plants, rubber trees, and giant bamboo. Between the biomes are outdoor gardens of temperate plants able to grow in the British climate.

FIGURE 1.20 Distinctive domes of the giant greenhouses now filling an old china clay pit in Cornwall

Therefore what was an open pit mine, and an eyesore on the landscape, has been transformed into a tourist attraction. At the same time it allows and encourages scientific and educational studies of plants. Other restoration projects in England (see Information Box) offer opportunities for different uses. In future, things will be different. Planning laws in the UK are now much stricter. Planning permission for a new quarry or surface mine will not be granted without a full study of how the landscape will be restored once work finishes.

INFORMATION BOX

Other examples of restoration projects in England

Stone Cove, Leicestershire

- An old granite quarry which filled up naturally with spring water
- Now the National Diving Centre with over 50,000 visitors a year

Cotswolds Water Park

- An old sand and gravel quarry quickly filled with water
- Unsuitable for landfill
- Now used for recreation—fishing, boating, water skiing, etc.

FIGURE 1.21 Inside the rainforest biome: tropical vegetation growing in the UK

ACTIVITIES

1 Make notes for a case study of mine restoration using the following headings as a guide:
   (a) information about the mine;
   (b) details of the restoration project itself;
   (c) advantages of the project.

2 (a) Make a list, with examples, of the different uses for old quarry and mine sites.
   (b) Choose what you consider to be the best and the worst. Explain your choices.

Sustainable use and conservation of rocks and minerals

INFORMATION BOX

Definitions

- *Sustainable* describes activities and economic growth which have a long future because people are working with the environment upon which they depend.

- *Sustainable resource* is something useful to humans which will last for ever or which can be replaced; renewable alternative energy sources such as sun and wind, and woodland which can be replanted are examples.

- *Sustainable development* considers the needs of future generations as well as those of people today. The aim is to have for coming generations the same conditions on Earth and its resources as they are at present.

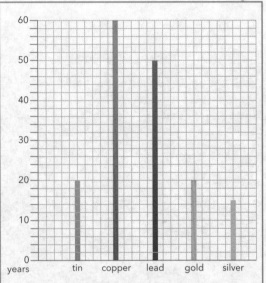

FIGURE 1.22 How long the known reserves of certain minerals are expected to last: estimated in 2015.

Present rates of mining and use of the Earth's mineral resources are non-sustainable for future generations. Figure 1.22 shows the 'life expectancies' of five mineral resources— estimates for how many years the known reserves will last at present rates of consumption.

Of course, these are only estimates. New deposits might be found, but the rate of consumption could also decrease. There are several strategies which will help to reduce the amount used. These include:

A Increased efficiency in use: This is where companies through their own Research and Development departments can make a big difference. New jet engines for aircraft are not developed unless they can work more efficiently and save fuel. Car manufacturers seek more efficient engines which increase the number of kilometres per litre of fuel. In developed countries, such as the UK, governments insist on labels on electrical goods, such as washing machines and fridges, which indicate to the customer how energy-efficient the product is.

B Reduce, reuse, and recycle: This is where individuals can make a big difference. Lights and machines can be switched off when not in use to reduce energy consumption. Broken items can be repaired instead of being thrown out. Glass and plastic bottles can be refilled and used again. Glass, aluminium cans, paper, cardboard, rags, and plastics can be collected and recycled. Some are remade into the same product, such as waste paper (pulped down and made into new paper goods) and aluminium cans (melted down and made into new containers). Others are made into different products, such as clothes and textiles (made into furniture covers and blankets) and plastics (made into clothing).

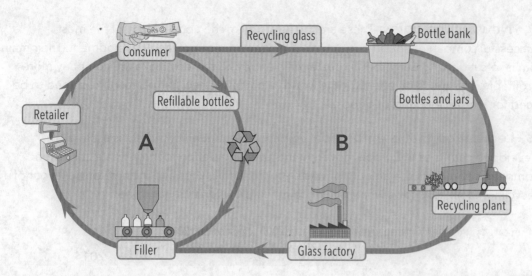

FIGURE 1.23 Recycling glass bottles: why is option A more environmentally friendly than option B?

Recycling as an idea for saving natural resources is not new. Some industries have recycled for many years. The steel industry is a good example; scrap iron is collected and reused in electric furnaces, saving on the amount of new iron ore needed. Electric arc furnaces themselves are the most efficient way to make steel, increasing the cost benefits for companies. Recycling aluminium cans is very energy and cost efficient. Reprocessing of the cans only needs 5 per cent of the energy needed to produce aluminium from its raw material (bauxite).

FIGURE 1.24 Garbage disposal system in a US supermarket

In big cities in the developing world, plenty of individuals make their living by going through what other people have thrown out as waste in order to collect metals and other materials than can be recycled. In most European countries, as well as in developed Asian countries, there are separate collecting bins in public places for paper, plastics, and textiles.

C Increased efficiency in extraction and refining: The greater the percentage of a mineral that can be extracted from mineral ore, the less waste and the greater the profit for the mining company. Also less new ore needs to be mined to satisfy the demand. When only about two per cent of useful copper is obtained from copper ore, even an improvement of half a per cent in the amount of copper retrieved will significantly extend the life of the known reserves of copper (Figure 1.22). The life expectancy of many oil wells has been extended by new technology which allows a higher percentage of the oil in the well to be forced out.

D New technologies: These are the key to all of the above. Many of the most successful companies spend huge sums of money on research and development. Their main aim is to cut down costs through greater efficiency, and thereby make the company more profitable. The knock-on effect for the world is that fewer new natural resources need to be used for the same output of goods.

E Legislation that is enforced: Legislation without enforcement is useless. In developed countries in Europe, governments used legislation to force waste collection companies to reduce the amount of waste sent to landfill sites and incinerators in favour of recycling. Table 1.3 shows what happened in the UK when this was done.

TABLE **1.3** How the UK managed its domestic waste (2000 compared with 2014)		
	2000	**2014**
Total waste (m. tonnes)	28	25
Methods of disposal (%)		
Landfill	75	32
Incineration (burning)	11	24
Recycled	14	44

ACTIVITIES

1 (a) Give a definition of recycling.

   (b) Describe how recycling can reduce the amount of mining and extend the life expectancy of minerals.

   (c) Explain why new technology is essential to reduce mineral use.

2 Look at Figure 1.23. Which is more environmentally friendly A or B? Explain your choice.

3 Refer to Table 1.3.

   (a) Draw pie graphs for 2000 and 2014 to show methods of disposal.

   (b) State the main differences for total waste and its disposal between 2000 and 2014.

   (c) Has waste disposal in the UK become more environmentally friendly? Explain your answer.

4 Look back to the example of Cerro de Pasco.

   (a) What is different about the Cerro de Pasco mine and open pit compared with the mining pit in which the Eden Project is located?

   (b) What seems to be different about the attitudes of the authorities between Peru (a developing country in South America) and the UK (a developed country in Europe)?

   (c) Suggest two reasons why they are different.

CHAPTER 2

Energy and the environment

OBJECTIVES

In this chapter you will learn about

- fossil fuel formation
- energy resources and generation of electricity
- factors affecting energy demand
- conservation and management of energy sources
- impact and management of marine oil pollution

FIGURE 2.1 Rush hour traffic jam: what are the consequences for people and the environment?

INTRODUCTION

Among the many mineral resources provided naturally by the Earth are highly valuable fossil fuels (coal, oil, and natural gas). They are hugely important to people because they were and are the basis for industrial and economic growth, and they led to a transport revolution.

The Industrial Revolution began in the UK in about 1750. It was based on coal. The technological breakthrough came with the invention of the steam engine, capable of driving railway engines, ships, and factory machinery. However, economic growth in the second half of the 20th century depended more and more on oil instead of coal.

Being a liquid rather than a solid gives oil many advantages over coal. It is cheaper to obtain by drilling than by mining, cheaper and easier to move long distances by pipelines and tankers, and easier to control in use in engines and machinery. In particular, oil enabled the 20th century transport revolution (cars, trucks, container ships, and aircraft) to grow. Together, these developments have allowed local, national, and global movements of people and goods on a scale not known, nor ever imagined, in previous centuries.

Only in the last 25 years have there been serious attempts to break away from total dependence on fossil fuels by searching for alternative sources of energy, most of them renewable. Reasons for this change in attitude are a mixture of negative and positive.

Negative factors:

- Concern about the local and global effects of unrestricted fossil fuel use (air and water pollution, global warming)

- **Finite** (non-renewable) nature of fossil fuels, which will run out if current rates of use are continued for another 50 years or more (Figure 2. 2)

Positive factors:

- Human ingenuity, by research and development (R&D), to harness what the Earth provides in abundance, notably wind and sunshine

- Not only will these renewable resources last forever, but they are cleaner and much more widely available. Fossil fuels were formed only in certain places on the Earth's surface.

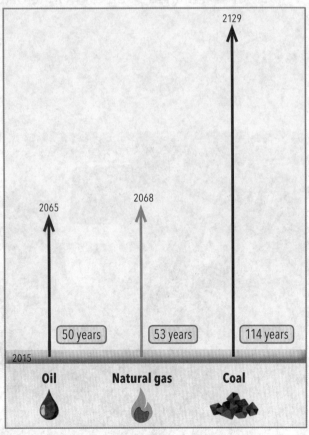

FIGURE 2.2 Life expectancies of coal, oil, and natural gas from the year 2015

Formation of fossil fuels

Fossil fuels have two characteristics in common for their formation.

- They were formed from the decomposition of the remains of plants and animals.
- It took millions of years for them to accumulate and form deposits which are large enough to be exploited for human use.

Formation of coal

Where today there are seams of coal, once there were dense forests. About 300 million years ago, in the Carboniferous (Information Box), dense forests were widespread. They must have been similar to those found near the Equator in the Amazon and Congo Basins today. As older trees and plants died, the dead vegetation decomposed on the swampy forest floors. In time, it formed a thick layer of peat (Figure 2.3A). Later, rivers covered the peat with deposits of mud and sand; over millions of year, mud and sand were compressed into sedimentary rocks and the peat hardened into coal (Figure 2.3C). Coal is a black rock, so useful because it gives out heat when it burns.

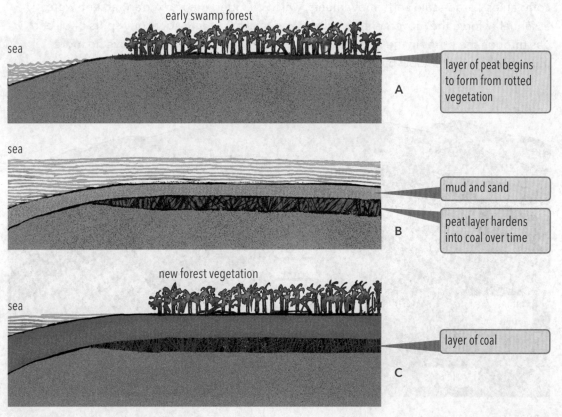

FIGURE 2.3   Stages of formation of coal

Formation of oil and natural gas

Oil and gas were formed from the decomposition of plants and dead creatures which collected in layers on the sea bed. Each one rotted to form a tiny spot of oil. Their remains were covered by mud and sand. As the sand was compressed into hard sandstone rock, the oil and gas separated, and rose through the sandstone, filling in the spaces (or pores) between the particles of rock. The lighter gas rose to the top (Figure 2.4). Below the oil is a layer of more dense water.

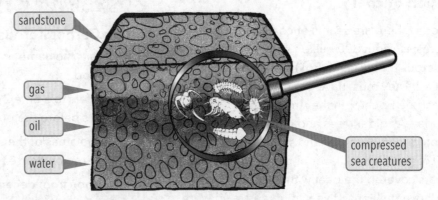

FIGURE 2.4 Formation of oil and gas

Only where the arrangement of the rocks is favourable, as in the anticline oil trap shown in Figure 2.5, are the oil deposits sufficiently large to be of commercial interest to the oil companies. Large-scale earth movements, which changed the rock arrangement, were essential to force the movement of millions and millions of individual tiny spots of oil and gas through the pores in the rock. They accumulated when they could move no more, trapped above and below by impermeable rocks such as shale.

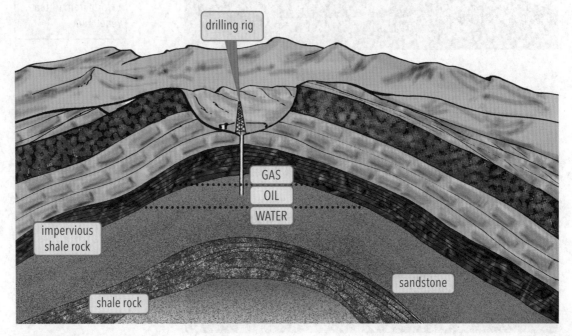

FIGURE 2.5 Anticline oil trap

Once geologists have worked out how they think rocks are arranged underground, engineers drill down into the porous rock, which they believe contains oil. Drilling is the only certain way of finding out whether oil and gas are present. Many drill holes are found to be dry, and the oil company loses its money, which can be as much as a million dollars per hole. Where test drilling suggests that large enough deposits exist, a drilling rig is set up above the oil trap. Oil and gas are forced up to the surface through pipes.

ACTIVITIES

1   Explain the formation of coal.

2   (a)   State two similarities between coal, oil, and natural gas.

    (b)   In what ways are they different?

3   (a)   Draw a labelled sketch of an oil trap.

    (b)   Explain why oil is trapped.

    (c)   Describe how oil is discovered and extracted.

4   Suggest reasons why the oil trap shown in Figure 2.5

    (a)   was difficult to discover;

    (b)   might have been missed by the oil company.

Energy resources and the generation of electricity

Figure 2.6 shows the main commercial energy sources in the world for the twenty years up to 2015 and their relative importance. What are the important features of world energy supply and use that are shown?

- World energy demand continues to increase.

- The world still relies greatly on energy from fossil fuels.

- Nuclear energy and hydroelectricity (HEP) are the only non-fossil fuels in widespread use.

- Hydroelectricity is the only renewable source with a large enough use to be named and separated out.

- Renewables (other than HEP) make only a small contribution, but it can be seen to be increasing.

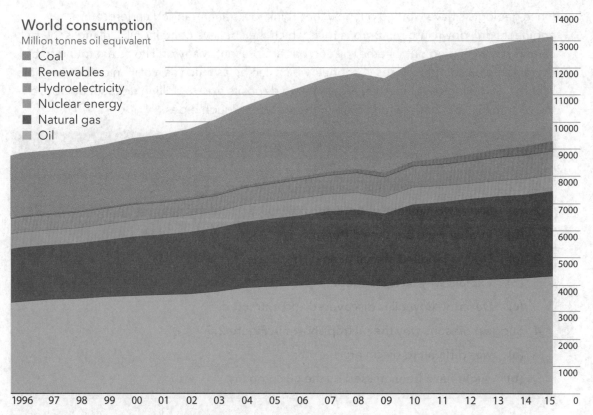

World consumption
Million tonnes oil equivalent
- ■ Coal
- ■ Renewables
- ■ Hydroelectricity
- ■ Nuclear energy
- ■ Natural gas
- ■ Oil

FIGURE **2.6** World commercial energy consumption (1996 – 2015)
Source: BP Statistical Review of World Energy, 2015

TABLE **2.1** World energy consumption, 2015

	(million tonnes oil equivalent)	
Total	13,140	100%
of which:		
oil	4330	33.0%
natural gas	3140	23.9%
coal	3840	29.2%
nuclear	580	4.4%
hydroelectricity	890	6.8%
renewables	360	2.7%

Note that Figure 2.6 does not give a complete picture of world energy supplies, because energy sources that people obtain for themselves are not included. In rural areas of Asia and Africa biofuels are often the main energy source. The simple label biomass is often used to include fuelwood (firewood), animal dung, and crop wastes, which villagers use for cooking. Biofuels are much less important in the developed world, and it is here that about two thirds of world energy consumption takes place.

ACTIVITIES

1   Use the information in Table 2.1. Draw a pie graph to show the contribution of different energy sources to total world energy consumption in 2015.

2   (a)   What percentage of the 2015 total was contributed by fossil fuels?

    (b)   What does this suggest about their importance?

3   Statements about what Figure 2.6 shows:

    A   Total world energy consumption keeps on increasing.

    B   Coal is the main fossil fuel used.

    C   Nuclear energy is as important in 2015 as it was in 1996.

    (a)   State whether, in your view, each of these statements is true or false.

    (b)   Briefly explain each of your answers using the graph information in support.

Different methods of generating electricity

These are many and various (Figure 2.7). Their number, range, and importance keep on increasing. Of the commercial energy sources in Figure 2.6, most of the coal, some of the oil and gas, and all of the nuclear, hydro-electric power, and renewables are used for generating electricity.

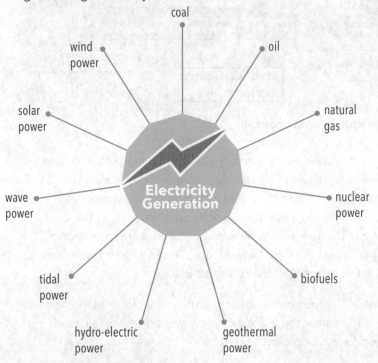

INFORMATION BOX

Definitions of energy terms

Alternative energy source:
Energy source to replace fossil fuel use

Renewable energy source:
Energy resource that is replaced naturally, so that it never runs out

Sustainable energy source:
Energy source that can be used for a long time; the environment or resource on which it depends is not being used up

FIGURE 2.7   Energy resources used for generating electricity

At present electricity is of limited use for transport. Trains and trams are the main users, although some believe that electric cars will be the transport of the future. What electricity is most important for is lighting and for operating machinery.

Non-renewable energy sources and electricity generation ■

Thermal (coal, oil and gas) and nuclear (uranium) are non-renewable resources used to generate electricity. They are not inexhaustible. In use, electricity is clean energy. However, making electricity using fossil fuels, and coal in particular, is a dirty business. It is a major cause of air pollution. How does Figure 2.8 show this?

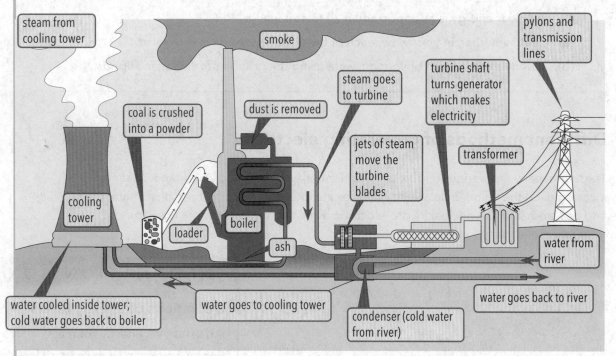

FIGURE 2.8   Coal-fired power station–how electricity is made from coal

The process for making electricity is the same as shown in Figure 2.8, whatever fuel source is used to heat water and make steam in the boiler. Coal use in power stations is more widespread than oil and natural gas, especially in countries with large coal deposits like China, India, and the USA. The use of oil is most likely in oil-rich countries such as the Gulf States. Natural gas use is increasing in Europe, where environmental concerns are strong, mainly because it gives off fewer pollutants than coal when burnt. Among the biofuels, wood pellets, waste, and biogas can be burnt instead of one of the fossil fuels.

Nuclear power is produced by 'fission'. At the centre of each atom is a nucleus; as an atom is split using the metal uranium in a nuclear reactor, a great deal of heat energy is released. Heat from this reaction is harnessed for making electricity.

One way of doing this is shown in Figure 2.9. A gas takes the heat from the reactor to the boiler, where water is turned into steam. The steam is used to drive the turbines, which work the generators and make electricity. The radiation shield around the reactor is made of concrete and is up to four metres thick to protect workers from the dangerous radiation.

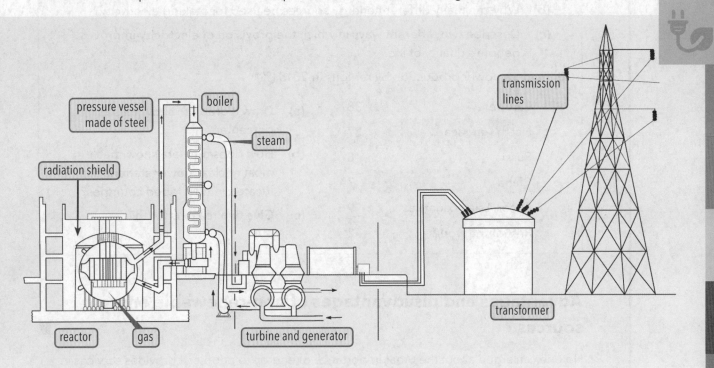

FIGURE 2.9   How electricity is made in a gas-cooled nuclear reactor—what is similar to electricity production using fossil fuels instead of uranium? What is different?

Although nuclear power only contributes between four and five per cent of the world's commercial energy consumption, in a few countries it is the main way of making electricity. France is the prime example; the country's lack of fossil resources encouraged its early take-up and widespread use (Table 2.2).

TABLE 2.2   Nuclear power, 2015: the world's top five producers

	Country	m tonnes of oil equivalent	Comment
1	USA	190	Big economy, huge demand for power
2	France	99	No coal left, very little oil and gas
3	Russia	44	Developed when it was the USSR
4	China	38	Growing economy, huge demand for power
5	South Korea	37	Rapid economic growth, has no oil or gas

ACTIVITIES

1 (a) Describe how electricity is made, whatever energy source is used.

   (b) Why can many different energy sources be used for making electricity?

   (c) Describe two different ways in which the provision of electricity improves people's quality of life.

2 Nuclear power production by regions in 2015 (%)

Europe	38
North America	37
Russia	8
China	7
Other Asian countries	9
Rest of the world	2

   (a) Draw a graph to show these percentages.

   (b) How does the data show that most nuclear power stations are located in developed countries?

   (c) Give two reasons for this.

Advantages and disadvantages of non-renewable energy sources

No one can argue about the great importance of energy to people. It provides services in the home, such as lighting, refrigeration, and heating, which improve people's quality of life (social advantages). It is vital for the economic development of countries; energy is needed to power machinery for industrial production (economic advantages). Machines are increasingly doing the work that people had always done in farming. The transport revolution allows local, national, and international movement of people and goods (social and economic advantages).

Definitions useful for exam questions which ask for **advantages** and **disadvantages, impacts,** and **effects**

EXAM TIP

Social—about people (relationships, quality of life, standard of living, way of life)

Economic—about money and income (wealth, activities which generate income)

Environmental—about the natural world (air, water, land, and sea) and its plants and wildlife (both on land and in the sea)

Human ingenuity developed the new machines, but this was only possible because **fossil fuels** were available to power them. The unfortunate thing about fossil fuels is that they cause environmental problems at every stage—from mining, to transportation, to use (Table 2.3).

TABLE 2.3 Fossil fuels–a summary of environmental problems

Mining	■ Opencast mining leaves great scars on the landscape. ■ Both opencast and deep mining produce surface waste heaps. ■ Some oil drilling takes places in environmentally sensitive areas. ■ There is an ever present risk of oil spills (e.g. Gulf of Mexico).
Transportation	■ Pipelines break and oil seeps into the ground, causing land pollution. ■ Tankers crash or sink in coastal areas and leak thick black oil, killing animal and plant life and covering tourist beaches (e.g. Tasman Spirit disaster in 2003).
Use	■ Burning fossil fuels (in power stations, factories, cars and trucks, etc.) causes air pollution; city dwellers in particular are exposed to dirty air. ■ Coal-fired power stations are the main cause of acid rain, which devastates forests and acidifies lakes to the point where aquatic life disappears. ■ Carbon released into the atmosphere when fossil fuels are burnt increases greenhouse gas concentrations and the threat of global warming. ■ Possible environmental effects of global warming include rising sea levels, flooding of low-lying coasts, land loss, increase in intensity and frequency of climatic hazards, upsetting the natural balance in ecosystems.

INFORMATION BOX

Hole in the ozone layer
- Fossil fuels do **not** cause ozone depletion.
- CFCs, **not** fossil fuels, cause and add to the ozone hole.
- Blaming fossil fuels for causing the ozone hole is one of the most common **mistakes** made by students in Environmental Management exams.

See Chapter 7, pages 205–208 for information about the ozone hole.

We don't contribute to global warming
We don't contribute to ozone depletion
We don't cause acid rain

Are we the friends of the Earth?

Nuclear power was seen by some in the 1960s and 1970s to be the clean power of the future. One nuclear power company made the following claim in its advertisement.

This advertisement focuses upon how much cleaner, and therefore how much more environmentally friendly, nuclear power is than fossil fuels. This is true. However, what the advertisement does not mention are the dangers to all forms of life from the radiation that is released during the nuclear process. Humans exposed to higher than average levels of radiation develop cancers and leukaemia. Waste is produced, which remains radioactive, and therefore dangerous to people and animal life, for thousands of years. No completely safe way has yet been found to dispose of this waste.

Scientists have repeatedly emphasized how safe nuclear power is, but they have not been able to convince most people of this. Public confidence in nuclear power was shattered by the great explosion in 1986, at Chernobyl in Ukraine (then part of the old Soviet Union), when one of its four nuclear reactors exploded. This killed workers, caused cancers in people living near the plant, and created a highly radioactive zone in the area around the works, making it unsafe for people to live there for hundreds of years. The nuclear fallout forced tens of thousands to leave their homes, never to return.

INFORMATION BOX

Nuclear reactors opened before and after Chernobyl

- In the 30 years before—over 400 opened (409)
- In the 30 years after—under 200 opened (194)

Some were just beginning to forget the dangers when the disaster at Fukushima in Japan happened in March 2011. A very strong earthquake out at sea caused a giant tsunami wave which smashed against the power station, flooded it with sea water, and triggered a triple meltdown at the Fukushima Daiichi nuclear power station—a freak event for which Japan's nuclear industry was not well prepared.

FIGURE 2.10   The Fukushima Daiichi Nuclear Power Plant after the March 2011 earthquake and tsunami

160,000 people fled from the zone of high radiation around the station. Until this disaster, one third of Japan's electricity was produced by nuclear power. Following the disaster, the government of Japan stopped all nuclear production.

There have been knock-on effects. In the wake of Fukushima, the German government examined their own nuclear future; it decided to speed up plans to close all its old nuclear power stations, and not to build any new ones to replace them. Instead, Germany has committed its future to renewables.

ACTIVITIES

1 One student's assessment of nuclear power is given below:

Renewable	✗
Does not emit carbon-dioxide	✓
No air pollution	✓
No local environmental problems	?
Safe	✓
Cheap	✗
Known technology	✓
Low level technology suitable for developing countries	✗
Always available because it does not rely on the weather	✓

(a) Suggest why this student could not decide how to answer the question about local environmental problems for nuclear power.

(b) Comment on what the assessment shows for nuclear power.

(c) State two pieces of evidence which show that nuclear power is not seen as the power of the future by many governments and people.

2 (a) Do your own assessment for a fossil fuel, such as coal, using the same headings as for nuclear power.

(b) Comment on what the assessment shows for using fossil fuels.

3 Look at Figure 2.20 on page 48. Draw two spider diagrams like those to show the advantages and disadvantages of using fossil fuels.

4 Look at the two power stations in Figures 2.8 and 2.9. Which one is cleaner and more environmentally friendly? Explain your answer as fully as you can.

OXFORD
UNIVERSITY PRESS

environmental management

Renewable energy sources and electricity generation

Hydro-electric power (HEP) is different from the non-renewables because no fuel is used. Instead, fast-running water drives the turbines that work the generators and produce electricity. The greater the force and amount of water, the greater the amount of electricity produced. However, certain favourable physical conditions are essential. These include:

- fast-flowing water (for example, a waterfall)
- high rainfall (preferably well distributed during the year)
- a natural water store (such as a lake)
- a narrow, deep-sided valley suitable for building a dam (to make a reservoir)

Countries without high mountains, or big rivers, or high rainfall cannot generate HEP.

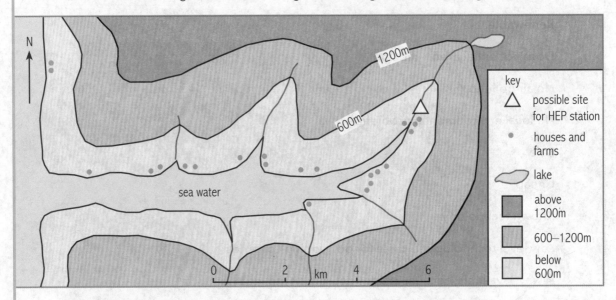

FIGURE 2.11 An area in southern Norway with favourable physical features for generating HEP
What other information about the area does a company need before it decides whether to build a HEP power station here?

Once up and running, it is one of the cheapest ways of producing electricity. The natural flow of water allows continuous generation of electricity without any pollution. Because the water is neither consumed nor contaminated to produce HEP, it can be used downstream for other purposes such as for drinking and irrigation.

Many problems and disadvantages are, however, associated with setting up a hydro-electric power station. A dam is often needed to store water in order to guarantee a year-round water supply. Possible problems are economic, environmental, and social.

- Large dams are expensive; developing countries may get into debt.
- The best physical conditions are often remote from places where people live; long distance power lines need to be built.
- Forests and other types of natural vegetation are affected and destroyed, as also are wildlife habitats.
- People already living in the valley that is going to be flooded are forced to move into new settlements.

The larger the dam, the greater the possible environmental and social problems. The Three Gorges Dam in China (Chapter 4, page 123) illustrates this well.

Like hydroelectricity, **geothermal power** makes use of a natural source for its generation. This time heat from the ground is used. In Iceland, as in many other volcanic areas, there are many hot springs and steaming geysers on the surface, as well as pools of hot water under the surface lava fields. Holes are bored deep into the ground to allow steam to reach the surface, where it is taken through pipes to a power station. The steam turns the turbines, which generate electricity, just as in all other types of power stations.

Dig deep enough anywhere into the Earth's crust and there is heat. However, at present it is only economic to use this heat for geothermal power where it is at or near the surface. This restricts geothermal production to areas of present or recent volcanic activity, such as New Zealand and Kenya.

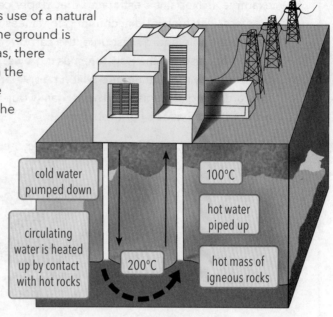

FIGURE 2.12   How a geothermal power station works

ACTIVITIES

1 (a)   Look at Figure 2.11. Give reasons why point △ seems to be a good site for the location of a HEP station.

   (b)   Figure 2.13 below shows the climate in southern Norway.

          Describe the features of its climate which are favourable for the generation of HEP.

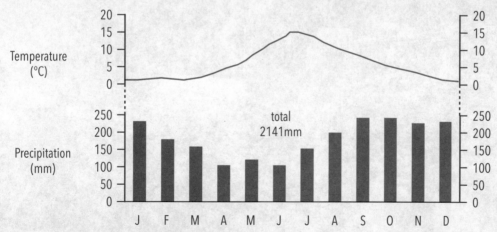

FIGURE 2.13   Climate for a weather station in southern Norway

2 (a)   Do your own assessment of geothermal power, as in Activity 1 on page 39.

   (b)   Comment on what your assessment shows.

Biofuels include wood, biogas, and bioethanol. There is nothing new about power from biomass; in rural areas of developing countries fuelwood is the main energy source. For example, in Nepal it is estimated that 90 per cent or more of the energy used is from biomass, with fuelwood accounting for at least three quarters (Figure 2.14). Biomass should be a renewable energy resource; the carbon released into the atmosphere when it is burnt should be offset by the new forest as it grows, since it uses carbon from the atmosphere. Unfortunately, more than one billion people are consuming fuelwood resources faster than they are being replenished. This is mainly due to population pressure. In parts of Africa, drought also makes a contribution.

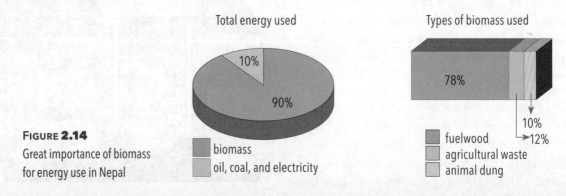

FIGURE 2.14
Great importance of biomass for energy use in Nepal

FIGURE 2.15 Drax power station in the UK

The use of biomass for making electricity is largely confined to a few developed world countries. Environmental groups such as WWF (World Wildlife Fund for Nature) have thought that for many years biomass has been overlooked by developed countries as a renewable source of electricity. The big advantage of biomass over wind and solar energy is that it can be stored and used when needed.

It does take a larger amount of wood pellets to produce the same amount of energy as coal, but the carbon footprint of the biomass is far less. When coal is burnt, it is stored carbon from millions of years that is being added to the atmosphere today, producing a net increase in carbon. On the other hand, if the forest is being well managed so that every tree cut is replaced, carbon released by burning biomass is being offset by new tree growth taking carbon from the atmosphere.

Look at Figure 2.15: the emissions from the cooling towers are harmless steam. The pollution is from the oxides of nitrogen and sulphur dioxide coming out of the tall chimney near one of the towers.

Example: Drax power station in the UK

Time line

1986: Completed; coal fired using coal from nearby coalfields; the UK's largest thermal power station, producing 7% of its electricity. Its large size also meant that it was the UK's largest emitter of CO_2.

1995: Flue gas desulphurization equipment was fitted; this was expensive technology to reduce harmful SO_2 emissions.

2004: Began converting some of the six units from coal to biomass, using mainly wood pellets from sustainably managed forests in the USA; economically it was helped by government subsidies for renewables.

2012: Three of the six units now being converted to biomass; once complete, Drax will be using 1.5 times of the UK's total wood production each year.

2015: Question marks over its future; UK government renewable subsidies have been greatly reduced; government policy is to phase out coal-fired power stations (too dirty and the government has international CO_2 emissions targets to meet).

Comment
Power stations using wood emit more carbon than those burning coal, but this is ignored in carbon emission calculations because, unlike coal, trees will grow back and absorb carbon over their growth life; more carbon is used by young trees than old ones. Biomass in the UK costs more to buy than coal.

Another way to produce electricity from biomass is by burning waste (see Figure 2.28, page 58). Otherwise, biofuels in liquid form, made from crops, are mainly used directly for transport. They are obtained either from vegetable oils (methyl esters) for use in diesel engines, or from fermented and distilled products of crops such as corn and sugar cane (ethanol) for use in petrol engines. The country which pioneered the use of these as early as 1975 was Brazil. It seemed to be a mineral-rich country without oil—that was until the quite recent massive discoveries of offshore oil in the south-east.

OXFORD
UNIVERSITY PRESS

There are some issues about biofuels such as:

- Should land that could be used to feed people be used to provide raw materials for biofuels instead?
- Will this cause food shortages?
- Will it increase food prices?
- Will biofuels limit the demand for fossil fuels, helping to stop increases in fuel price?

ACTIVITIES

1 (a) Make two columns. List the advantages and disadvantages of biofuels as energy sources.

(b) Which is the stronger: advantages or disadvantages? Explain your choice.

2 Look at the example of the Drax power station in the UK.

(a) (i) Identify two changes made at Drax since the power station began generating electricity.

(ii) Suggest reasons why they were made.

(b) In 2015 there were rumours that the power station could soon be closed, even though it generates so much electricity. Suggest reasons why this might happen.

The commercial importance of **wind power**, **solar power**, **tidal power**, and **wave power** is on the increase. This is shown in Figure 2.7, where they are included under the heading 'Renewables', even if their overall contribution to total world energy consumption is still small.

Two of them, wind and solar, are now in widespread use. It is increasingly likely that you will have seen wind turbines and solar panels in your home area (Figure 2.16). Tidal and wave are more specialized, and restricted to certain areas where physical conditions are suitable, just like hydro and geothermal.

The modern **wind turbine** stands over 30m high and has blades made out of fibreglass, 35m or more across (Figure 2.16). Where several turbines are placed together, they make what is called a 'wind farm'. Locations are chosen where strong winds are most frequent, such as

- on hill tops and other areas of open high ground;
- onshore, next to the coast on land;
- offshore, in the sea but close to the coast.

Solar panels

Wind turbines

FIGURE 2.16 Solar panels and wind turbines

Wind turbines like those shown in Figure 2.16 are now a common sight in some European countries such as Denmark, Germany, Spain, and the UK, where average wind speeds associated with the prevailing westerly winds are high.

Although the cost of setting up a wind farm is high, wind turbine technology has been developed to a point where land turbines in some favourable locations can produce electricity more cheaply than by using fossil fuels. What is more, this is a pollution-free way of making electricity. Turbines take up little land and the spaces between them can still be used for farming.

The downside is that many turbines are needed to produce the same output as one coal- or gas-fired power station. On calm days, no power is produced, which means that other power stations must be kept open to take over on days without strong winds. People living close by complain about noise and spoiling the view. Some consider large groups of turbines to be eyesores.

Solar panels and photovoltaic cells (PVs) (Figure 2.16) absorb sunlight and generate heat. This can be used either directly for heating water or indirectly for making electricity. For a time, solar power was much more expensive than wind power, but research and development have allowed the costs of photovoltaic cells to fall. In 2016, solar panels in Europe were 80% cheaper than five years ago. China, the main manufacturer of PVs, greatly reduced prices in 2014, leading to a surge in use worldwide (in both developed and developing countries).

Tidal power, unlike hydro, wind, and solar power, can be guaranteed. Every day coastal areas experience two high and two low tides. Tidal power works on the simple principle that sea water, by flowing in and out all the time, can drive a turbine to make electricity. In order to harness the energy of the tides, a dam or barrage must be built across an estuary with spaces in it, through which the water of the tides is funnelled. The turbines to generate electricity are placed here (Figure 2.17).

The cost of building dams across river estuaries is enormous. To make the project economically viable there needs to be a big tidal range—a great difference in height between water levels at high and low tide.

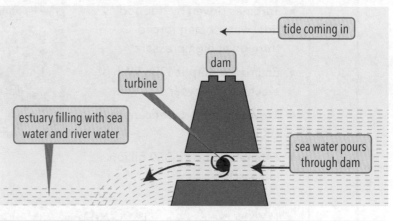

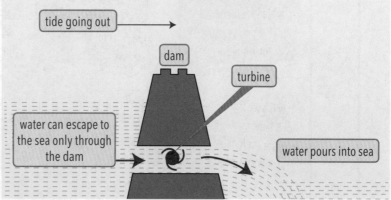

FIGURE 2.17 How the tides can be used to generate electricity (side view)

The world's first tidal power station was built across the Rance estuary in northern France. Similar high tidal ranges are found in estuaries such as the River Severn in south-west England. For many years, a scheme to dam this estuary has been proposed, but not acted upon. Why? The cost was high, but could be afforded. And it would provide a lot of electricity, upto six per cent of the UK's needs. The main issues have been environmental. Many are worried about the dam's possible effects on water flows, currents, and wildlife. These are difficult to predict accurately. Others say that the opportunity to make use of the great potential for tidal power around the coasts of the UK is being wasted. Not only is it carbon free, but also reliable (not intermittent like other renewable sources dependent on the weather).

INFORMATION BOX

Severn Estuary Tidal Power Scheme

- Tidal range 14 metres (second highest in the world)
- 10 mile (16km) long dam needed
- Open and close sluice gates in the dam with over 200 turbines
- Turbines driven by trapped tidal water being forced through at high pressure
- Estimated output 17bn kWh of electricity per year
- Providing for 5-6 per cent of UK needs
- Estimated cost US$30 billion (at least)

This scheme is in the right place for tides, but the wrong place for the environment.

Mudflats at low tide, which are great feeding grounds for birds, will be lost.

Better to build four or five smaller tidal schemes such as across Swansea Bay instead of one big one.

Interfering with natural water flows will increase coastal erosion in some locations and silt deposition in others.

It will have the output of 8 large coal-fired power stations, or 3 nuclear stations.

It will cut the UK's carbon emissions by 16bn tonnes per year compared with using coal.

The UK government needs an energy mix, and tidal is new and different.

FIGURE 2.18 Arguments for and against building a barrage (dam) across the Severn Estuary for tidal power

Wave power is electrical energy generated by wave movement. It is still in the early stages. Several companies in Europe are engaged in research to discover a reliable method to harness the great potential of big Atlantic waves reaching the coast of Western Europe. Many of the machines being tested look like giant worms floating on the sea surface (Figure 2.19). The electricity is generated by wave (water) movement. By 2016, some have been shown to work on a small scale. The research goal is to develop wave machines capable of generating sufficiently large amounts of electricity to make them commercially viable (companies can make a profit).

Until then, wave power remains largely a potential source of power. Perhaps in 2017 it is at the point where solar power was 20 or 30 years ago.

FIGURE 2.19   Experimental machine for using wave energy

ACTIVITIES

1   Show that you understand the difference in meaning between each of the following pairs of terms:

   (a)   renewable and non-renewable;

   (b)   sustainable and finite;

   (c)   fossil fuels and alternative energy sources.

2   At present, wind and solar power are more important sources of energy than tidal and wave power. Give as many reasons for this as you can.

3   Many of the world's poorest countries are located in the Tropics. Explain why solar power offers the best hope for electricity for people living in remote rural areas.

4   **(a)**   In two columns, list the arguments for and against building a large tidal power station like the one proposed for the Severn estuary.

   (b)   In your view, should the UK government go ahead and build the Severn Tidal Power Station? Explain your choice.

Advantages and disadvantages of renewables for electricity generation

These are summarized in Figure 2.20.

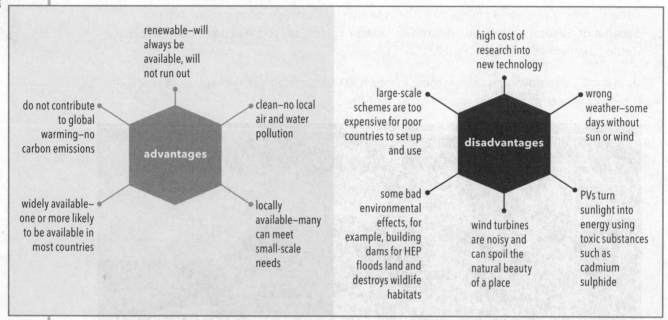

FIGURE 2.20 Advantages and disadvantages of renewable energy sources

The two biggest **advantages** of renewables compared with fossil fuels are:

- they will last forever (sustainable);
- they are clean (non-polluting).

This is why environmentalists are always expressing their disappointment at how slowly countries are changing from using fossil fuels towards renewable alternatives. Why has it been so slow? The main reasons are that fossil fuels have been used for a long time, they are easy to use, and everyone is used to using them. They are also cheap. When oil prices rise, this merely encourages the big companies to look for new deposits of oil and gas. The era of high oil prices (around US$100 per barrel) between 2011 and 2014 encouraged further oil exploration into environmentally sensitive areas like the Arctic, as well as by **fracking** (Figure 2.29, page 60).

Therefore, although known deposits of oil and gas are finite (look again at Figure 2.2 page 28), when the price is high, more will be searched for and discovered. At the same time improved technology is allowing resources located in areas previously considered too difficult, such as the cold Arctic or deep ocean waters, to be exploited. It is the same with fracking. This means that oil and gas are not going to lose their world energy dominance anytime soon, even though interest in renewables will keep on increasing. And there are some examples of dramatic changes, which perhaps give a glimpse of the future (Figure 2.21).

Use of renewables is on the increase.

Developed World

Portugal-electricity production (%)		
Type	2013	2016
Fossil fuels	50	25
Nuclear	27	27
Renewables	23	48
(hydro, wind, solar)		

Denmark

2015-Denmark produced 42% of its energy from wind turbines, the highest percentage in the world.

2 September, 2015-no fossil fuel power stations were switched on; all power came from solar cells, wind turbines, heat, and power plants using local and imported waste.

Developing world

Morocco	
Noor 1-a sea of solar mirrors near Ouarzazarte in the Sahara Desert	
Opened	2016
Cost	$709m
Power output	160MW (megawatts)
Cost of power production	$0.19/kWh
Comment	Almost as cheap as fossil fuels
Unique feature	Molten sand underneath can store energy for up to 8 hours.

Kenya	
Geothermal hot spot	
Source	Underground water at 300°C where the Earth's crust is thin on the side of Africa's Great Rift Valley
Output	609MW after new plants opened in 2015, the world's fifth largest geothermal producer
Potential	Estimated 10,000MW
Comment	The geothermal plants run on a 24-hour basis, 365 days a year.

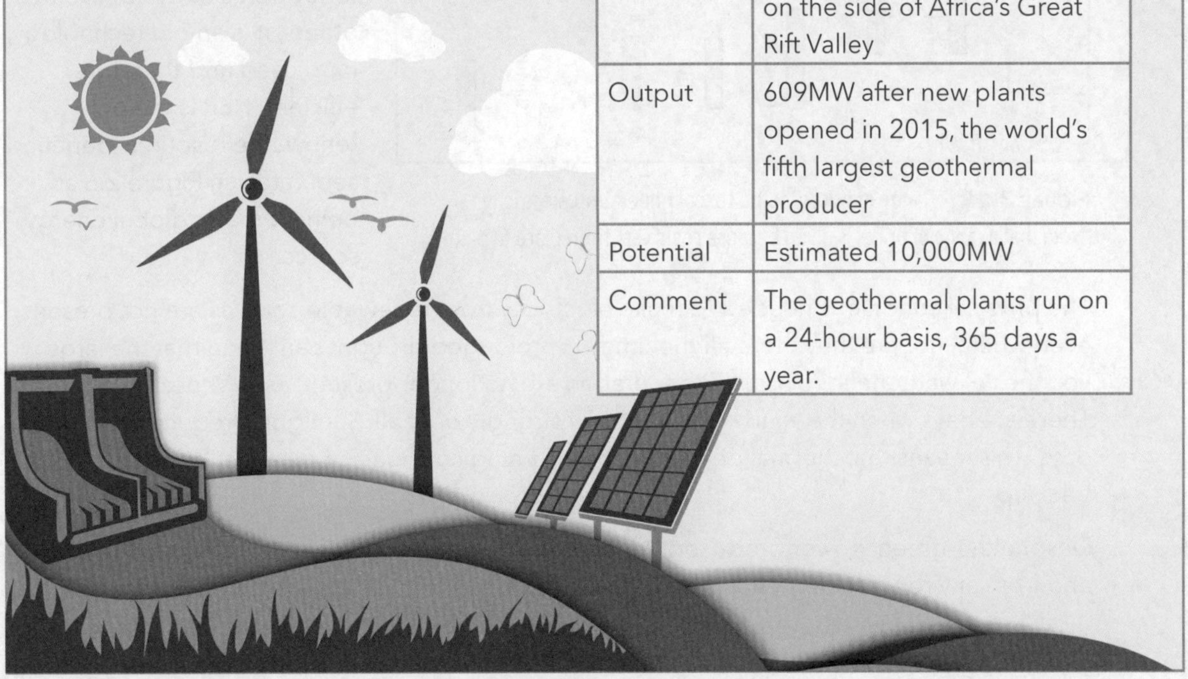

FIGURE **2.21**   Use of renewables is on the increase.

So what is holding back the greater use of renewables, even at a time when more and more people are aware of, and concerned about, the environmental damage fossil fuels are causing? The two biggest disadvantages of renewables compared with fossil fuels are:

- high cost (more expensive to set up and operate);
- most are intermittent (only produce full power from time to time)

Research is a gamble. New technology is expensive to develop and all the money spent can be lost. Finding the technology to harness wave power is proving particularly difficult. Of course, once a new technology is shown to succeed, costs of production can drop quickly with more widespread use and higher demand. In some favourable locations in Europe, electricity produced from wind turbines and solar panels is now almost cost competitive with that from fossil fuels. However, this stage was only reached because of generous government subsidies (in Germany, the UK, Spain, etc.) in response to environmental concerns and EU targets limiting carbon dioxide emissions.

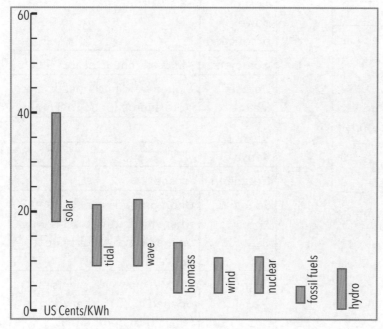

Trying to compare costs of electricity production between fossil fuels and renewables, and between different renewables, is notoriously difficult. World oil prices fluctuate greatly, while physical conditions for renewable production vary between locations. Undoubtedly, HEP gives us the cheapest energy from renewables. Why? Unlike the others, it is an old technology, long used and therefore efficient. HEP is the only renewable resource identified separately in Figure 2.6 as being a major global energy source.

FIGURE 2.22 Range of prices for the cost of generating electricity. [Note that a range of prices is given because costs vary from place to place.]

The physical conditions needed to make electricity from renewable sources are not present everywhere, nor are they there all the time. A prolonged drought can mean that the large volumes of water needed for HEP generation are no longer present, as in Venezuela in 2016. There are days when the wind does not blow strongly or at all. Sunlight is reduced on cloudy days. This means that thermal power stations burning coal, gas, or oil are still needed as back-ups.

Despite the 'green' power produced, renewables can still arouse opposition from the public and from environmental groups due to

- habitat losses from dam and reservoir construction,
- loss of scenic beauty with wind farms,
- use of toxic substances such as cadmium sulphide in making PVs.

Much of the electricity generation from renewables is small scale. This gives them the big advantage that they can be local. This is most valuable in rural areas of developing countries, where the grid infrastructure is unaffordable. A small dam, or a few wind turbines, or a cluster of PVs may be able to generate enough electricity for village or small town needs, and lead to great improvements in quality of life for the inhabitants.

ACTIVITIES

1 (a) Two big disadvantages of renewable sources of energy are high cost and intermittent output. State the evidence from Figure 2.20 which supports this statement.

   (b) Is it possible to have energy from renewable sources, which is not intermittent? Explain your answer.

2 Look at Figure 2.22.

   (a) Describe what the graph shows about the cost of power from renewables compared with fossil fuels.

   (b) Does the graph suggest that fossil fuels are going to continue to dominate energy production for many more years? Explain your views on this.

3 Study the views and comments about wind power in the UK in Figure 2.23.

> Prevailing westerly winds bring the best wind resources in Europe to the UK.
> **Weather forecaster**

> We now know that migrating birds are hit by the rotating blades of wind turbines.
> **Bird Protection Society**

> Wind turbines generate so little energy compared with the landscape damage they cause.
> **Wind farm objector**

> If we are serious about tackling climate change, we must look at renewables, and wind is one of them.
> **Government Energy Department**

> 80% of the UK people are in favour of wind power.
> **Opinion Poll Survey**

> Even if we covered the whole of the UK with turbines, we could not close a single nuclear or fossil fuel power station.
> **Economic advisor**

FIGURE 2.23 Comments about wind power and wind farms from people and organizations in the UK

   (a) State the arguments in favour of the greater use of wind power in the UK.

   (b) How strong are the arguments against the use of wind power in the UK? Explain your view on this.

4 Are renewable sources of energy being used in your home country?

   If yes, name them, and explain where and why they are being used.

   If no, explain why they are not being used.

EXAM TIP

It is good practice to refer to actual / specific examples in your answers in examinations to illustrate general points you are making, even when not directly asked for by the question.

Brief references are all that is needed, unlike in case study answers, in which much more detail is expected; but you still need to give details that are precise.

Here are some short examples which might be useful in answers to questions about renewable energy sources.

Remember also to use examples from your home country, whenever possible, to illustrate your answers.

A Venezuela–over-dependent on HEP for its electricity

April 2016: great shortage of electricity, leading to daily cuts (outages) and compulsory closures of places of work. Over 60% of the electricity is from HEP. There was winter drought blamed on El Niño. Water levels behind the Guri Dam, which alone produces 44% of the country's electricity, were in danger of becoming too low to spin the dam's turbines.

B Iceland–is it the world's most green country?

The only country in the world with 100% of electricity from renewables:

87% hydro from its glaciated mountainous interior, helped by its wet climate

13% geothermal from its 26 high-temperature geothermal fields; it has more than 600 hot springs.

Also 100% of the heating of water and space (inside buildings) is geothermal. Fossil fuels are only used for transport and as power supply back-up.

C Freiburg (South Germany)–is it Europe's most green city?

'Green' transport

Over 400km of planned cycle ways

70% of people live within 500m of a tram stop

Car use in the city fell from 38% of journeys in 1982 to 29% in 2016

Energy saving

New building design standards add 3% to the cost of a house, but reduce energy consumption by 50%.

Use of renewables

Solar: over 400 photovoltaic sites on public and private buildings

Biomass: use of waste wood chips from the Black Forest woodworking industries

Biogas (methane): organic household and industrial wastes are fed into a digester to produce electricity

Energy demand

The message from Figure 2.24 is clear. World energy consumption has increased massively over the years, and is still increasing.

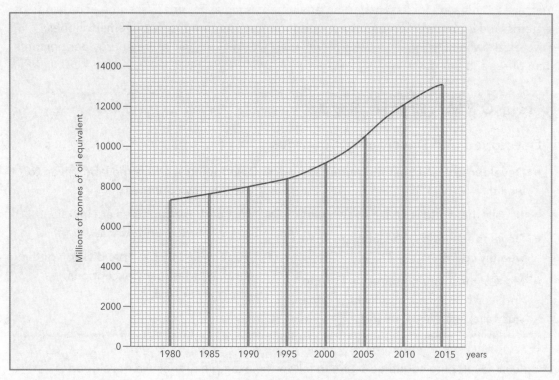

FIGURE 2.24   World commercial energy consumption, 1980-2015

There are three basic reasons for increasing world energy demand:

■ growing world population, increasing domestic and industrial demand;
■ higher levels of economic development, accompanied by increased personal wealth;
■ advances in transport technology (private cars, trucks, aeroplanes, container ships, and supertankers).

The **total world population** has increased progressively over the centuries. What is noticeable is how growth has speeded up, especially during the second half of the twentieth century (see Chapter 8, pages 224–240). It took almost 100 years for the world's population to double from one to two billion, but then it doubled again from two to four billion in less than 50 years. Today there are over seven billion people in world consuming energy. Population growth has not stopped. By 2050 the estimate is that the world population will be above nine billion.

Higher levels of economic development date back to 1750 and the coal-fired Industrial Revolution. Although it began in the UK, knowledge of the Industrial Revolution soon spread to Europe, then North America, and now many other parts of the world. In the last 50 years some of the fastest, and most impressive, rates of economic development have been in Asia. During the last 100 years the number, variety, and diversity of manufactured goods has increased dramatically. Many are made for individuals to buy to improve the quality of their lives; there has been a Consumer Revolution as well.

As **personal wealth** has increased, first in countries of the developed world, and now increasingly in countries of the developing world, people have sought an improved standard of living. Homes in the developed world are full of electrical and electronic goods. Some of these goods do jobs formerly done by hand, such as food processors and washing machines; others are for leisure and entertainment, such as PlasmaTVs, home entertainment systems, and for knowledge and communication, such as computers and smartphones. Private car ownership increases with more family wealth. Cars use more energy per person than buses and trains.

INFORMATION BOX

Developed and Developing Countries

- Development is almost the same as wealth.

- Usually the world is split into two parts.

- **Developed world** is the label given to wealthy countries.

- Most of these are countries in Europe and North America, and include Japan, Australia, and New Zealand.

- **Developing world** is the label given to less wealthy countries.

- Most of these countries are in Asia, South America, and Africa.

- The term is only a simple division of the world. It hides many exceptions, especially in Asia.

People in developing countries aspire to follow the example of those in developed countries. Once a home is linked up to an electricity supply, the minimum needs besides light fixtures and fans are a TV and a fridge. In those Asian countries that have experienced rapid economic development since the 1970s, homes, factories, offices, and transport are consuming more and more energy. China (1.35 billion people) and India (1.3 billion people), the world's population giants, have also experienced high rates of economic growth.

ACTIVITIES

1   Describe what Figure 2.24 shows about world energy consumption since 1980.

2   (a)   Using Figure 8.3, Chapter 8, page 225, make a list of the number of years needed for world population to grow by one billion (1-2 billion, 2-3 billion, etc.).

    (b)   Explain the relationship between world population growth and increased world energy consumption.

3   Look at Figure 2.25. Answer the three questions below sketches A and B.

OXFORD
UNIVERSITY PRESS

FIGURE 2.25 Building sites, past (A) and present (B): How have the sources of power changed? Why has it been possible? What are the consequences for world energy use?

Factors affecting variations in energy demand

Energy use per head is regarded as a reliable indicator of a country's level of economic development. More people in richer countries can afford cars and electrical and electronic goods than those in poorer countries. Their personal wealth is higher. However, remember that not everyone within a developed country is rich, nor are all people in a developing country poor. But in general, a farmer and his family living in a village without electricity have a low energy demand. At the same time, their quality of life is low.

In all developed countries, demands for energy are high from well-developed manufacturing and service sectors, high levels of transport, and many movements of goods and people (for both work and leisure). In Canada and the USA, consumption of energy per person is double that in Europe. The **climate** helps to explain this. Many places in North America experience huge seasonal differences in weather, between very cold winters (much heating needed) and very hot summers (air conditioning considered a necessity). Seasonal variations in temperature in Europe are less extreme. Likewise, in oil-rich Gulf States such as the UAE and Qatar, energy use per head is amongst the highest in the world. Only air conditioning, a massive user of energy, makes modern living bearable in the desert in summer, with daily temperatures always above 40°C. Lack of rain means that much of the fresh water is obtained from sea water by desalination, another process for which is much energy is needed.

ACTIVITIES

1 From the text above on variations in Energy Demand, make notes for how energy demand is affected by these factors named in the syllabus:

   (a) domestic demand; (b) industrial demand; (c) transport; (d) personal wealth; (e) national (country) wealth; (f) climate.

2 (a) What kinds of fuel and power do you use at home, and for what purposes?

   (b) Do you think that you and your family use more or less power than others living in the same city or area as you? Explain your answer.

3 (a) Briefly describe the climate in the area where you live.

   (b) Explain how the climate affects you and your family's energy demand.

Conservation and management of energy resources

Many of the strategies needed for the conservation and management of energy resources are the same as those already described in Chapter 1 for conserving rock and mineral resources (page 24). **Reduce, reuse,** and **recycle** apply here as well.

Reduced energy consumption can be achieved in a variety of ways. One of these is by R & D (research and development). Makers of car and aircraft engines, for example, keep searching for increased efficiency that allows more power to be produced from lower energy consumption. This allows more kilometres to be travelled for every litre of fuel used. Since car and aircraft use is increasing everywhere, and since most car owners are unwilling to give up their cars or stop travelling to other countries, the only way is to make car and aircraft engines more energy efficient and cleaner. Figure 2.26 shows that cars built since 2000 in Europe can be up to 90 per cent cleaner than older ones, while travelling up to 50 per cent further. The big breakthrough came around 2000 with the use of catalytic convertors, highly successful in reducing emissions of pollutants such as oxides of nitrogen, carbon monoxide, and hydrocarbons. What would you expect to have changed since 2000?

Individuals as well as manufacturers can also make a big difference. Lights and machines can be switched off when not in use. Energy efficient light bulbs can be used. In the cool climates of Europe and North America, householders are urged to place layers of insulation in the loft space below the roof so that less heat from the home is lost during winter. Other measures widely used to stop heat loss from housing are double glazing of windows and cavity wall infilling between the bricks to reduce heat loss through the walls. Likewise in hot countries, homes and flat-roofed buildings use insulation or light-coloured paint on the roofs and walls to deflect the Sun's rays and reduce heat by conduction.

In developed countries there is increasing pressure on companies to go green by installing energy efficient lighting, heating, and air conditioning systems. In well-designed supermarkets in Europe, heat given out by freezers and fridges is fed into offices and other parts of the store that need heating. This is an example of recycling heat and saving energy. A few hotels advertise themselves as 'green hotels'. Few do better than the Hotel Victoria in Freiburg, Germany, which tries to be CO_2 free (Figure 2.27).

	1987	2000
Amount of pollution		
Number of cars making this amount of pollution		
Kilometres per litre for a small car	9	13

FIGURE 2.26 Cleaner and more energy efficient cars in Europe in 2000

FIGURE 2.27 Hotel Victoria–a 'green hotel'; note the wind turbines and solar panels.

OXFORD
UNIVERSITY PRESS

Also in Freiburg, the city authorities sponsor a 'Green Transport' policy (Exam Tip, page 52). They want as many people as possible to walk, cycle, or use public transport to travel to work, school, or the shops. The only hope of persuading people to leave their cars at home is by providing a network of safe footpaths and cycle ways, and a cheap, clean, and efficient public transport system of buses, trams, and trains.

Recycling and **re-use** as ideas for saving natural resources are not new. In recent years burning waste to make electricity and to heat buildings has increased (Figure 2.28). Instead of tipping the waste collected in the city into a landfill site, which has many environmental drawbacks (Figure 1.19, page 20), it can be incinerated. Heat from burning the waste in an incinerator makes steam, which can be harnessed to drive a turbine to generate electricity. The hot water produced by this process can have a second use: it can be piped to houses, shops, offices, and public buildings to benefit people in the nearby city which produced the waste. This saves on fossil fuel use.

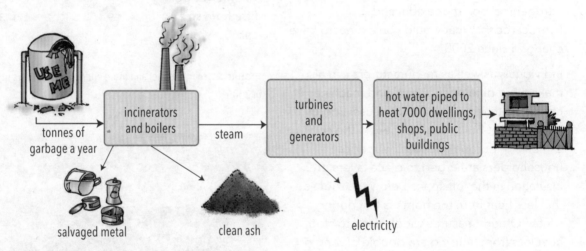

FIGURE 2.28 Electricity and heat produced from burning garbage

SUMMARY COMMENT

Renewables

- Change from fossil fuels to renewables has been slow.

- But it is persistent and will continue.

- Everyone is waiting for the next big technological breakthrough.

- What will it be? Who knows?

- One suggestion is cheap, light, long-life batteries.

- What great problem with renewables will that solve?

Another way of making power from recycling is to collect waste oil, for example, from fast food outlets and restaurant kitchens. This can be filtered and cleaned to become biofuel. Then a small percentage can be added to new fuel oil for use in engines and machines.

In all these examples, education is important. Most people (individuals and companies), once they are well informed about recycling, are willing to cooperate, especially if governments and city authorities take the lead and provide recycling facilities. Pressure from environmental groups and the EU is strong in Europe and is growing elsewhere. Not only are businesses required to draw up their own targets for conservation and reducing emissions, but they are now under greater pressure to deliver what they have promised.

ACTIVITIES

1 Make a large version of the table below and fill it in.

Terms	Definition and examples	Advantages	Problems
Recycling			
Energy efficiency			
Energy conservation			

2 **(a)** Describe the methods that hotels, like the Hotel Victoria in Freiburg, can use to conserve energy use.

(b) Suggest reasons why many hotels, shops, and offices do little to conserve energy use.

3 Investigation

(a) At present what do **(i)** you and your family and **(ii)** the authorities in your home area do to reduce energy consumption?

(b) Can anything be done to reduce energy consumption further? Explain your view.

4 TABLE **2.4**   How electricity was generated in four Asian countries in 2015(%)

Country	Thermal			Nuclear	Hydro-electric	Other renewables
	oil	gas	coal			
Saudi Arabia	64	36	-	-	-	-
Pakistan	32	50	6	1	11	-
India	28	7	58	1	4	2
Japan	42	23	27	-	5	3

Choose **two** of the countries.

(a) Draw two pie graphs to show the percentages for each of them.

(b) What is similar about electricity generation between the two countries?

(c) State one difference and suggest reasons for it.

Fracking is very controversial. The term fracking refers to how shale rock is fractured (forced) apart by high pressure to release the gas and oil inside it. Water, sand and chemicals are injected into the rock at high pressure, widening the spaces in the rock, which allows the trapped gas and oil to flow out to the top of the well (Figure 2.29). Ninety per cent of what is forced down the well is water, hence the use of the term hydraulic fracturing on the diagram.

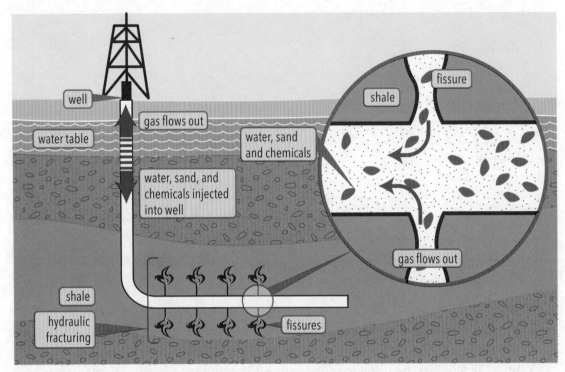

FIGURE **2.29**   Shale gas extraction by fracking

This is cutting-edge technology (i.e. new, beyond anything that has been achieved previously, and is still being developed and improved). The big technological breakthrough was horizontal drilling so that the well could follow the gas-bearing layer of shale rock. Environmental campaigners say that fracking is encouraging more reliance on fossil fuels at the expense of renewables. Obtaining more oil and gas by fracking will increase the number of years other resources will last compared with the estimates in Figure 2.2.

INFORMATION BOX

Advantages of fracking

- Allows drilling of hard-to-reach gas and oil resources.
- It has significantly boosted oil production in the USA and Canada.
- Increased supply contributed to the fall in world market prices of oil and gas from 2014.

Disadvantages of fracking

There are significant environmental concerns including:

- use of vast amounts of water;
- chemicals used may escape and contaminate ground water.

There are worries that the fracking process can cause small earth tremors.

ACTIVITY

1 **(a)**   Explain what is meant by fracking.

   (b)   How is it different from drilling for oil and gas?

   (c)   People either love it or hate it: what makes fracking such a controversial energy issue?

Impact of oil pollution

Although the increasing signs of pollution in the open oceans are a great concern, many parts are still relatively clean compared with coastal regions. This is because over 75 per cent of marine pollution comes from the land: the rest mainly comes from dumping from ships, and from offshore mining and oil production.

TABLE 2.5   Sources of marine oil pollution

Sources	Examples
Land (about 50%)	transport, heavy machinery, and industry
Shipping (about 33%)	oil tanker operations and other shipping discharges
Offshore oil industries	drilling and well leaks, transport spills

For as long as oil has been drilled, there have been accidents and oil spills. The mining industry has always been associated with making a quick profit and moving on before the environmental damage becomes obvious to all. For many years environmental issues were given a low priority by the oil companies in their drive to make money. Over the years, however, although often as a result of pressure from environmental groups plus government safety regulations, the oil companies have had to become more safety conscious and risk averse. In one way new technology has helped; leaks and spills are more avoidable than ever. In another way, it has allowed drilling operations to move into more challenging environments, such as deep-water ocean drilling, where risks are higher. One result was the Deepwater Horizon well blowout in the Gulf of Mexico in 2010 (Case study, pages 68–70).

The risk of oil pollution is present at all stages of oil company operations.

A Drilling for oil—from well leaks, oil seeping to the surface, well blowouts

B Transporting the crude oil—from pipeline leaks, pipeline sabotage (deliberate breaking of the pipes due to war, terrorism, or hostility of local communities), tanker accidents (especially in coastal areas)

C Oil refining—leaks into coastal waters and explosions

OXFORD
UNIVERSITY PRESS

(millions of gallons)

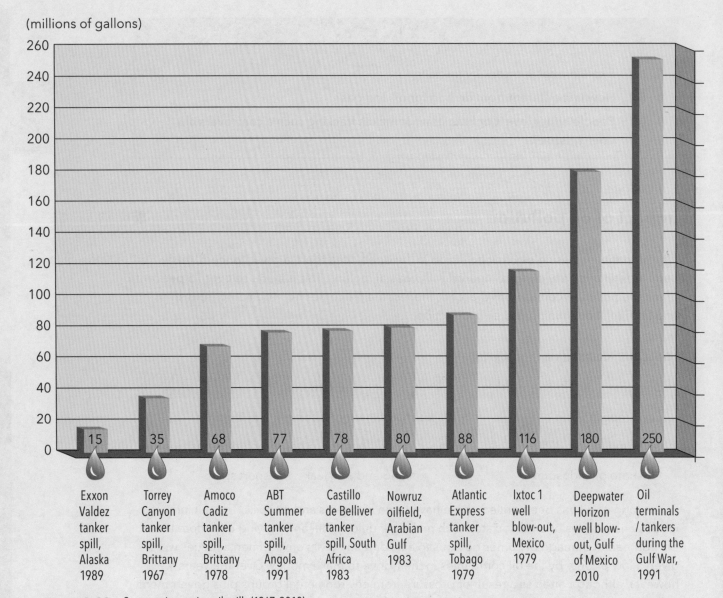

FIGURE 2.30 Some major marine oil spills (1967–2010)

The impact of marine oil spills is immediate and easy to observe (Figure 2.30). Marine life is devastated throughout the area affected. Tourist beaches are ruined; the smell is strong and unpleasant, and lingers for a long time, keeping visitors away. Fishing is another coastal economic activity which is wiped out by an oil spill. Look at the Deepwater Horizon case study to discover the many impacts (environmental, economic, and social) that a large oil spill can cause.

The impact of oil spills lasts longest in cold environments, where ecological recovery is slow. Long-term consequences are serious because only slow growth is possible, for a short period each year. The amount of oil spilled from the Exxon Valdez into Prince William Sound in Alaska in 1989, one of the richest fishing areas in the world, was relatively small (Figure 2.30). Yet 25 years later, the coastal and marine ecosystems have not made a full recovery.

FIGURE **2.31**   Beach pollution in Peru

INFORMATION BOX

Impacts of oil spills on ecosystems

- Birds: oil covers their feathers, reduces insulating properties, impedes flight, and the ability to seek out food.

- Marine mammals: oil can smother small mammals, reducing insulating properties of fur; most affected are sea surface animals like sea otters.

- Coral reefs: oil can kill or impede reproduction and growth, depending on amount of spill and length of time the spill lasts; it also affects many species of fish and crabs that live in and around the reefs.

- Beach life: oil spills smother shoreline creatures like shellfish, and stop many bird species from feeding; flight and mobility of shore-based wading birds are greatly reduced.

Which areas are most at risk? Pollution risks are highest in sheltered bays and river estuaries, where wave action is weak so that pollutants can concentrate more easily. Narrow and enclosed seas and gulfs are at high risk because water flows are restricted. The Arabian Gulf and Mediterranean Sea are examples.

The Arabian Gulf is the world's largest oil producing region; its many oil rigs and tanker terminals are potential sources of marine pollution on a large scale. Political instability in the region is another factor: deliberate sabotage of Kuwaiti oil fields by Iraq during the Gulf War in 1991 showed how vulnerable the Gulf is to a major pollution disaster. The Mediterranean is an almost enclosed sea. It is one of the world's most important shipping routes for oil tankers between the Suez Canal and Straits of Gibraltar. Egypt has recently increased the size of the Suez Canal enabling more, and larger, super-tankers to pass through. Large rivers such as the Nile and Rhone empty pollutants as well as water into the sea. Since the Mediterranean Basin is highly populated and a great tourist destination, risks to economic activities are ever present.

OXFORD
UNIVERSITY PRESS

ACTIVITIES

1 Study Figure 2.30 and answer these questions.

   (a) Which happens more frequently—tanker spills or well blow-outs?

   (b) Which leaks the most oil—tanker spills or well blow-outs?

   (c) Suggest reasons for the answers to these two questions.

2 Use information from here, and from later case studies of Deepwater Horizon in the Gulf of Mexico and Niger Delta. Describe with examples the impact of oil spills on (a) the natural environment and (b) natural ecosystems.

Management of oil pollution

Marine pollution is a global problem. All the world's oceans are linked and ocean currents transfer water between them. Therefore international agreements are essential. The IMO (International Maritime Organization) is a United Nations agency. In order to prevent and reduce pollution from ships, the MARPOL (International Convention for the Prevention of Pollution from Ships) Protocol of 1978 was issued. It was a response to a number of serious tanker accidents. Since then it has been amended and updated. One of the most important amendments was made in 1992, making it compulsory for all new tankers to be built with double hulls (Figure 2.32). Previously, over half of the world's tankers were single-hulled. This meant that oil began to spill out as soon as the hull was breached after hitting a rock or colliding with another ship.

Prevention is always better than cure. Looking at Figure 2.30, is there any evidence that the MARPOL Protocol has helped to reduce oil pollution from tanker spills?

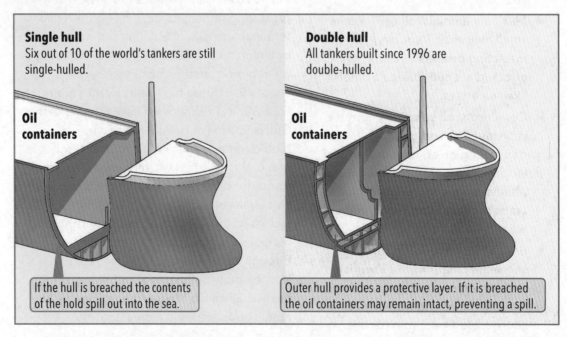

Single hull
Six out of 10 of the world's tankers are still single-hulled.

Oil containers

If the hull is breached the contents of the hold spill out into the sea.

Double hull
All tankers built since 1996 are double-hulled.

Oil containers

Outer hull provides a protective layer. If it is breached the oil containers may remain intact, preventing a spill.

FIGURE 2.32 Single and double hulls in tankers

OXFORD
UNIVERSITY PRESS

Dealing with oil spills

The main methods are illustrated in Figure 2.33. The immediate task is damage limitation by confining the oil slick using booms. The next job is to disperse the larger slicks by using detergent sprays. Some of the remaining oil can be removed by skimmers. All three methods were used to manage the pollution in the Deepwater Horizon event (see Managing the pollution, A, B, and C, page 70).

The clearing-up operation

Booms
Floating inflatable tubes prevent slicks from spreading.

Detergent sprays
Chemicals break up oil into droplets, dispersing larger slicks.

Skimmer
Oil drawn up absorbent belt; rollers scrape and squeeze oil into collecting tank.

FIGURE 2.33   Methods of tackling an oil spill

ACTIVITIES

1   A high percentage of oil tankers now in use have double hulls.

   Explain why tankers with double hulls are less likely to cause oil pollution than those with single hulls.

2   (a)   Explain how each of the three methods of dealing with oil spills in Figure 2.33 works.

   (b)   Why is more than one method needed for dealing with large oil spills?

   (c)   How environmentally friendly are these three methods? Explain what you think.

3   Why is prevention of oil pollution always better than cure?

OXFORD
UNIVERSITY PRESS

Case Study: Oil pollution in the Niger Delta region of Nigeria

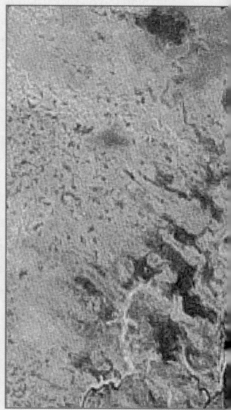

The problem

- An area with enormous oil and gas deposits but with up to 300 oil spills (large and small) per year, and occasional very big leaks like Shell's Bomo well blowout in 2009.

- Pipelines are old; frequent leaks from the Trans Niger pipeline to the port of Bonny

- Sabotage is a problem; groups blow up pipelines, people steal oil.

- Many terrorist attacks on pipelines in 2016; estimated losses 700,000 barrels

The impact

- Some are highly visible: black lakes, black waterways, deposits of black tar

- Spills like Bomo have affected thousands of hectares of mangroves.

- Residents in the town of Bodo complain of headaches and eyesight problems.

- Local water courses needed for drinking water are contaminated.

- Dead fish; fishermen lose their livelihoods, prices of fish (the main food) shoot up.

- Farmers complain about 75% reductions in oil palm yields.

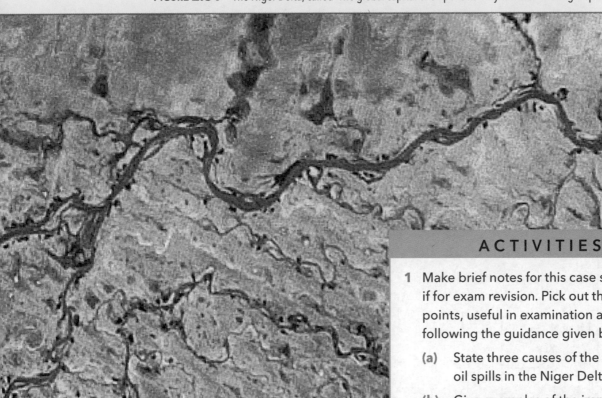

FIGURE **2.34** The Niger Delta, called 'The global capital of oil pollution' by environmental groups

Management

- Environmental laws and regulations are weak in Nigeria.

- Those which exist are not properly enforced; officials are bribed.

- Local people complain that pipeline and well maintenance standards are low.

- Unlike the Gulf of Mexico, there is little independent monitoring of oil spills.

- After the Bomo leak, it took Shell six years to admit liability and agree on compensation.

- Only in 2015, after years of legal battles, did individuals in the Bodo community receive compensation from Shell for their economic losses. And only then did the oil company pledge to clean up Bodo Creek.

ACTIVITIES

1 Make brief notes for this case study, as if for exam revision. Pick out the key points, useful in examination answers, following the guidance given below.

   (a) State three causes of the frequent oil spills in the Niger Delta.

   (b) Give examples of the impact of oil spills using these headings:

      (i) environmental

      (ii) economic

      (iii) social

   (c) Give three reasons why clean-up of the oil spills has been slow and poor.

2 Look ahead to the Deepwater Horizon case study.

   (a) Identify similarities and differences between the oil spills in the Niger Delta and in the Gulf of Mexico from the Deepwater Horizon disaster.

   (b) In which location was management of the oil pollution more effective? Explain your answer.

Case Study: Deepwater Horizon oil spill, Gulf of Mexico, 2010

This is the world's largest accidental oil spill to date. Oil from the drilling well owned by BP, which blew out in April 2010, flowed for 87 days until mid-June. Almost 5m barrels (over 909m litres) of oil were released into the sea. Eleven workers lost their lives.

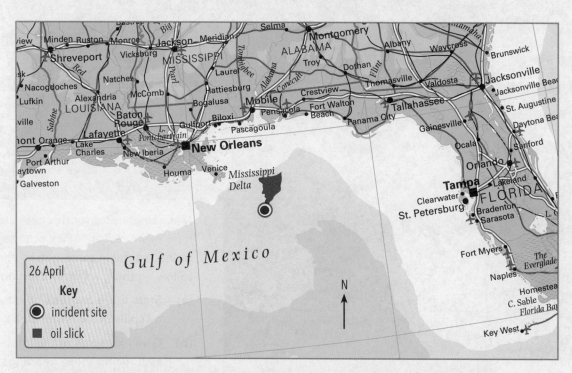

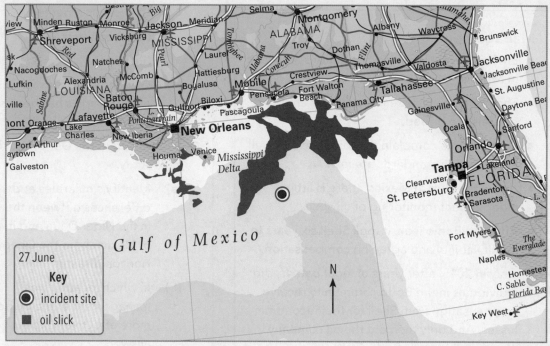

FIGURE 2.35 Location of oil well and extent of spill

It was an exploration well, 5600 metres below the sea bed, in water 1600 metres deep. It was close to the limits of known drilling technology; even so, if all the safety measures had worked as intended, the blowout would not have happened.

Impacts

Oil covered a large area in the Gulf of Mexico (over 180,000 sq km). It reached across 800km of the Gulf's Coast, affecting five Gulf states; most badly affected was the coast of Louisiana. Oil covered sandy beaches and penetrated mangroves and coastal marshes. The Gulf of Mexico's rich marine life was badly affected, especially young bottlenose dolphins and shellfish such as oysters.

These environmental impacts had severe economic consequences for the Gulf's main economic activities—offshore drilling, fishing, and tourism. The American government banned new drilling in the Gulf of Mexico until investigations were complete and safety was improved. The oyster fishing industry collapsed. Tourists kept away from the Gulf's oil-covered beaches.

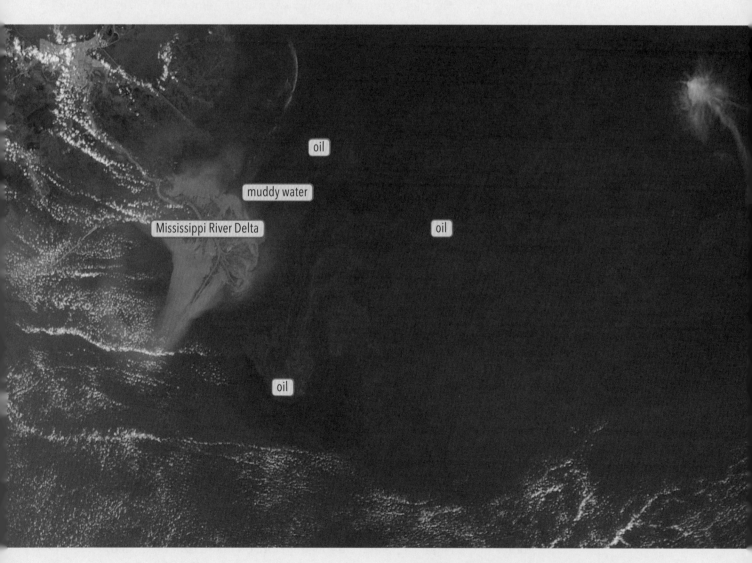

FIGURE 2.36   Oil slick in the Gulf of Mexico—bird's eye view

Managing the pollution

Three main strategies were employed; A: containment, B: dispersal, and C: removal.

A Booms were built to hold back (contain) the oil. Barriers were made to try to stop the oil reaching beaches, marshes, mangroves, shellfish farms, and other ecologically sensitive areas. They were partly effective, but some oil was washed over them by strong waves.

B Chemicals, especially Corexit, were sprayed on the slick to break it up. Dispersing the oil makes it easier for oil-eating microbes in the water to digest it. The microbes did a good job. Some Gulf residents, however, complained of health problems caused by these chemicals.

C Over two and a quarter billion litres of oil were collected from the surface by using skimmers. Some of the oil was set alight and burnt off (flared). It was worth doing so, but only a small part of the total spill could be skimmed up off the surface.

In addition there was the land-based clean up. On beaches, the sand was sifted and tar balls were removed. In the marshes, low pressure flushing was used to remove the oil. At the peak of the clean-up operations in the summer of 2010, 47,000 people and 7000 vessels were involved. The total clean-up costs for BP were over US$15bn. It was fortunate that the company was big enough to have the resources to limit the environmental impact and reduce the economic impacts for businesses in the Gulf of Mexico region.

Five years later, in 2015

The environmental catastrophe was not as bad, or as total, as was first feared. With time, nature is showing its resilience and gradually repairing the man-made damage. What has been destroyed and what has been recovered, however, is a matter for debate. It all depends who is doing the talking.

Some fishermen were reporting oyster catches back up to pre-disaster levels; others maintained that catches were so poor that it was not worth carrying on. There are residents who continue to believe that their ill-health was due to the chemicals used. Scientists studying the marine and coastal ecosystems have found it difficult to distinguish between the effects of the oil spill and pollution from the land which had been getting worse for years before the spill.

ACTIVITIES

1 Make short notes for the case study of a pollution event using these headings.
   (a) Causes
   (b) Impacts (effects)
   (c) Attempts to reduce impacts
   (d) Effectiveness of these impacts

2 Why do people in 2015 disagree about how great are the effects of the Deepwater Horizon oil spill that happened in 2010? Explain as fully as you can.

3 Using information from page 61 onwards (Impact of oil pollution) and from the case studies of the Niger Delta and Deepwater Horizon in the Gulf of Mexico, describe with examples the impact of oil spillages on (a) the natural environment and (b) natural ecosystems.

CHAPTER 3

Agriculture and the environment

OBJECTIVES

In this chapter you will learn about

- soil composition
- what makes soils suitable for plant growth
- different types of agriculture
- techniques used to increase agricultural yields
- impact of agricultural practices
- soil erosion (causes, impacts, and management)
- strategies for sustainable agriculture

FIGURE 3.1 Cattle rearing in Central America on land previously covered by tropical rainforest: what are the environmental risks?

INTRODUCTION

What is soil?

Stated in the simplest possible way, soil is what plants grow in. It is the loose material on the Earth's surface above the solid rock. The thickness of the soil layer varies greatly from place to place. In the hot wet tropics, where the rocks are weathered and broken down very quickly by heat and rain, the soil may be 10 or more metres deep. At the other extreme, on bare rock outcrops there is no soil at all.

Most soils have three layers called horizons. Figure 3.2 is a soil profile showing these.

The topsoil is known as the A horizon. This gains new material from the decomposition of trees and plants. However, minerals may also be washed out of this layer into horizons below by leaching (Figure 3.3).

The subsoil is the B horizon. This is where material accumulates from horizons above and below.

The bottom layer is the C horizon. This contains many loose pieces of rock, broken off from the parent rock below by weathering.

Soil is the topmost layer of the Earth's crust. It can be argued that it is the most important part of the Earth's crust for humans. Plants need it for growth. Plants, in turn, are the basis of the food chain which supports humans and all the land animals upon which humans feed.

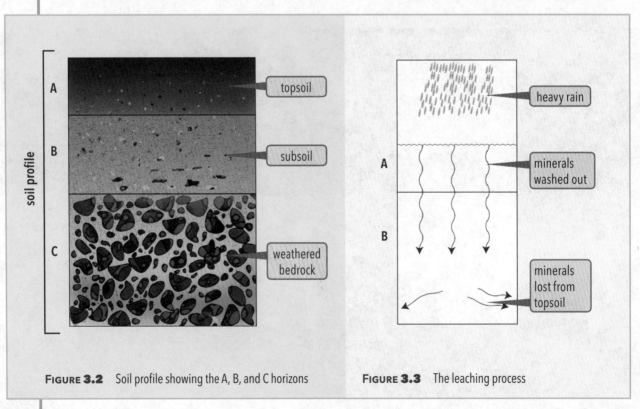

FIGURE 3.2 Soil profile showing the A, B, and C horizons

FIGURE 3.3 The leaching process

Soil composition

Soil has four basic constituents (Figure 3.4).

1   Organic matter: living plants and animals and their dead remains and waste

2   Mineral matter: mainly sand, silt, and clay

3   Water

4   Air

Although all soils are composed of these four elements, there are many different types of soil. This is because the percentages of the different constituents vary greatly from one soil to another.

Figure 3.4 shows average percentages of these basic materials for agricultural soils in Europe. The largest portion of soil is made up of mineral matter, mainly sand and clay. Organic material, though only in a small proportion, is very important. Most organic material is supplied on the surface by falling leaves and litter. Millions of soil organisms, including small animals, such as earthworms and insects, fungi, and microscopic bacteria, live in the soil, breaking down plant and animal remains. Decomposed plant material is mixed with the mineral soil near the surface; this is natural recycling on a massive scale (Figure 3.5).

About half of the soil, by volume, is not solid at all. It is made up of air and water in roughly equal parts, although the percentages keep changing depending on the weather. During the wet season the proportion of water increases to fill what were air spaces during the dry season. This explains why a wavy line is used to separate air and water in Figure 3.4.

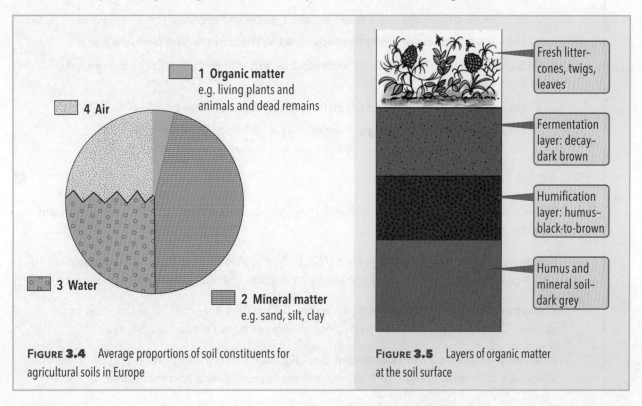

FIGURE 3.4   Average proportions of soil constituents for agricultural soils in Europe

FIGURE 3.5   Layers of organic matter at the soil surface

Mineral particles are formed by weathering of the rock that lies below the soil. Granite, for example, is made up of both hard minerals (mainly quartz) and soft minerals (mainly mica and feldspar). When the rock is weathered, quartz breaks down into sand and silt-size particles while mica and feldspar form clay. Minerals are distinguished mainly according to particle size (Figure 3.6).

Sand grains (mostly quartz) diameter: 0.05-2.00mm	Silt grains (mostly quartz) diameter: 0.002-0.05mm	Clay particles (iron oxides and silicates) diameter: < 0.002mm

FIGURE 3.6   Particles sizes of sand, silt, and clay

ACTIVITIES

1 (a) What is soil?

   (b) Name the four constituents of soil.

   (c) State the source for each constituent.

   (d) From Figure 3.4, state the approximate percentages of these four constituents in agricultural soils in Europe.

   (d) Why do these percentages vary from one soil to another?

2 (a) State briefly the main features of a typical soil profile.

   (b) Give two reasons why the topsoil is the most important part of a soil.

3 Explain why soil fertility is (a) increased by organic matter, and (b) decreased by leaching.

4 (a) What is (i) similar and (ii) different between sand and silt?

   (b) What are the two ways in which clay is different from sand and silt?

Soils for plant growth

Plants need minerals for healthy growth. They are absorbed through the roots as **mineral ions** dissolved in soil water.

Nitrogen is obtained from **nitrate ions (NO_3)**; they are needed to make amino acids, without which plants suffer from stunted growth. Amino acids are the building blocks of protein.

Phosphorus is obtained from **phosphate ions (PO_3)**; they are used for respiration and growth. Otherwise plants suffer from poor root growth and discoloured leaves.

Potassium is obtained from **potassium ions (K)**; their use is in respiration and photosynthesis. Without a sufficient quantity of these ions, there is poor flower and fruit growth.

In areas of natural vegetation, dead leaves and other waste matter are ruthlessly recycled to maintain levels of organic matter in the soil. This is the nutrient cycle (Figure 3.7). Farming a crop takes away some of **organic content** of the soil. For crop yields to be maintained, the farmer needs to make up this loss. In small-scale farming this might be done by composting waste; on larger farms which keep animals, their manure can be spread on the land. Large-scale commercial farmers are more likely to use fertilizers.

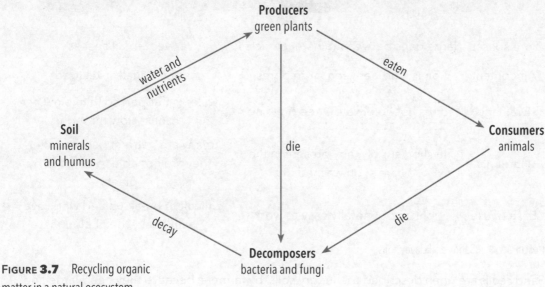

FIGURE 3.7 Recycling organic matter in a natural ecosystem

Soil acidity is measured by the **pH scale**. The concentration of hydrogen ions in a soil is measured and given a value on the pH scale from 0–14 (Figure 3.8). The ideal range for a soil used for farming is between 5.5 and 8.0. This favours plant growth and most soil processes, including nutrient availability and microbial activity. Below 5.5, acid soils restrict root access to water and nutrients. Above this, alkaline soils become too salty for most plants to grow well.

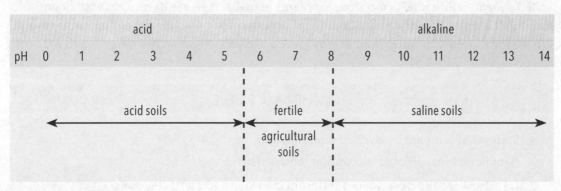

FIGURE 3.8 pH scale

Soil texture is important because it affects many of the factors which influence plant growth and farming. Texture is the balance of mineral particles in the soil, determined by the relative percentages of sand, silt, and clay in a soil. The two opposites are sandy soils and clayey soils (Figure 3.9). Neither soil is ideal for agriculture.

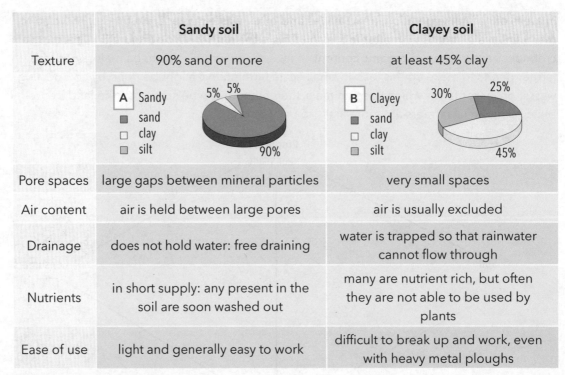

	Sandy soil	Clayey soil
Texture	90% sand or more	at least 45% clay
	A Sandy — sand, clay, silt — 5% 5% 90%	B Clayey — sand, clay, silt — 30% 25% 45%
Pore spaces	large gaps between mineral particles	very small spaces
Air content	air is held between large pores	air is usually excluded
Drainage	does not hold water: free draining	water is trapped so that rainwater cannot flow through
Nutrients	in short supply: any present in the soil are soon washed out	many are nutrient rich, but often they are not able to be used by plants
Ease of use	light and generally easy to work	difficult to break up and work, even with heavy metal ploughs

FIGURE 3.9   Sandy and clayey soils

Sandy soils are often described as 'hungry soils' by farmers, because they need large and frequent feeding with fertilizers for crops to be grown successfully. Clayey soils with their high water content can be good for grass growth, but expensive drainage work is needed to enable such soil to be ploughed and cultivated.

Therefore the best soil for farming is one somewhere between the two—one that has a good balance of sand and clay particles, so that it has both large and small pore spaces. This gives a supply of air (in the large pore spaces) and a supply of water (in the small pores). This is called a loamy soil. It retains moisture for plants to use, but allows excess water to drain through it in times of high rainfall. Loamy soils contain enough clay for holding nutrients and are reasonably easy to work. Their acidity level is likely to fall within the range 5.5 to 8.0 on the pH scale (Figure 3.8).

ACTIVITIES

1 State what is meant by each of the following:

   (i) mineral ions, (ii) organic content, and (iii) pH.

2 (a)   How are the pore spaces different between sand and clay soils?

   (b)   Explain how this affects drainage and air content.

   (c)   Why are these important soil characteristics?

3 (a)   Draw a graph to show the texture of a loamy soil.

       sand 33%   clay 33%   silt 34%

   (b)   State three reasons why loamy soils are good for farming.

Different types of agriculture

On some farms, only crops are grown; this type of farming is **arable** farming. Padi (wet rice) cultivation is an example (Figure 3.10). On other farms, only animals are kept; this is **pastoral** farming. Cattle ranching shown in Figure 3.1 is one example. These are the two basic types of farming. Some farmers grow crops and keep livestock as well. This is **mixed** farming. On many family farms in Africa, crops are grown on small plots in and around the village, while livestock (cattle, goats, sheep) are taken to land further away to graze.

Figure 3.10   Wet rice cultivation in Vietnam

In some types of farming everything is produced to be sold. This is **commercial** farming. Commercial arable farmers often concentrate on growing just one crop, or at best a limited number of crops. Tropical plantation agriculture is a good example (Figure 3.11). Typically it is one plantation, one crop. Bananas, pineapples, and coffee are widely grown on plantations in Central and South America for export worldwide (see Figure 6.16, page 173). Usually these plantations are owned and operated by big companies, some with headquarters overseas. Similarly on commercial pastoral farms, often only one type of animal is kept. The ranch shown in Figure 3.1 makes all its money from the sale of cattle.

Figure 3.11   Banana plantation in Central America owned by a big American food company

OXFORD
UNIVERSITY PRESS

The opposite of commercial farming is **subsistence** farming. Farmers grow crops and perhaps keep a few chickens and other animals to feed themselves and their family. Only when they have produce more than their family needs will they sell this in a local market. The photo in Figure 3.12 shows a subsistence farmer. Contrast this scene with commercial banana production on plantations.

One of the most traditional forms of subsistence farming is shifting cultivation, widely practised by indigenous (local) people in the tropical forests of South America and South-east Asia. This method of farming is summarized in Figure 3.13. No modern methods of farming are used—only traditional methods which have stood the test of time. Provided that there is no population pressure, the big advantage of this type of farming is that it does not lead to

FIGURE 3.12   Brazilian farmer taking home bananas, grown on his plot of land, to hang on the balcony for his family to eat.

serious forest destruction. The plots cleared are so small that it is easy for the forest to re-invade and take over again once cultivation stops. This means that in most areas it is a sustainable type of farming. The disadvantage is that the output per hectare is very low, not many people can be supported by it, and large areas of natural forest are needed for higher output.

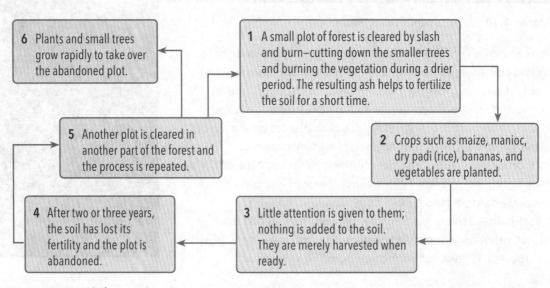

6   Plants and small trees grow rapidly to take over the abandoned plot.

1   A small plot of forest is cleared by slash and burn—cutting down the smaller trees and burning the vegetation during a drier period. The resulting ash helps to fertilize the soil for a short time.

5   Another plot is cleared in another part of the forest and the process is repeated.

2   Crops such as maize, manioc, dry padi (rice), bananas, and vegetables are planted.

4   After two or three years, the soil has lost its fertility and the plot is abandoned.

3   Little attention is given to them; nothing is added to the soil. They are merely harvested when ready.

FIGURE 3.13   Shifting cultivation

One crop commercial farms (e.g. tropical plantations, wheat farms on the Prairies and Great Plains of North America), and one-animal cattle ranches in the Americas, and dairy farms in Europe, could not be more different. Human inputs—capital (money), machinery, seeds, and chemicals—are high. The amount produced is also high: it has to be for the farmer to get back all money invested and still make a profit. These farms are the world's great food producers. They have used a variety of techniques to keep increasing crop yield and animal output, which will be identified and described in the next section.

ACTIVITIES

1   Make a table for Farming Types, like the one below. Fill your table in by
   (a)   adding ticks to indicate **(i)** whether the type of farming is arable, pastoral, or mixed, **(ii)** whether it is commercial or subsistence,
   (b)   naming examples of locations where it takes place.

TABLE **3.1**   Main farming types in the Tropics

Key: A = arable, P = pastoral, C = commercial, S = subsistence, L = Locations

Type of farming	A	P	C	S	L
Nomadic herding		✓		✓	savanna lands of Africa
Wet rice / padi cultivation					
Plantations (e.g. coffee)					
Shifting cultivation					
Cattle ranching					
Wheat farming					
Dairy farming					

2   Study Figure 3.14.
   (a)   Describe the different types of farming shown.
   (b)   Do you think the types of farming shown are commercial or subsistence? Explain the answer you give.

FIGURE **3.14**   Farming in Egypt

ACTIVITIES

3 Answer either part A or part B (depending on where you live, and whether or not you live in a farming country).

   A   For your home region or country:

   (a)   name the main types of farming;

   (b)   state whether it is mainly arable or pastoral farming, or both;

   (c)   state whether it is mainly subsistence or commercial;

   (d)   give reasons for the types of farming named by you.

   B   For your home region or country:

   (a)   give the reasons why farming is of little or no importance;

   (b)   state the five foods that you and your family consume the most;

   (c)   explain where in the world they come from.

Agricultural techniques to increase yields

Farming output had to increase just to keep pace with the growth in world population. One of the most remarkable things is that, despite many gloomy predictions, enough food is grown in the world to feed all 7 billion plus people. The fact that there are people suffering from malnutrition and starvation at the same time as there are food surpluses in Europe and North America has more to do with food availability in places where it is needed than with the amount produced in the world as a whole. However, impressive increases in world food production over the last 50 years have not been achieved without many environmental costs. In the opinion of many people, one of the greatest impacts on the environment has been the clearance of tropical rainforests to be replaced by cattle ranches and plantations (Figure 3.1).

Agricultural techniques used to increase yields are many and varied.

INFORMATION BOX

Changes 1970–2015

- World population has increased by over 3 billion.

- This means it has almost doubled.

- But the amount of agricultural land has increased by only 5%.

- Global famine that some predicted has not happened.

- Instead food output per hectare of staple crops has increased.

- Staple crops are the grains (rice, corn/maize, wheat) which most people eat.

- Grain yields per hectare have more than doubled.

- Thanks to farmers, agricultural scientists, and genetic engineers.

A **Irrigation** is the provision of a supply of water from rivers, lakes, reservoirs, or underground sources to farmland. More of the world's fresh-water supplies are used for this than for any other purpose. Typically, water is transferred from areas of storage to places of use by canals, from which water is drawn off into a criss-cross arrangement of small channels between the fields. In the case of field crops and certain fruit crops, water is sprayed onto the plants from giant sprinklers, which rotate around a central pivot to provide equal amounts of water over a wide area.

Examples of climates in which irrigation water is used:

- Hot desert—dry all year, so that growing crops is impossible without irrigation, such as in Egypt, the Middle East, California in the USA

- Savanna and monsoon—a dry season during which temperatures are high enough for crops to grow provided that water is made available, such as East Africa, India, and Pakistan

FIGURE 3.15   An oasis of cultivation in the Egyptian desert: 8 per cent of Egypt is cultivated; without irrigation it would be zero.

OXFORD
UNIVERSITY PRESS

B **Chemicals (fertilizers and pesticides)** are made to suit every farming need. Natural shortages of one or more mineral nutrients in a soil can be compensated for by adding inorganic fertilizers. Nitrogen fertilizers, ammonium nitrate, and ammonium sulphate, provide plants with soluble sources of nitrogen that can be absorbed through their roots. Crop-eating insects can be destroyed by spraying insecticides. Weeds that would compete with the crops for light and nutrients can be killed by herbicide sprays. Fungi can be controlled by using fungicides. In the past it was not possible to grow the same crop on the same piece of land year after year because of soil exhaustion and the spread of disease. Now one cash crop farming from tropical plantations supplies the world with bananas, sugar cane, cocoa, and coffee, thanks to chemicals.

Fertilizers and pesticides

EXAM TIP

- Make sure that you know the difference between them. Many students don't.
- Both fertilizers and pesticides are used to increase output and yield.
- Fertilizers add nutrients to the soil for better crop growth.
- Pesticides kill insects or weeds which reduce plant yield.

INFORMATION BOX

Biological control of insects
- This is the beneficial action of parasites and predators in reducing damage caused by insects.
- One way is to introduce or encourage a natural enemy.
- For example, parasitic wasps are the natural enemies of aphids, caterpillars, whiteflies, and other insects.

C **Mechanization** allows farming on a larger scale. Farm tasks, such as ploughing, adding fertilizers, planting seeds, spraying against insects, and harvesting using tractors and combines, can all be completed much more quickly and in a more controlled manner than by manual labour using primitive tools. Farmers can take maximum advantage of periods of good weather.

Capital is needed for agricultural improvements. Irrigation water, chemicals, and machinery do not come free; all of them have to be bought by the farmer. This is why yields have been increased most on large farms. Governments in some developed countries, notably the USA and EU, give subsidies to their farmers, which helps them to modernize and mechanize.

D **Selective breeding of plants**, especially the development of high-yielding varieties of seeds, has been responsible for spectacular increases in food output since the 1960s. New varieties of maize, wheat, and rice, which are staple foods, were developed, leading to what has been described as the 'Green Revolution'.

The Green Revolution started in the 1950s when American researchers working in Mexico developed a new hybrid strain of wheat which yielded three times more. It was so successful at solving Mexico's food shortage that these 'miracle seeds' were taken in the 1960s to Asia, where the Indian government was keen to feed its rapidly growing population. The seeds not only offered a reduced risk of famine, but also gave hope for improvements in living standards in rural areas, where the majority of Indians lived.

Since then, the Green Revolution has been mostly associated with Asia. New varieties of improved rice were developed in the Philippines. One of the best known varieties is IR 8, which resulted in a six-fold increase in yield compared with old seeds. Further improvements have developed new seeds which are more drought-resistant. One introduced into India gives an average yield of 5.0 tonnes compared with 1.5 tonnes per hectare from old seed varieties.

There is a catch, however. The Green Revolution is only successful when accompanied by capital investment in a package of new technology, including fertilizers, pesticides, and measures for water control and irrigation. Otherwise, the high yields are not achieved.

TABLE 3.1 Successes and failures of the Green Revolution

A Successes	B Failures
For farmers	**For farmers**
▪ Yields increase by three times or more for farmers able to afford high yielding variety (HYVs) and fertilizers.	▪ Yields do not change for many poor peasants unable to afford new seeds and fertilizers.
▪ Faster growing plants allow more than one crop per year (multiple cropping).	▪ Some, who borrowed money to buy seeds, find they cannot pay it back and end up in debt.
▪ Increased output creates a surplus for sale, raising rural incomes and standards of living.	▪ The gap between large-scale rich farmers and small-scale poor farmers widens.
For the country	**For the country**
▪ Food production is 'revolutionized', and in some cases surpluses for export are created.	▪ Environmental problems increase from the use of fertilizers and pesticides.
▪ Less dependence on imported food or food aid	▪ Salinization is a major problem in areas of widespread irrigation.
▪ Lower rates of malnutrition and reduced risk of food shortages	▪ The only way for some to pay off their debts is to sell out and move to the cities.
▪ Reduced rates of rural to urban migration due to higher standards of living in rural areas	

Selective breeding of animals has led to similar increases in meat and milk output. For example, the average dairy cow in the UK gives three times as much milk as 50 years ago. Most UK dairy farmers now keep only one variety, the Holstein. Selective breeding of the best of this breed has produced a cow that gives more milk per year than any other breed of cow. Manual milking was replaced first by machine milking, and now increasingly by machine robots, so that more milk is produced using less labour, although only after greater capital investment.

ACTIVITIES

1 **FIGURE 3.16** Problems for farmers which reduce crop yields

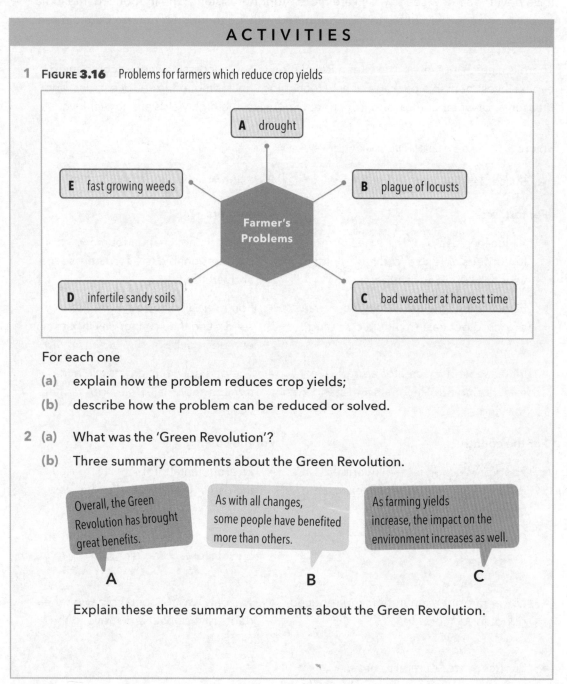

For each one

(a) explain how the problem reduces crop yields;

(b) describe how the problem can be reduced or solved.

2 (a) What was the 'Green Revolution'?

(b) Three summary comments about the Green Revolution.

> Overall, the Green Revolution has brought great benefits.
> **A**

> As with all changes, some people have benefited more than others.
> **B**

> As farming yields increase, the impact on the environment increases as well.
> **C**

Explain these three summary comments about the Green Revolution.

Two more techniques to increase agricultural output are more recent in their widespread use.

E Genetically modified organisms are now, for some people, the big hope for increasing future food supplies to feed a world population expected to reach 9 billion by 2050 or shortly afterwards.

Genetic engineering is the process of altering the genetic composition of an organism by modifying its own genes or introducing genes from a different species. It involves the transfer of genes from one organism to an unrelated species. This does not happen in the natural world, which is why the word 'engineering' is used to describe it.

Biotechnology is the use of living organisms or biological processes for industrial, agricultural, or medical purposes. The names of certain huge biotechnology companies, notably Monsanto and Syngenta, have become internationally known in recent years. This is partly because of the publicity surrounding GM crops—genetically modified crops—created by scientists and research workers in biotech companies using techniques of genetic engineering.

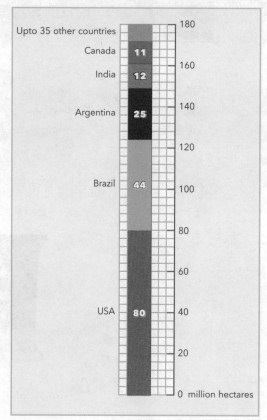

FIGURE 3.17 Countries growing GM crops in 2015

The main GM crops (in terms of area planted in 2015) were soya beans, cotton, corn (maize), and canola (oilseed rape). The five countries named in Figure 3.17 dominate world production, although trials of GM crops have taken place in more than 40 countries.

TABLE 3.2 The different types of GM crops

1 Pest resistant Bt crops	2 Herbicide tolerant
Plants are protected against insect damage by producing a toxin, found in the common soil, bacterium Bacillus thuringiensis, or **Bt**, which kills caterpillars and other insect larvae. This also reduces the need for pesticide use.	Some otherwise useful herbicides kill crops as well as weeds. By breeding into a plant the ability to tolerate herbicides, weeds can be sprayed and killed while the crop continues to grow.
3 Disease resistant	**4 Modifying plant products**
Plants can be armed with a 'vaccine' that stops them being destroyed by viral plant diseases.	Food could be produced that offered higher levels of nutrients and vitamins, or to keep longer (e.g. tomatoes), or to be more useful for making other products (e.g. vegetable oils from oilseed rape to be used in cars instead of petrol).

OXFORD
UNIVERSITY PRESS

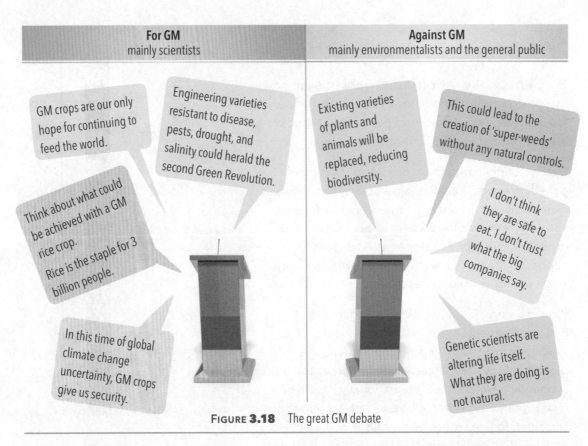

For GM	Against GM
mainly scientists	mainly environmentalists and the general public

GM crops are our only hope for continuing to feed the world.

Engineering varieties resistant to disease, pests, drought, and salinity could herald the second Green Revolution.

Think about what could be achieved with a GM rice crop. Rice is the staple for 3 billion people.

In this time of global climate change uncertainty, GM crops give us security.

Existing varieties of plants and animals will be replaced, reducing biodiversity.

This could lead to the creation of 'super-weeds' without any natural controls.

I don't think they are safe to eat. I don't trust what the big companies say.

Genetic scientists are altering life itself. What they are doing is not natural.

FIGURE 3.18 The great GM debate

F Controlled environments, such as greenhouses (glasshouses), are used mainly in countries with cool climates, as in Northern Europe, to extend the length of the growing season, and provide additional warmth for high value crops such as tomatoes, cucumbers, and peppers. These crops grow in the fields in Southern Europe. Greenhouse costs of production for tomatoes in the Netherlands are higher than out of doors in Spain, but Dutch producers are closer to big city markets. Lower transport costs offset higher production costs.

FIGURE 3.19 Greenhouse cultivation–useful for supplying local markets

Hydroponics is an extreme form of glasshouse production. Soil is replaced by a mineral solution pumped around the plant roots. This is a highly scientific form of farming as the concentrations of minerals in the solution need to be constantly monitored and regularly adjusted according to plant needs. Although this technique allows crops to be grown in places without soil, costs are high and it is only used where a high price can be obtained for fresh produce such as tomatoes in the oil-rich Arabian Gulf States.

Farming in controlled environments is not going to feed the world. Water from hot springs in volcanic Iceland heats greenhouses and even allows oranges and bananas to be grown near the Arctic Circle. However, they are never going to put the banana plantation owners in Central America out of business!

OXFORD
UNIVERSITY PRESS

One of the best techniques for maintaining good yields from the soil is one of the oldest. This is **crop rotation**. It was practised by farmers in the Middle East 8000 years ago; they grew a cereal crop followed by a legume crop. With rotation, crops grown on any plot of land change from one growing season to the next. Growing the same crop on the same land, year after year, depletes the soil of certain nutrients, leads to progressively lower yields, and destroys the soil structure. When one crop is replaced by another, minerals taken out by one crop can be replaced by another. Cereals use up nitrates, whereas legumes are nitrate fixing. If you rotate cereal crops (wheat, barley, oats) with leguminous crops (beans, clover, alfalfa), what one takes out, another returns. Legumes used for animal grazing are particularly useful, since animal grazing fertilizes the land with organic manure. Therefore, a good rotation system

- maintains soil fertility and structure,

- increases crop yield,

- reduces the risk of soil erosion.

ACTIVITIES

1 (a) What is meant by genetic engineering?

  (b) How is it different from cross-breeding?

2 (a) From Figure 3.17, calculate the percentage of GM crops grown in the USA. Show your working.

  (b) Suggest reasons why the USA dominates world GM crop production.

3 With the help of examples, explain why higher yields and outputs are expected from GM crops than from non-GM crops.

4 (a) From Figure 3.18, choose one of the comments from each side of the argument, for and against GM crops, which you consider to be the strongest and best.

  (b) Explain your two choices.

  (c) With which one do you agree most? Explain your view about GM crops.

5 A farmer grows crops (wheat, barley, beans, and clover), and keeps cattle and sheep.

  (a) Name the type of agriculture on this farm.

  (b) Suggest a four-year rotation plan by naming the order of crops grown in one of the fields in years 1, 2, 3, and 4.

  (c) Explain the benefits of your rotation plan for the farmer.

The adverse effects of modern agricultural practices

In the drive to increase food output, impacts on the environment and other people were rarely considered. Some of the negative effects are summarized in Figure 3.20. Then they are described in more detail below.

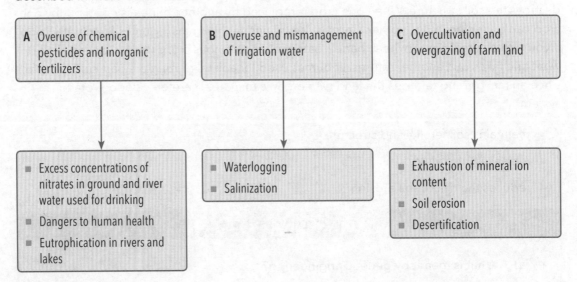

FIGURE 3.20 Adverse environmental effects of modern agricultural practices

A Overuse of chemical pesticides and inorganic fertilizers

Natural ecosystems can be badly affected. Nitrates and phosphates speed up the natural process of **eutrophication**. What happens is shown in Figure 3.21. In extreme cases of eutrophication, rivers and lakes are no longer able to support aquatic life. Warm water released from power stations causes thermal pollution. In cold climates, as in the UK, this can be harmful to temperature-sensitive fish such as trout and salmon. In general, the higher the water temperature, the less desirable are the types of algae that grow in it. Worst of all are the blue-green algae, which develop into heavy blooms.

> **DEFINITION**
>
> **Eutrophication** is the process by which a water ecosystem increases in productivity, leading to the formation of algal blooms. This is due to increased nutrient input, often nitrogen and phosphorus from human sources.

River, lake, and groundwater stores, upon which people depend most for water supplies, are being increasingly contaminated with biological and chemical wastes. At best, polluted water causes sickness and diarrhoea, greatly reducing the ability of people to work. More serious is the long-term damage, such as the development of certain cancers. For human health, the metals of greatest concern are probably lead, mercury, arsenic, and cadmium. If they find their way into drinking water supplies, some, such as arsenic and mercury, are poisonous. It is known that high lead levels can cause brain damage.

Pesticides contain toxic chemicals and have to be used with great care to reduce risks to human health and life. There have been many incidents in developing countries, where up to 25 million farm workers are estimated to experience pesticide poisoning each year, resulting from lack of instruction, fewer safety regulations, and use of faulty equipment. Workers in developed countries can also be affected: labourers in the cotton fields of the USA suffer from skin disease and disfiguration. Land fauna is most at risk from pesticides. They are blamed for the rapid decrease in the UK's bee and butterfly populations.

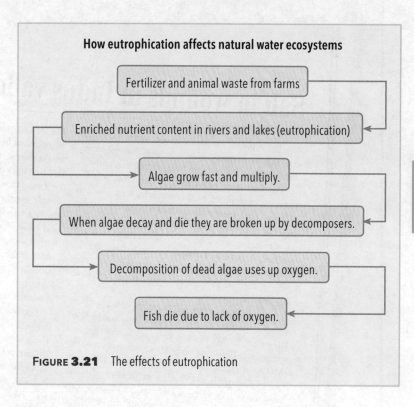

How eutrophication affects natural water ecosystems

Fertilizer and animal waste from farms

Enriched nutrient content in rivers and lakes (eutrophication)

Algae grow fast and multiply.

When algae decay and die they are broken up by decomposers.

Decomposition of dead algae uses up oxygen.

Fish die due to lack of oxygen.

FIGURE 3.21   The effects of eutrophication

B Overuse and mismanagement of irrigation water

It is quite normal to find soils containing salt in dry areas of the world. The big worry is that in some places farming activities are increasing the amount of salt in these soils, thereby reducing crop output (Figure 3.22). Salinization is a particular problem on irrigated land (Figure 3.23). It occurs when excessively large quantities of water are spread over the soil surface. Due to poor management, the surface becomes waterlogged. Some of the world's worst affected areas are in the Middle East and surrounding countries. For example, it is estimated that between 20 and 40 per cent of irrigated land in Egypt, India, Iran, and Pakistan is affected by salinization. As long ago as 2003, a newspaper report in Pakistan revealed the scale of the problem in the Indus Delta (Figure 3.24), and it has worsened since then.

Concentrated areas of irrigation water on the surface

↓

Salts are drawn up to the top of the soil as moisture is evaporated.

↓

Further evaporation leaves the salts behind in the topsoil.

↓

A hard crust of salt is deposited on the surface.

↓

Salt concentrates around plant roots.

↓

As most plants and crops cannot tolerate high salt levels, they wither and die.

FIGURE 3.22   Cropland affected by salinization

FIGURE 3.23   How and why salinization occurs

OXFORD
UNIVERSITY PRESS

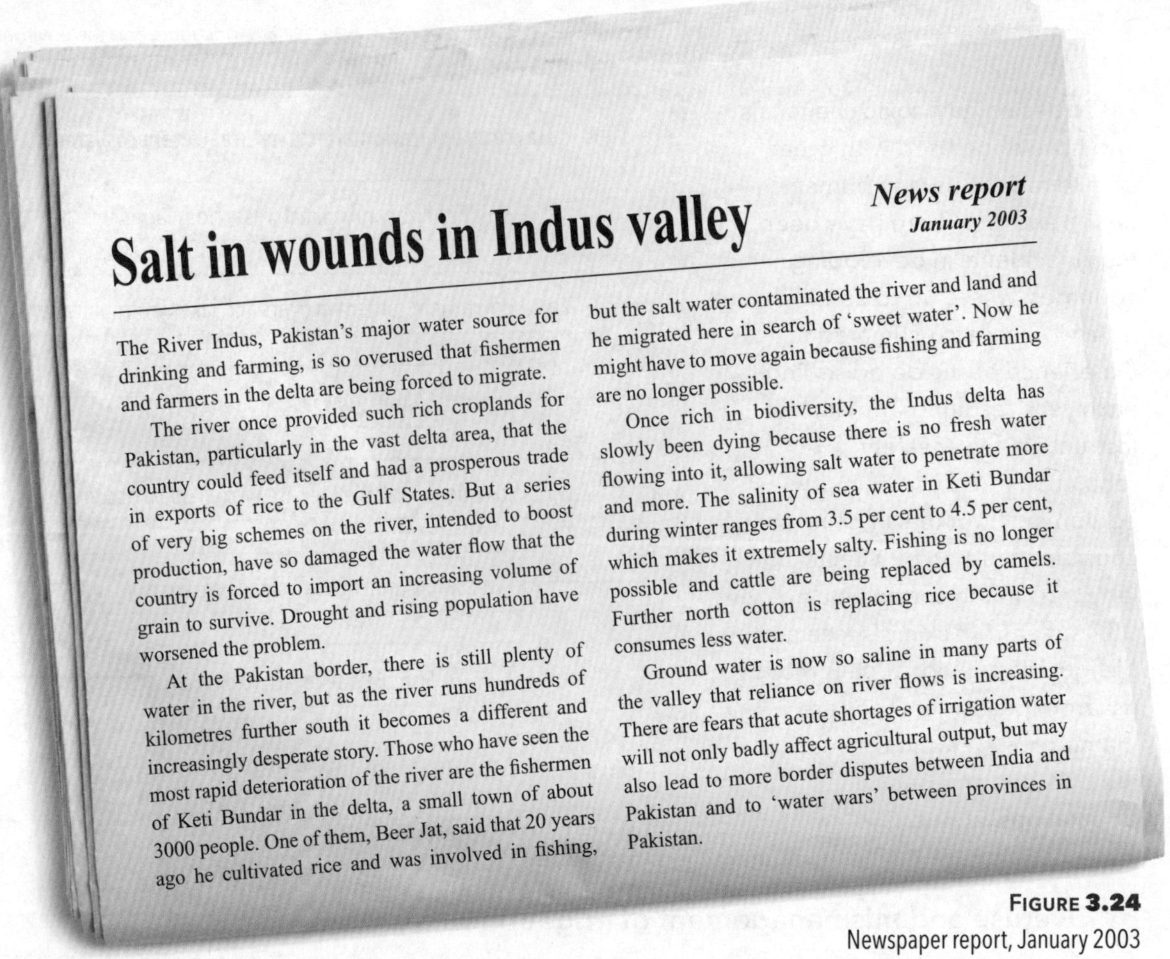

Salt in wounds in Indus valley

News report
January 2003

The River Indus, Pakistan's major water source for drinking and farming, is so overused that fishermen and farmers in the delta are being forced to migrate.

The river once provided such rich croplands for Pakistan, particularly in the vast delta area, that the country could feed itself and had a prosperous trade in exports of rice to the Gulf States. But a series of very big schemes on the river, intended to boost production, have so damaged the water flow that the country is forced to import an increasing volume of grain to survive. Drought and rising population have worsened the problem.

At the Pakistan border, there is still plenty of water in the river, but as the river runs hundreds of kilometres further south it becomes a different and increasingly desperate story. Those who have seen the most rapid deterioration of the river are the fishermen of Keti Bundar in the delta, a small town of about 3000 people. One of them, Beer Jat, said that 20 years ago he cultivated rice and was involved in fishing,

but the salt water contaminated the river and land and he migrated here in search of 'sweet water'. Now he might have to move again because fishing and farming are no longer possible.

Once rich in biodiversity, the Indus delta has slowly been dying because there is no fresh water flowing into it, allowing salt water to penetrate more and more. The salinity of sea water in Keti Bundar during winter ranges from 3.5 per cent to 4.5 per cent, which makes it extremely salty. Fishing is no longer possible and cattle are being replaced by camels. Further north cotton is replacing rice because it consumes less water.

Ground water is now so saline in many parts of the valley that reliance on river flows is increasing. There are fears that acute shortages of irrigation water will not only badly affect agricultural output, but may also lead to more border disputes between India and Pakistan and to 'water wars' between provinces in Pakistan.

FIGURE 3.24
Newspaper report, January 2003

C Overcultivation and overgrazing of farm land

Overuse of the soil depletes the store of mineral ions. Not only does this lead to lower yields, but it also damages soil structure. Poorer crops also mean less vegetation cover to protect the ground surface. Together these increase the risk of heavy rain and high winds removing topsoil; this is **soil erosion**. On desert fringes, soil erosion is one of the processes contributing to **desertification**. This occurs where deserts spread and engulf areas that formerly carried surface vegetation cover and faming settlements. The causes, impacts, and management strategies for soil erosion are covered in some detail in the next section.

ACTIVITIES

1 (a) What is meant by the process of eutrophication?

(b) Describe what happens at the end of the process.

(c) Explain how modern agricultural techniques are increasing rates of eutrophication in rivers and lakes.

2 (a) With the help of a labelled diagram, explain what is meant by salinization.

(b) Why is it worse in some countries than in others?

3 From Figure 3.24, identify and explain (a) environmental, (b) economic, and (c) possible political problems in Pakistan's Indus Valley.

Human impacts

'The rich get richer, the poor get poorer'. This is perhaps the worst **human impact** of modern agricultural practices.

In developing countries, modern agricultural practices favour large-scale operators over small-scale farmers. Owners of large farms are likely to have the capital needed to buy seeds, irrigation water, fertilizers, and machinery, or else be in a better position to borrow the money needed. Using tractors and mechanical seed drills is economic only on large rice farms, where more land means that they can be used for more of the time, which justifies the high costs of buying them. Big farmers benefit from 'economies of scale': this means the larger the farm, the less it costs to cultivate one hectare of land. Look at Figure 3.25 to see the cycle of what happens next.

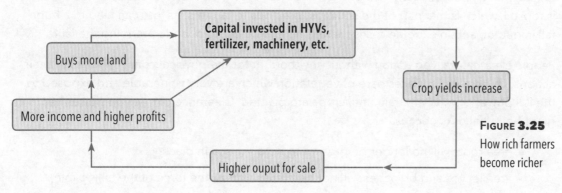

FIGURE 3.25
How rich farmers become richer

Another trend in world agriculture is favouring big farmers and companies at the expense of both the environment and people. This is replacing food crops with cash crops. Big landowners can often make more money by specializing in growing one crop (monoculture) instead of many crops (polyculture) and selling to companies serving the large urban or overseas markets instead of in local markets with low rural prices. Food supply is no longer local. Farmworkers and villagers are forced to go to town markets to buy their food.

Monoculture is less good for the soil than polyculture. Without crop rotation, it is necessary to rely more and more on chemicals to maintain yield and control diseases. When world demand and prices are high, as they were for palm oil between 2005 and 2015, pressure increases for clearing more of the natural vegetation cover, replacing rainforest with palm oil plantations. Now there are kilometre after kilometre of oil palms in the west and centre of the Malaysian peninsula.

ACTIVITIES

1 Make another version of Figure 3.25 to show how poor farmers become poorer.

2 (a) Suggest reasons why small-scale farmers are more likely to practise crop rotation than large-scale farmers.

   (b) Make a list of the environmental problems which result from one crop cultivation (monoculture).

   (c) Why, despite all these problems, is monoculture a common farming practice?

OXFORD
UNIVERSITY PRESS

Soil erosion: causes and impacts

This is the loss of topsoil by wind and water. It is a natural process, happening all the time, but usually slowly because of the protective covering of vegetation. New soil formation from weathering of rock surfaces can generally keep pace and replace what is being lost. Rates of soil erosion are highest either in dry climates where there is little surface vegetation to shelter the soil against wind, or on steep slopes in wet climates where the gradient increases the speed of surface water flows during heavy rainfall.

What most people really mean by soil erosion is 'accelerated soil erosion' i.e. soil erosion speeded up by the activities of humans. Wrong farming practices greatly speed up the processes of erosion (Figure 3.26). It has been estimated that farming has increased the natural rate by 250 per cent—two and a half times—over the centuries. The soil that is lost first is topsoil, which is that part of the soil most precious to farmers. Its loss can lead to a huge fall in output, and in extreme cases there is no choice but to abandon farming the land.

People clear natural vegetation without any thought for the physical consequences of their actions. This creates surfaces bare of vegetation which are very vulnerable and exposed to the full power of wind and rain until crops are planted. Clearance of trees on slopes has great potential risks because

- tree roots will no longer be present to hold the soil in place;
- tree leaves and branches will not be there to break the force of the falling rain;
- obstructions like the tree trunks will no longer be available to restrain surface-water flows down the slope.

On steep slopes, many farmers plough up and down the slope because it is easier, but by doing so they are creating natural channels in the furrows for rainwater to flow down the slope, carrying away the soil particles.

Farmers overexploit their land without taking precautions to stop the likely effects of heavy rain and strong winds. The desire to make money and pressure from population increase for more food have both contributed to overgrazing and overcultivation. When too many cattle and other livestock are grazed beyond the carrying capacity of the vegetation, patches of bare soil appear. These gradually increase in size as the animals pull out grasses by the roots to the point where there is nothing left to hold the soil particles together. Overcultivation is often seen at its worst in areas of monoculture. Growing the same crop year after year drains the soil of certain nutrients. Over time, nutrient loss means less plant growth; less plant cover increases the risk of further erosion.

Misuse of soil, of whatever type, always has the same net effect: surface soil humus is lost, which weakens the soil structure by loosening the individual soil particles. In turn, this makes removal by wind and rain more likely. Eventually, all plant remains in the soil are lost, further increasing risks of erosion to the soil that remains. In other words, the situation just goes from bad to worse.

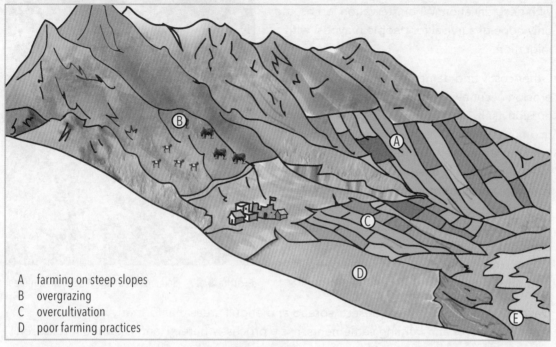

A   farming on steep slopes
B   overgrazing
C   overcultivation
D   poor farming practices

FIGURE 3.26 Causes of soil erosion in a mountainous area

ACTIVITIES

1 **(a)** State how the few centimetres of topsoil are different from the rest of the soil below.

   (b) Why is it the most valuable part of the soil to farmers?

2 Study Figure 3.26.

   (a) Explain why more of the land like that labelled A is being used for farming.

   (b) Why is the risk of soil erosion high in area A?

   (c) Give more details about the causes of soil erosion in areas B, C, and D.

   (d) Describe the likely consequences of soil erosion upon area E.

Impacts of soil erosion

Crop yields go down. Pasture land becomes less productive. Farmers respond by buying and using fertilizers to try to stop the decline in yields. Farmers' incomes go down while costs of farming go up. For farmers in developing countries, feeding the family becomes even more of a struggle; buying fertilizer is not an option for many of them.

The environment suffers. Faced with the prospect of famine, more trees will be cut down where available. Instead of being left in the soil to improve soil structure and retain moisture, crop stubble is removed from crop land for livestock feed. By this stage, the situation goes from very bad to even worse. A point can be reached with soil erosion where the land degradation becomes so severe that it goes beyond the point of no return. This happens with desertification. When starvation looms, the only hope of survival for people may rest with migration.

Other costly and damaging effects of soil erosion occur away from the scene of the erosion itself. Most of the eroded topsoil ends up in rivers, increasing the amount of sediment. With more sediment filling the channel bed, rivers more readily overflow their banks and flooding becomes more frequent. Eventually, rivers drop their load which silts up HEP dams and damages fish breeding areas. It costs port and harbour authorities more time and money to keep their deep water channels open to shipping.

Figure 3.27 Soil erosion in the Malaysian rainforest

Desertification occurs where deserts spread and engulf areas that formerly had surface vegetation cover and farming settlements. It is a process whereby land is turned into desert as a result of human activity, although natural processes such as climatic change may also contribute. Soil erosion and salinization are two processes that may result in desertification because both can create land surfaces unable to support vegetation. A summary of the causes of desertification is given in Figure 3.28.

Areas most at risk are the semi-arid regions where rainfall is concentrated in one season and the amount that arrives is very variable from year to year. When two or three dry years occur together, human pressures on the natural vegetation increase. The relentless rise in human populations means that subsistence farmers can no longer accumulate a food surplus in wet years for use in dry years. They need the same high output from crops and animals every year, and have to hope that every year will be a wet year, which it will not be. In dry years, overcultivation, overgrazing, and further deforestation for fuelwood begin the train of events that end with soil erosion.

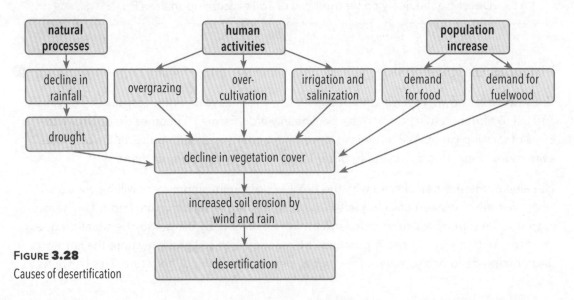

Figure 3.28
Causes of desertification

TABLE 3.3   Symptoms of desertification and their effects

Symptoms of desertification	Effects
Reduced crop yields	Less food, more hunger, and malnutrition
Reduced total biomass	Less available feed for livestock
Reduced wood biomass	Less wood for fuel and longer searches for fuelwood supplies
Reduced water availability	Longer searches for surface / underground supplies
Advancing sand dunes	Farmland, settlements, water holes, etc. overwhelmed
Increased disruption to life	People's need for relief aid increases; some migrate, becoming refugees

ACTIVITIES

1 Study Figure 3.27.
  (a) Describe what it shows.
  (b) Explain how it happened.
2 (a) State (i) the human and (ii) the physical causes of desertification.
  (b) Describe the (i) physical, (ii) economic, and (iii) social effects of desertification.
3 Where and why in your home country or world region is soil erosion a problem?

Soil erosion: management strategies

The aim of soil conservation is the prevention of soil erosion so that the fertile topsoil is retained. A variety of strategies can be used, based on mechanical methods, changes in farming practices, and community solutions.

Mechanical methods

The main strategy used for soil conservation in mountainous areas is **terracing**. Terraces built across slopes hold the soil on flatter land. These are needed most in tropical lands where most rain falls in heavy storms, capable of dislodging large amounts of soil on slopes. On a smaller scale there are **bunds** or embankments, for which stones are placed across the lower ends of steep slopes to hold back soil and water. Farmers themselves can help by using **contour ploughing** i.e. ploughing around or across the slope instead of up and down.

Figure 3.29 Cultivation terraces in Northern Pakistan: how high are the risks of soil erosion in an area like this?

Ridges formed by ploughing block the downward movement of water on slopes. Planting trees in lines, either as **windbreaks** for the farm or as shelter belts between the fields, checks wind speeds and protects against wind erosion.

Changes in farming practices

Rates of erosion are low when the soil is covered; one simple strategy is to use a system of **mixed cropping** or **inter-cropping**. For example, a field crop like maize (corn) can be planted between a bush or tree crop like coffee. Rather than leaving the bare soil between crop plantings open to the wind, the bushes will provide shelter. **Crop rotation** can help in the same way if crops of different sizes and periods of growth are planted in neighbouring fields.

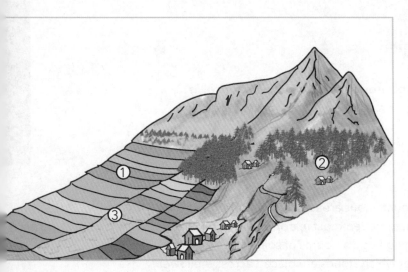

Figure 3.30 Methods used to prevent soil erosion in a mountainous region

However, the main advantage of crop rotation is maintenance of soil fertility. This is based on the principle that not all crops use the same nutrients: what one takes out of the soil, another will give back. A four-field system of cereals, root crops, vegetables, and grass is one example. Using grass as one crop in a system of rotation is helpful because it maintains a surface cover all year, as well as giving soil nutrients a rest between more demanding crops. An additional advantage is that grass increases the humus content. Maintaining soil fertility is crucial; **adding organic matter** to the soil is the best way to retain water and promote a stable soil structure. The main farm sources are animal manure, crop stubble, and straw.

Community solutions

Some strategies for soil maintenance need to be led and funded by governments. One of them is **tree planting** on slopes in and next to farming areas, in order to replace trees already cleared. Planting schemes without community support are not always successful. If local people view the new plantations as a resource instead of a protection against erosion, they may be invaded for fuelwood and for wood for sale. Today it is more widely recognized that the participation of the community increases chances of success.

This is now happening more in Nepal than previously. Local people are allowed to harvest

FIGURE 3.31   Mixed cropping in the Tropics: note the variety of crops and small quantities of each one.

grass and other-low level vegetation from within the forest plantations. These are taken back to the village and fed to animals, now kept in pens so that they cannot eat and destroy the shoots of young trees. Animal dung is used to fertilize the land. When supported by training and help from the government's agricultural extension service, schemes like this can form part of an integrated rural development programme. Soil conservation is integrated with agricultural change to increase food output and improve rural standards of living.

ACTIVITIES

1   Seven strategies for reducing soil erosion are highlighted in bold in this section.

   For each one, briefly state what it is, and how it works.

2   (a)   Name the soil conservation methods in use in areas 1 and 2 in Figure 3.30.

   (b)   Describe the methods farmers might be using in the agricultural areas marked 3 on the same figure to reduce the risks of soil erosion.

3   (a)   Explain why, in areas like the one shown in Figure 3.26, soil erosion will always be a risk.

   (b)   Name the methods of soil conservation that may be used in areas A, B, C, and D. Justify your choices.

   (c)   Make another sketch of Figure 3.26 to show what the area might look like with soil conservation methods in use.

Case Study

Case study of Niger in the Sahel: soil erosion and desertification

Niger is in the Sahel, a broad belt of land across Africa on the southern side of the Sahara desert, extending from the Horn of Africa in the east upto the west coast on the Atlantic Ocean. In the 1970s and 1980s, virtually every year was drier than average. Great numbers of people were affected by famine, particularly in Ethiopia. In the 1980s, at the height of the drought, United Nations Environmental Programme (UNEP) claimed that the Sahara was advancing southwards by 6–10km per year.

Plentiful evidence exists for desertification within the belt. Take the example of Niger, a country in West Africa, where about 250,000 hectares are being lost to desertification each year. Average yields of staple crops such as millet and peanuts are down to under 20 per cent of what they were 50 years ago. The slash and burn techniques that farmers use have destroyed the trees and other perennial bushes that once sheltered the millet and added to soil fertility. Dunes form from the soil eroded off agricultural land, and there is nothing to stop them from being blown across more farmland now that the trees have gone.

The region began to receive normal and above average rainfall again in the mid and late 1990s, and clear evidence is emerging that desertification can be reversed. The Eden Foundation is working in the Tanout region in Niger. The strategies being used include

- research in field stations;
- passing on advice and giving demonstrations to farmers;
- providing farmers with new seeds;
- returning some vegetation cover by spreading seeds of perennial plants that will naturally re-seed and regenerate in future years.

Sustainable environmental management is what the region needs. Once the perennial plants take root again in Tanout, they will stabilize the soil against erosion, improve its fertility, and become a potential resource for wood for fuel and building materials. Halting desertification should be permanent, provided that the resources are protected from predatory use and managed so that the amount consumed each year is less than the amount produced.

FIGURE 3.32 A view of the North African desert

Cause	Method
Overcultivation	▪ higher yielding / drought resistant seeds ▪ crop rotation
Overgrazing	▪ reduce numbers of cattle by using higher-yielding breeds ▪ rotate grazing land
Deforestation	▪ tree planting schemes ▪ alternatives to fuelwood, for example, biogas plants
Population pressure	▪ policies for reducing birth rates ▪ alternative employment, for example, tourism and craft industries

FIGURE 3.33 Methods for tackling the causes of soil erosion and desertification

However, all that was hoped for has not come about. There have been years of good rains, but drought years keep returning as they did in 2010 and 2012. Recovery from droughts for both the land and the people is taking longer. Population pressure is major factor. At almost 44.2 per 1000 people, Niger's birth rate is the highest in the world, with little chance of a meaningful reduction soon. This is due to a mix of cultural, economic, and political factors (Figure 8.16, page 239). No end is in sight to overuse of the land in an effort to feed more and more mouths. The inevitable result? More soil erosion during and after the next drought period in the Sahel, which can only increase the knock-on effects shown in Figure 6.36 (page 194).

ACTIVITIES

1 Draw a labelled flow diagram, based on the one used in Figure 3.28, to show the causes of soil erosion and desertification in Niger.

> **Guidance:**
> ▪ Under 'natural processes' write in dates for Sahel droughts.
> ▪ Under 'human activities' write in details of farmers' activities.
> ▪ Under 'population increase' include population data from Figure 8.16.

2 Describe some of the methods used in the Tanout region of Niger to reduce soil erosion.

3 Explain why policies begun in the 1990s have not achieved all their aims.

environmental management

Strategies for sustainable agriculture

Behind the concept of sustainable agriculture is the idea that we should not be putting at risk tomorrow's food supplies from the land because of today's short-term economic greed. Nor should we be piling up environmental debts which will burden our children, and their children, and all future generations. Six strategies helpful to sustainable agriculture are shown in Figure 3.34. Three have already been described. Follow the page reference links.

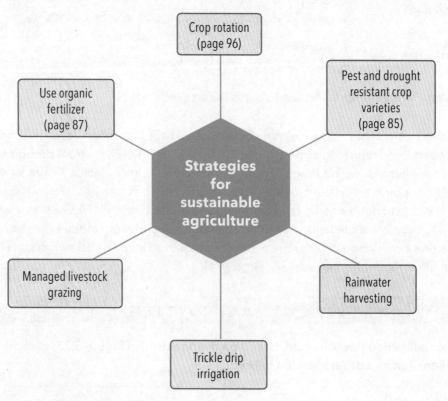

FIGURE 3.34 Strategies for sustainable agriculture

Managed grazing is practised in two ways, although in the end, they really come down to the same thing—do not have too many animals for the amount of vegetation available. One way is to rotate where the animals are allowed to graze by moving them from field to field. Fences (wooden or electric, or something similar) are needed for this to be effective. A 'no grazing' period gives the grass time to grow without being trampled down. Another way is to leave the animals to graze the same land all year, but to ensure that the number of animals is well short of the carrying capacity of the vegetation. Rotation is better.

The carrying capacity of the land is not constant. It is lower in dry seasons or during cold winters, and it drops like a stone during droughts. Good management is needed most during times of low carrying capacity. Giving the animals supplementary feed, such as hay, is one way. Another is to reduce numbers by selling off some of the animals. These solutions are often possible for farmers in developed countries, who have built up some cash reserves in the good years, but less likely for those living in developing countries, especially where population pressure is high—hence overgrazing, soil erosion and desertification, and non-sustainable agriculture.

Trickle drip irrigation is an example of appropriate technology capable of being used by local people with limited resources, which will bring long term (i.e. sustainable) benefits. This is a more efficient way to irrigate crops than surface channels and sprinklers, which are widely used on large farms, and more likely to lead to salinization (Table 3.4).

TABLE **3.4** Efficiency of different irrigation systems for corn (maize) production	
Irrigation method	**Productivity** (kg of corn per m³ of water)
Surface channels (basin irrigation)	0.7
Sprinkler	0.9
Trickle drip	1.4

Pipes are laid on the surface between or around the crops. Short side pipes, or holes in the main pipe, direct the water at the plant roots, exactly where it is needed (Figure 3.35). This means more water is used by the plant and less is evaporated. Water is no longer wasted on the bare soil between the crops, thus reducing weed growth.

FIGURE 3.35   Trickle drip irrigation

Rainwater harvesting is another example of appropriate technology. This is trapping, collecting, and storing rainwater which would otherwise have been lost as runoff down the drains or into streams. The main aim for farmers is to increase and store the amount of water they need to use for irrigation during dry periods. It is clean, non-contaminated water. However, there are other benefits too. Reducing runoff during heavy rains decreases the risk of floods and soil erosion. It saves on the amount of water that is needed from underground wells, thereby allowing groundwater levels to be sustained. For small farmers, this is a win-win situation.

Most often, rainwater is collected from the roofs of buildings, where it is redirected to a store. This may be a pond on the surface, but it is better if the store is in a deep pit such as a well-shaft or borehole. In particularly dry areas, where every drop of water is valuable, nets can be used to collect dew or fog, from which the trapped water drips into a store below. Even an upturned umbrella, with a pipe in the middle (instead of a handle) leading to a container, will collect a good amount of water in a storm.

The beauty of rainwater harvesting is that these things can be done by individuals or community groups. Even so, people in rural areas often need a lead or a push. In all the rural areas of the Indian state of Tamil Nadu, it has been compulsory since 2001 for new buildings to include rainwater collection facilities. It is an important source of water in Brazil's drought zone in its dry north-east as shown in Figure 6.30 on page 189.

ACTIVITIES

1 (a) Give a brief definition for each of the following:

      (i) organic fertilizer   (ii) crop rotation

      (iii) managed grazing   (iv) resistant crop varieties.

  (b) Describe how they can make agriculture more sustainable.

  (c) Suggest reasons why they are not used by more farmers.

2 (a) Draw a labelled diagram of trickle drip irrigation.

  (b) What are the advantages and disadvantages of trickle drip irrigation for crop growing, compared with the other two methods of irrigation in Table 3.4?

  (c) Why is trickle drip irrigation considered to be more sustainable than the other two methods of irrigation?

3 (a) What is meant by rainwater harvesting?

  (b) State three environmental benefits of rainwater harvesting.

  (c) Why can it be described as an example of appropriate technology?

4 Investigation: Rainwater harvesting in your home region or country

  (a) Describe the main features of the climate in your home area.

  (b) Is rainwater harvesting used in your home area?

     If yes, then where, how, and why?

     If not, why not?

CHAPTER 4

Water and its management

OBJECTIVES

In this chapter you will learn about

- global water distribution
- the water cycle
- sources of water supply for people
- water usage, quality, and availability
- multipurpose dam projects
- sources of water pollution
- impact and management of water pollution
- managing water-related diseases

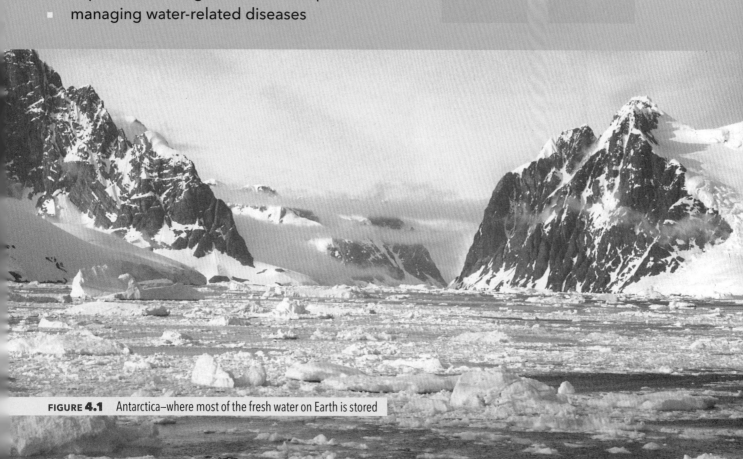

FIGURE 4.1 Antarctica–where most of the fresh water on Earth is stored

INTRODUCTION

Without water, there would be no life on Earth. Without a supply of fresh water, there would be no plants and animals. One of the main reasons for scientists sending space probes to Mars is to discover whether there is any evidence for the existence, past or present, of water that could allow life on the Red Planet.

Look at the Information Box. Are you surprised by how little fresh water is present on the Earth's surface? Figure 4.2 shows you where the fresh water is stored. Essentially there are only two major stores for all the Earth's fresh water resources—locked up in surface ice sheets, and locked away underground in spaces in permeable rocks. Add up the total amount of water from all the other stores and it is less than 0.5 per cent. What percentage of fresh water is readily available for human use?

INFORMATION BOX

Water on Earth

- Oceans cover 71 per cent of the surface.
- Oceans and seas contain 97 per cent of all the water.
- This means only 3 per cent is fresh water.
- Most of this fresh water is stored frozen in ice sheets (Figures 4.1 and 4.9).

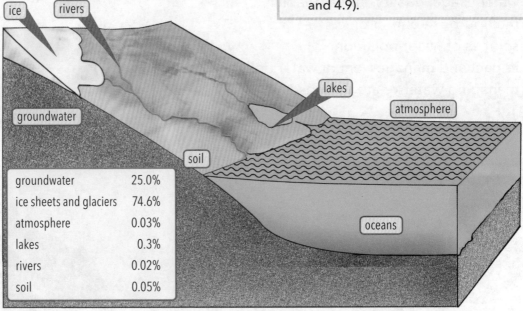

groundwater	25.0%
ice sheets and glaciers	74.6%
atmosphere	0.03%
lakes	0.3%
rivers	0.02%
soil	0.05%

FIGURE 4.2 Global fresh water stores

ACTIVITIES

1 Draw pie or divided bar graphs to show percentages of **(i)** land and water surfaces on Earth, **(ii)** salt water and fresh water, and **(iii)** fresh water in different types of store (use ice sheets and glaciers, ground water, and others).

2 Explain the importance of what your graphs show.

The water cycle

This is one of the Earth's great natural systems. The system consists of inputs, stores, flows, transfers, and outputs.

Inputs: precipitation from the atmosphere

Stores: surface stores such as oceans, seas, and lakes, and underground stores such as aquifers

Flows: rivers transport water from land to sea

Transfers: surface water is evaporated and transferred to the atmosphere as water vapour

Output: precipitation from the atmosphere as the cycle continues

The main water cycle processes are shown in Figure 4.3.

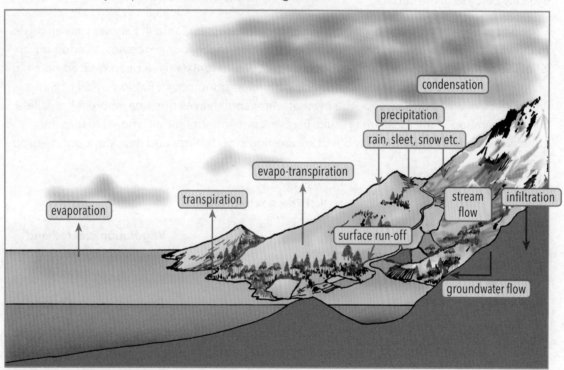

FIGURE 4.3   The water (hydrological) cycle

Solar heating drives the system. **Evaporation** takes place due to heating of the surface. Water from ocean, sea, and lake surfaces is changed from water droplets to water vapour in the atmosphere. Water is also lost from vegetation (trees, plants, crops), mainly from their leaves. This is **transpiration**. It is difficult to separate out amounts lost between water and vegetation covered surfaces, therefore the term **evapo-transpiration** is used to cover all water losses from land surfaces.

Air temperatures decrease with height. As water vapour is carried upwards by air currents, it is cooled, leading to **condensation**. This is the process by which the water vapour (an invisible gas) is turned back into a liquid (water droplets) or a solid (particles of ice). When you see clouds, you are observing the results of condensation. Further cooling leads to **precipitation**, which is all the moisture which reaches the Earth's surface, irrespective of type. Rain is the most common type, but snow and hail are included as well.

OXFORD
UNIVERSITY PRESS

What happens to precipitation after it falls on the Earth's surface? Some is prevented from falling directly on the ground by trees and plants; this is **interception**. Some flows over the ground surface, eventually finding its way into streams and rivers; this is **run-off**. From both surfaces there is some immediate water loss back into the atmosphere, especially on hot days, by evapo-transpiration. Have you seen a road surface steaming after a downpour as soon as the Sun comes out again? This is evaporation in action.

The remainder seeps underground, downwards by **infiltration** and sideways by **groundwater flow**. In other words, there is **through-flow** through soil and rocks. The rock type has a big influence on the amount that seeps underground. Permeable and porous rocks, such as limestone and sandstone, have gaps or spaces (pores) between the grains of rock which allow water to pass through. However, little infiltration is possible where impermeable rocks like clay outcrop at the surface.

Changes in surface land use can affect water cycle processes. Table 4.1 shows how changes to the vegetation cover of an area affect the operation of the four processes. In addition to what the table shows, there is some evidence that where forests have been cleared on a big scale over large areas, the amount of precipitation has gone down. Rapid run-off of water into surface rivers after clearance means that water soon leaves the area where it has fallen. Less evaporation in the local area results in less water vapour feeding moisture into the atmosphere, which could be capable of supporting clouds large and heavy enough to drop showers.

TABLE 4.1 How changes to vegetation cover affect water cycle processes

Area of dense vegetation			Vegetation cleared and replaced by farming (crops and cattle)	
Process	Rate	Reasons	Process	Change
Interception	High	Much foliage to hold and block falling precipitation	Interception	Decrease
Evapo-transpiration	High	Plant leaves are the main source of water loss; water held for longer on leaves and stems after rainfall	Evapo-transpiration	Decrease
Run-off	Low	Rainwater delayed or stopped from reaching ground surface by trees, which obstruct free water flow	Run-off	Increase
Infiltration	High	Water reaches the ground slowly and in small amounts; this gives time for soil and rocks to soak up water reaching the surface.	Infiltration	Decrease

ACTIVITIES

1 Briefly show that you understand the difference between each of these pairs of processes:

(a) evaporation and transpiration;

(b) interception and infiltration;

(c) infiltration and ground water flow;

(d) evaporation and condensation.

2 Name the eight processes shown in Figure 4.4.

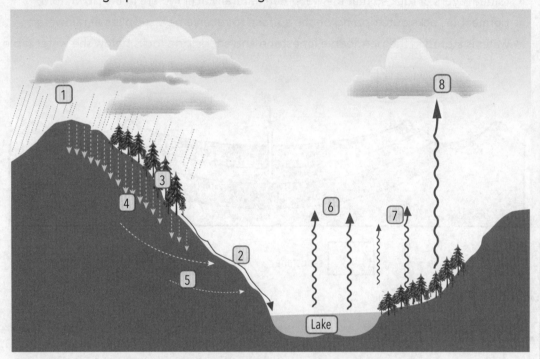

FIGURE 4.4 Processes in the water cycle (1-8)

3 Changes in the amount of surface run-off in an area

Year	Run-off	Land use
	(mm of rainfall equivalent)	
1995	90	mainly grazing land
2005	180	partly urban
2015	310	all urban

(a) Draw a graph to show the changes in run-off.

(b) Give reasons for these changes.

Water supply

Although one quarter of all fresh water is stored underground, not all of this is accessible for human use. Most of it is too widely dispersed within the many holes in permeable rock; a lot of it is simply too deep underground to be easily reached. Some of the best sites for water supply are above **aquifers**, places where favourable geological conditions have concentrated underground water in one place, within reach from the surface.

One example is shown in Figure 4.5. The favourable geological conditions are:

- alternating layers of permeable and impermeable rocks to trap water in the permeable rock;
- folded layers of rock so that the water can naturally accumulate in the down fold;
- permeable rocks outcropping on the surface to receive new supplies of rainwater;
- water is stored in the permeable limestone and sandstone rocks below the water table.

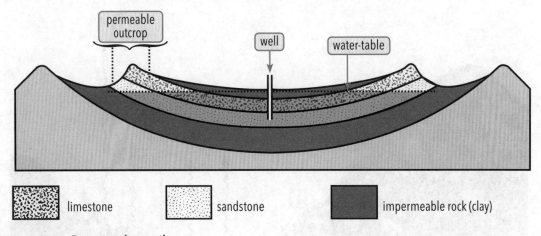

limestone   sandstone   impermeable rock (clay)

FIGURE **4.5**   Formation of an aquifer

INFORMATION BOX

The water table

- **What is it?**

  Level below which the ground is saturated; the soil and rock cannot hold any more water.

- **Why is it important?**

  Where the water table reaches the surface, natural springs will flow; these bring underground water to the surface without the need of pumps.

  Where the water table is below the surface, wells must be sunk below the water table before water can be pumped out.

In this example, once the well has been dug, the water pressure will be sufficient to force the water to flow out without any need for pumps. There are places where water naturally reaches the surface. This is at points where water-bearing permeable rocks meet impermeable rocks, which will not allow water to pass through; hence surplus water emerges at the surface in **springs**. This is as clean, reliable, and cheap a source of fresh water as it is possible to have. More often a well needs to be dug to reach water-bearing rocks. Mechanical pumps or human labour are used to raise the water to the surface.

Oil-rich Gulf countries like Saudi Arabia, UAE, and Kuwait have another alternative—**desalination**. A great amount of energy is needed to change seawater into fresh water by taking out the salt. Only plentiful energy supplies and a desperate need for fresh water can justify the high costs.

Supply

- Desert climate—limited surface sources

Riyadh	J	F	M	A	M	J	J	A	S	O	N	D
Precipitation (mm)	3	20	23	25	10	0	0	0	0	0	0	0

- Three quarters of fresh water comes from underground aquifers.
- Aquifers filled up when the climate was wetter (about 20,000 years ago).
- It was estimated that in 2010 the aquifers contained 40 per cent less water than they did in 1985.

Demand	(billion cubic metres)	Use	(%)
1980	2.4	Domestic	12
1990	12.0	Industry	2
2000	16.0	Agriculture	86
2010	20.0		

- Some people ask whether Saudi Arabia would not be better off importing more of its food needs.

FIGURE 4.6   Water supply and demand in Saudi Arabia

FIGURE 4.7   A desalination plant in Saudi Arabia

INFORMATION BOX

The process of desalination
Reverse osmosis

- Sea water is pumped from the ocean.
- It is forced at high pressure through semi-permeable membranes.
- These block the passage of salt and minerals.
- Only fresh water flows through the membranes.

INFORMATION BOX

Definitions of key terms

- Aquifer: underground store of water
- Desalination: producing fresh water from sea water
- Impermeable rock: rock which does not allow water to pass through it
- Permeable rock: rock with spaces and gaps so that water can pass through
- Reservoir: artificial lake used to store water for human use
- Spring: point where underground water re-emerges at the surface
- Well: shaft, sometimes lined with stone, sunk into the ground for water

ACTIVITIES

1 Study Figure 4.8.

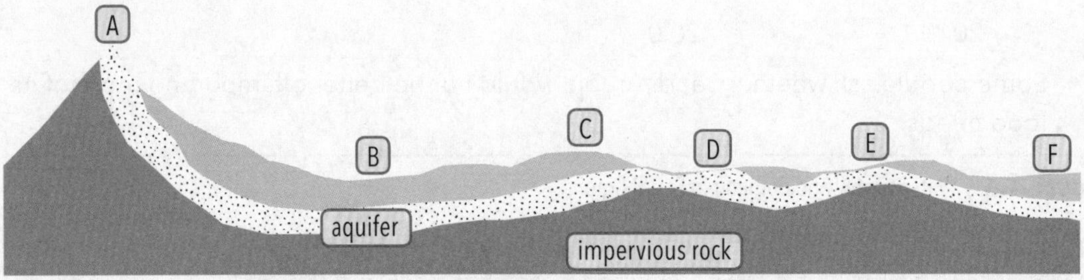

FIGURE **4.8**   Cross-section of an aquifer

(a) Why is what happens at A very important?

(b) Choose a letter at a good place for digging a well. Explain your choice.

2 With the help of labelled diagrams, explain how people can obtain underground water supplies.

3 Example of water in Saudi Arabia: study the information about Saudi Arabia in Figure 4.6 and write under these headings:

(a) Water supply sources

(b) Water demand and use

(c) Water supply problems (now and in the future)

(d) Suggestions for reducing future problems of water supply

Use graphs and diagrams where appropriate.

Surface water supplies and transfers

Most people rely on surface water sources. These are overwhelmingly concentrated in mountainous regions for three good reasons.

- Totals of precipitation are usually higher here than in the surrounding lowlands, because air saturated with water vapour is forced to rise more strongly over high land.

- Summer heating melts ice and snow in the mountains and releases fresh water.

- Many lakes are found at the bottom of steep-sided mountains, often carved out by glaciers in earlier times.

Glacier in the Andes in southern Chile   Lake formed by Andean glaciers between Chile and Argentina

FIGURE 4.9   Natural surface water stores in the mountains

The big problem is that few people live in mountainous areas where water availability is greatest. Fortunately, rivers provide surface transfers of water to lowland areas where farms, villages, towns, and cities are concentrated. Drawing water directly from surface rivers is the easiest and cheapest way of obtaining fresh water. It is not by chance that some of the world's most densely populated areas are along the banks of big rivers (Information Box).

In earlier times, water as a resource was taken for granted. People lived and farmed only where local water supplies were available from rivers, lakes, or aquifers. The cost of building pipelines

INFORMATION BOX

The great rivers of Asia

- The Tigris and Euphrates flow into the Arabian Gulf.
- The Indus in Pakistan flows into the Arabian Sea.
- The Ganges in India flows into the Bay of Bengal.
- The Yangtze and Hwang-Ho in China flow into the Yellow Sea.
- Mekong in Laos, Cambodia, and Vietnam flows into the South China Sea.

These rivers have been homes of ancient civilizations.

- They are used for intensive and productive farming.
- They have densely populated floodplains.
- They provide drinking water, irrigation, and transport.

OXFORD
UNIVERSITY PRESS

and pumping stations to move water over long distances could not be justified. There were exceptions to this general rule. The growth of farming, industry, and population in California, in the dry west of the USA, would not have been possible without a network of pipelines transferring water from hundreds of kilometres away in the Rocky Mountains.

Now government attitudes have changed. Populations and levels of economic activity have grown so fast that in many places they have outstripped local water supplies to the point of threatening further economic growth. The Indian government has put forward the India Rivers Interlinking plan to transfer water from 14 flood-prone Himalayan rivers in the north to 17 rivers in the drought-prone south. The Chinese government is building tunnels and canals to transfer water from behind the Three Gorges Dam to its water-poor yet highly populated north (see the case study, page 123).

In Pakistan, the River Indus is a managed river (Figure 4.10). Dams, such as the Tarbela Dam, are built in the mountains along the Indus and its four major tributaries. Here deep, steep-sided valleys provide favourable sites for dam construction. Most water reaches the rivers in summer, from ice and snow melt in Himalayan glaciers and the summer monsoon rains. Dams store the water which is released during the rest of the year, when it is dry. Barrages in the lowland hold back the water flow so that it can be distributed to irrigation canals and people in the cities. Karachi, the country's biggest city with around 20 million inhabitants, and located at the southern end of the Indus River system, has a desert climate.

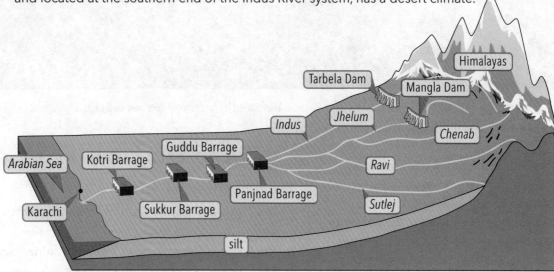

FIGURE 4.10 Indus River system management

The world demand for water has increased fourfold since 1950. Dam building has been the only way of meeting the increasing demand for water. There were only about 5000 dams in the world in 1950: by 2000, there were about 45,000, a nine-fold increase. Not only are there more of them, but the reservoirs held back by them have become larger and larger, and the Three Gorges Dam along China's Yangtze River dwarfs the rest. All the big, well-known dams (Hoover Dam, Aswan High Dam, Kariba Dam, Three Gorges) are **multi-purpose**: they need more than one purpose to justify the high construction costs. Not only do they supply water for domestic needs, irrigation, and industrial use, but they can also provide hydroelectric power (HEP), control floods in wet seasons, and help with year-long river transportation.

ACTIVITIES

1 Explain as fully as you can why most dams are built in the mountains.

2 Study Figure 4.10.

   (a) The River Indus is described as a managed river. Explain what is meant by a managed river.

   (b) Describe how the River Indus and its tributaries have been managed.

Water usage

For the purposes of gathering statistical data about the uses of fresh water, world organizations like the UN subdivide water use into three sectors:

- domestic – in the home and for waste disposal; about 10% of total water use;
- industrial – in factories and for power; about 20% of total water use;
- agricultural – mainly for irrigation; about 70% of total water use.

Large variations in importance exist between these three sectors (Figure 4.11). In the majority of countries within the continents of Africa and Asia, farming is still the main activity; many people grow their own food (subsistence farmers). Populations are still increasing, demanding higher food output. One way of achieving higher food output is to use more irrigation water. This boosts crop yields and allows crops to be grown in dry seasons. In dry countries, land can be reclaimed from the desert to increase in the area of land being farmed, as in Egypt (water from the Aswan High Dam) and southern Pakistan (water from the Indus River system).

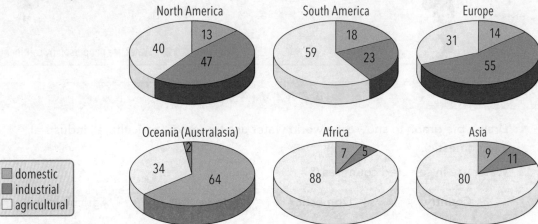

FIGURE 4.11 Percentage of water use for the three sectors by continent

In contrast, in North America and Europe, the percentage of water supply used in factories and industries is noticeably higher. On both continents there are areas of irrigated farmland; California is one example and countries around the Mediterranean Sea, such as Spain and Italy, are others. Considerable amounts of water are used in industrial processes for cooling (as in power stations and steel works), for mixing and making products like dyes and paints in chemical works, and for bottling and canning in food and drink industries.

Variations in the amount of water use

Average water use per head in the world is very unequal. This is the main message from Figure 4.12. The majority of people in Africa live in rural areas. Typically, they must seek out their own daily supplies. This can involve a long walk to the nearest stream or hours in a queue to await their turn to use the well. Except across the centre around the Equator, Africa is a dry continent (see key to Figure 4.13). Water is a truly scarce resource which needs to be used sparingly. In contrast, in European countries taps and flushing toilets are standard fittings in houses; electrical items such as automatic laundry and dish-washing machines consume a lot more water than washing by hand.

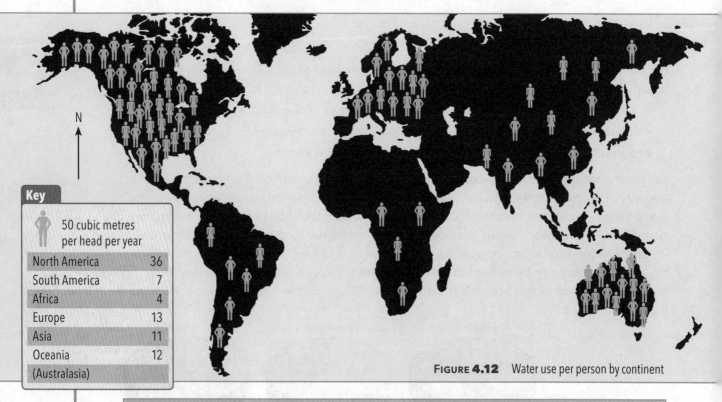

Key

	50 cubic metres per head per year	
North America		36
South America		7
Africa		4
Europe		13
Asia		11
Oceania (Australasia)		12

N

FIGURE **4.12** Water use per person by continent

ACTIVITIES

1 Draw a pie graph to show total world water use by sector (agricultural, industrial, and domestic).

2 Water use in selected countries (%)

Country	Domestic	Industrial	Agricultural
Bangladesh	3	1	96
India	6	4	90
Pakistan	3	2	95
UK	20	77	3
USA	15	44	41
China	8	28	64

Suggest reasons why:

(a) percentages for all three South Asian countries are similar;

(b) percentages for one of the other three countries are different.

3 (a) Describe what Figure 4.11 shows about water use per person in North America and Europe as compared with the other continents.

(b) Suggest why their water use is different from that in other continents.

4 (a) List the ways in which water is used in your home in order of importance.

(b) Is water use by you and your family increasing? Explain.

Water quality and availability ■

Precipitation fills surface rivers, other surface stores, and underground stores (aquifers). Precipitation, however, varies greatly from place to place across the Earth's surface (Figure 4.13). Notice that many of the world's driest and wettest places are found in tropical latitudes. Deserts are defined as places with an average rainfall of less than 250mm per year. They tend to be located on the northern and southern edges of the Tropics as well as in the interior of continents. The largest continuous area of hot desert is the Sahara in North Africa, which continues eastwards to the Arabian Gulf and the western edges of South Asia.

INFORMATION BOX

Extremes of precipitation

The world's driest place

- Atacama Desert in northern Chile
- No rainfall here for most years
- Average rainfall 0mm per year

The world's wettest place

- Cherrapunji in north-east India
- Average rainfall above 10,000mm per year

FIGURE 4.13 World annual precipitation

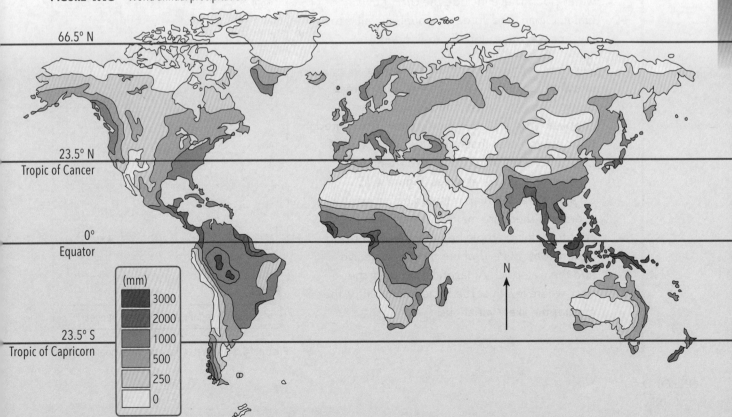

Water-rich countries ■

These are countries with plentiful fresh water supplies. The world's top 10 water-rich countries (for countries with more than 10 million inhabitants) are shown in Figure 4.14A. Some of them are very large countries with plenty of land surface for rain to fall on. In terms of land area, Russia is largest, followed by Canada, while Brazil is the world's fifth largest country. Others have large amounts of rainfall compared with the size of their total population. Small areas of desert in Peru and Chile are more than compensated for by heavy rainfall in other areas. For example, part of the vast Amazon Basin with its wet equatorial climate not only covers eastern Peru but also parts of five other countries listed in the top ten. These are Bolivia, Colombia, Venezuela, Brazil, and Ecuador.

Water-poor countries ■

The list of the 10 most water-poor countries in Figure 4.14B is dominated by desert countries in the Arabian Peninsula and North Africa. Indeed, many of the smaller countries (with under 10 million people) in the same areas are even more water-poor. These include the UAE, Kuwait, Qatar, Oman, and Jordan. Annual rainfall is too low and too infrequent for their needs.

Water-poor countries are the ones most likely to suffer from what is now called **water stress** i.e. worries over present and future water supplies. They are not the only ones. The United Nations estimates that one third of the world's population lives in countries experiencing medium to high water stress (Figure 4.15). Be aware that the map is based on national averages. There are many variations within countries, for example between the water-poor desert coast of Peru where most people live and the water-rich Amazon lowlands in the east, where few live. The larger the country, the greater the likely variations.

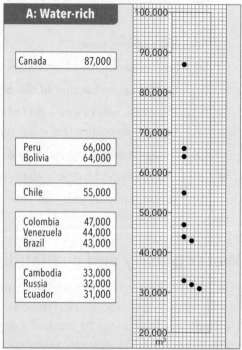

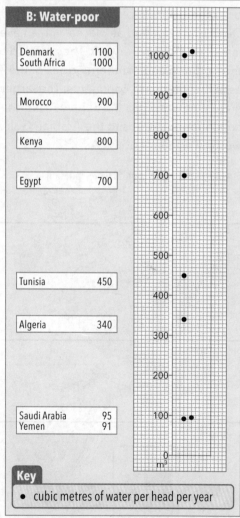

Key

● cubic metres of water per head per year

FIGURE 4.14 Water-rich and water-poor countries

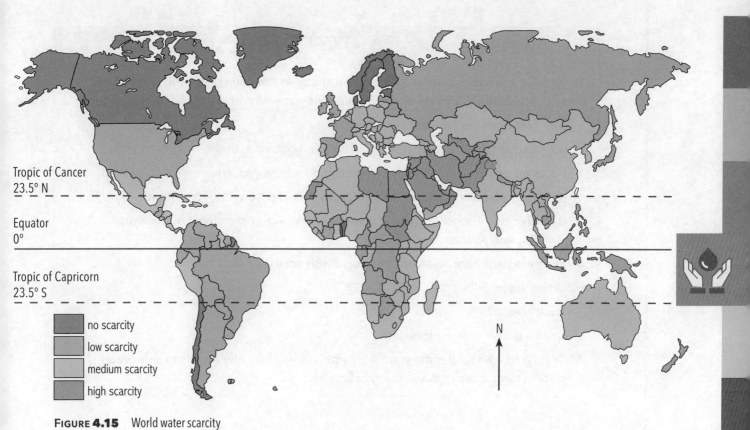

FIGURE 4.15   World water scarcity

Differences in water availability within countries

Not only are there differences in water availability between countries, but there can be equally large variations in water quality and access to clean water between different parts of the same country. Since 100% access to piped supplies of clean drinking (potable) water is taken for granted in developed countries of Europe and North America, the big differences are in developing countries. The biggest difference is between urban and rural areas. Some of the reasons for greater access in urban areas are shown in the spider diagram in Figure 4.16.

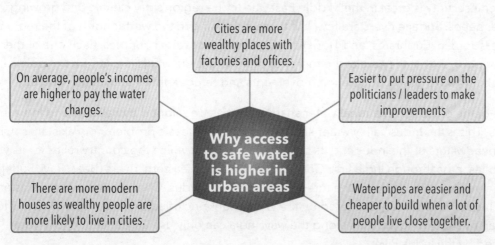

FIGURE 4.16   Access to safe water in urban areas

OXFORD
UNIVERSITY PRESS

environmental management

ACTIVITIES

1 (a) On a world outline map, colour or shade in the countries named in Figure 4.14A and B. Use different shading for water-rich and water-poor countries.

   (b) Describe the two distributions.

   (c) Explain the main differences in location between them.

2 Focus on your country and the world region where you live.

   (a) Describe what Figures 4.13 and 4.15 show for your country and world region.

   (b) Decide whether you live in a water-rich or water-poor part of the world. Explain your answer.

3 Percentage of people across the world with access to clean water:

   Urban areas: 94%

   Rural areas: 72%

   Draw a graph to show this data.

4 Draw your own spider diagram with labels to explain why access to safe water is poor in rural areas in developing countries.

Potential for water conflicts between countries

How do water-poor and water-stressed countries with high scarcity obtain their water supplies? Many rely upon **aquifers**. Rain water that has accumulated during hundreds or thousands of years is used to satisfy people's present day needs. Unfortunately, many countries are taking out more water each year than is naturally replaced by precipitation. In the long term, reducing the size of groundwater reserves is unsustainable. Saudi Arabia (Figure 4.6) is an extreme example of this.

Water insecurity is great in the Middle East due to the region's dry climate and growing water needs. Surface rivers are few, but those beginning in the wetter north of the region (Rivers Jordan, Euphrates, and Tigris) all pass through several countries, each one of them water-poor, so that they are at the mercy of their neighbours. This is in an area of political instability with massive population movements and refugee flows between countries.

One of the oldest international water sharing treaties was signed by Pakistan and India in 1960. This is the Indus Valley water sharing scheme. The basic problem for Pakistan is that the headwaters of the Indus and its big tributaries, upon which the country relies for its water supplies, pass through India first. Control over the three 'eastern' rivers (Beas, Ravi, Sutlej) was given to India, and over the three 'western' rivers (Indus, Chenab, Jhelum) to Pakistan. The Indus Waters Treaty, brokered by the World Bank, included precise do's and don'ts for Indian river-building projects along the way. India can only use 20 per cent of the water carried by the Indus River.

Since 1960 India and Pakistan have not engaged in any water wars. Nevertheless, there have been tensions, disagreements, and disputes—almost inevitable because both countries have never trusted each other, and both are water-stressed and in desperate need of increased water supply. Most issues have been settled using the legal procedures provided for within the treaty.

Egypt is one fortunate desert country to have a large river flowing through it which carries water from other countries with wetter climates. The White Nile rises from close to Lake Tanganyika below the Equator where it is wet most of the year. The Blue Nile begins in the mountains of Ethiopia where heavy monsoon rain falls in summer. It was the ancient Greeks who described Egypt as 'The Gift of the Nile'. This label fits just as well today. Without Nile water stored in the Aswan High Dam, opened in 1971, water-poor Egypt could not feed and support its over 90 million people. The dam provides reliable water and electricity supplies for the whole country.

However, fresh water supply is a growing international issue. The Nile flows through nine other countries before it reaches Egypt. For centuries, Egypt has viewed the Nile as its own river. Why should Egypt consume so much of the Nile's water? Upstream, Sudan and Ethiopia have their own desert areas and increasing populations. For many years, they demanded a fairer share of Nile water; both countries are far behind Egypt in levels of development. Egypt realized that it needed to cooperate instead of complaining and making threats about what action it would take if less Nile water reached Egypt.

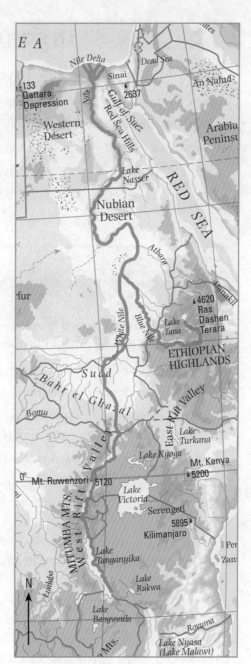

FIGURE 4.17   Nile River Basin

This is why the Nile Basin Initiative (NBI) was set up in 1999 with the aim of coordinating new dam developments along the Nile. Tensions still remain between Egypt and its neighbours, none more so than with Ethiopia over the Grand Ethiopian Renaissance Dam. Once complete in 2018, this will be the biggest HEP station in Africa. Egypt is worried that it would receive too little water for its needs while the enormous reservoir was being filled up. When the reservoir is full, Ethiopia insists that the water will only be used to drive the turbines, not for irrigation. Hence amounts of water carried by the Blue Nile to Egypt should not be affected.

INFORMATION BOX

Main countries of the Nile River Basin

Egypt: 84 million
- GDP per head US$ 6610
- Aswan High Dam supplies water and electricity to all Egypt
- Water resources fully used

Ethiopia: 87 million
- GDP per head US$ 1110
- Repeated droughts
- Plans for greater use of water potential of the Blue Nile

Sudan: 35 million
- GDP per head US$ 2160
- Suffers from drought
- Many old dams silting up

ACTIVITIES

1 Identify and explain two reasons why the potential for water conflict between countries is high in the Middle East.

2 (a) Why was the Indus Waters Treaty needed?

(b) How successful has it been? State and explain your view on this.

3 (a) Describe the differences between Egypt and its Nile Basin neighbours for (i) location, (ii) wealth, and (iii) water needs and use.

(b) (i) State two reasons why Nile Basin countries need to cooperate.

(ii) Why is this cooperation not easy to achieve?

Multi-purpose dam projects—how sustainable are they?

Large dams are always controversial. In all cases it is possible to put forward great advantages. Look at the benefits the Aswan High Dam has brought to Egypt. Water supplies are assured throughout Egypt, one of the world's most water-poor countries (Figure 4.14). The cultivated area of Egypt has doubled from four to eight per cent. More farmland is being reclaimed from the desert. Farmers can grow crops all year; two or three crops per year is now normal, compared with only one during the Nile flood season previously. The flood risk to crops and people has gone away. HEP from the dam provides electricity for homes, factories, and water pumps. Since 1971, Egypt has been a different place, so surely no one can complain. One of the complaints, though, is that Nile silt, instead of maintaining the natural fertility of the soil, is building up behind the dam. Farmers need to spend more on fertilizers to maintain crop yields.

Also, HEP production is always one of the main reasons for large dam building, among the many other uses that make them multi-purpose schemes. The energy produced is renewable and clean; it reduces fossil fuel use. It helps governments to meet their CO_2 reduction targets. There are no contributions to global warming.

Some of the environmental, economic, and social problems associated with dam building schemes in general were mentioned in Chapter 2 (page 40). More of these are covered in the case study of the Three Gorges Dam. The message on the dam wall in Figure 4.18 was used in an advertisement from an environmental organization—what do you think it is referring to? Figure 4.19 gives the policy recommendations from the same organization— how would implementing these recommendations make dam building more sustainable?

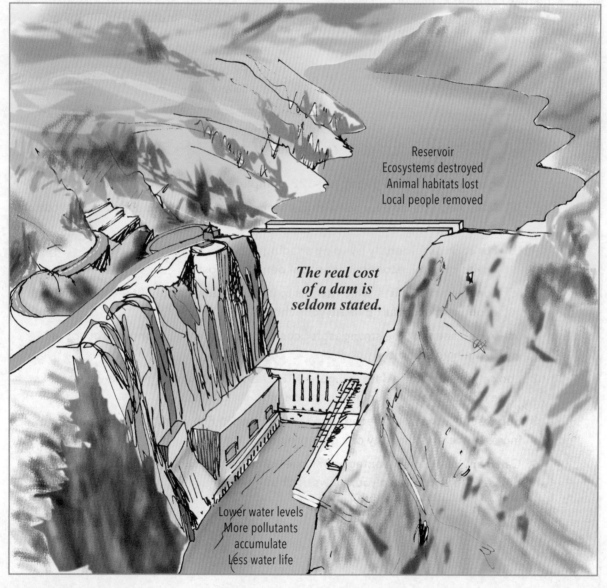

FIGURE 4.18   Message from an environmental organization about building large dams

The underlying problem with most dam building projects is that governments tend to focus on the economic advantages, for what they perceive as the national good. More often than not governments look only at potential economic benefits for the country as a whole, and not at the effects on the local people and region where the dam is located. People forced to move from land about to be flooded are usually promised new homes and land, but promises are not always kept. Often the new farmland higher up, on steeper slopes, is not as good quality as was their old land on the valley floor.

- Do an environmental survey of costs and benefits first.

- Discuss relocation and compensation with local people.

- Investigate alternative sites to discover whether building more but smaller dams will give similar advantages.

- Cooperate with other countries where rivers flow across national boundaries.

FIGURE 4.19   Policy recommendations for building dams

ACTIVITIES

1 Using information from pages 120-122, complete tasks **(a)**, **(b)**, **(c)**, and **(d)**.

   (a) Make two lists, one for advantages (benefits) and one for disadvantages (costs) of building large dams.

   (b) For each one, identify by using shading or symbols whether it is an environmental, economic, or social benefit or cost.

   (c) Looking at your lists, which seems to be strongest for benefits—environmental, economic, or social? Explain your choice.

   (d) Which seems to be strongest for costs—environmental, economic, or social? Explain your choice.

2 Look at the site of the dam in Figure 4.18. Describe as fully as you can why it looks to be a good site for building a large dam.

3 Suggest how the policy recommendations listed in Figure 4.19 would be likely to increase the sustainability of a dam project.

4 Can many of the disadvantages of large dams be avoided by building more small dams? Give and explain your views on this.

Case study: A recent multipurpose dam scheme

The Three Gorges Dam in China—this scheme is massive. It is the world's largest hydro power project. Look at the facts about it in the Information Box.

INFORMATION BOX

Three Gorges Dam

- Dam: height 185 metres, length 2000 metres
- Reservoir: width over 1km, length over 600km
- Cost: US$24bn +
- Construction: started 1992, finished 2012

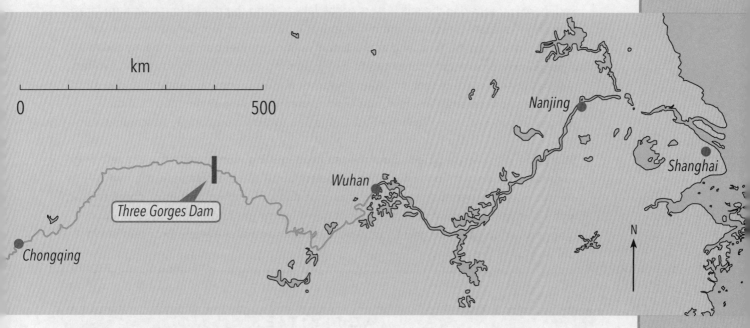

FIGURE 4.20 Three Gorges Dam

Advantages

The Chinese government believes that the scheme brings enormous benefits. In a country hungry for power, it supplies about 2% of the country's electricity. The great storage of water helps to control Yangtze floods downstream, meaning that big cities like Wuhan and Shanghai are less at risk from the effects of 'superfloods'. Some of the stored water is being transferred by tunnels and canals to the water-poor north of China. No longer do large ships from Shanghai need to pass through narrow and dangerous gorges; navigation inland to Chongqing along the Yangtze has been much improved.

124

Case Study

Disadvantages

As with all big schemes, there are drawbacks. Thirteen cities and 1500 smaller settlements were flooded. Over 1.2 million people were forced to move from their homes; not all were successfully resettled and adequately compensated. The destruction of the natural environment led to significant losses of plant and animal habitats, reducing diversity, and threatening rare species such as the dawn redwood and giant panda. Erosion of the banks of the reservoir as water levels go up and down is causing more landslides.

Environmental issues

Sediment is trapped in the still waters of the lake behind the dam. Here it accumulates, meaning that there is less sediment in the river downstream. Not only is less natural fertilizer spread on the farmland of the lower valley, but river banks are being eroded more quickly. Biodiversity continues to be threatened as the dam floods some habitats, reduces water flow in others, and alters weather patterns. Less rain and more droughts have been noticed since the dam was built. Lower water flow at the mouth of the Yangtze allows salt water from the East China Sea to penetrate further upstream.

Some scientists, very worried about these effects getting worse with time, are referring to this as 'China's looming environmental catastrophe'. On the plus side, the hydro-electric power generated saves the burning of about 30 million tonnes of coal per year, with significant reductions in emissions of greenhouse gas and oxides of sulphur and nitrogen. Air pollution caused by coal-fired power stations is a major problem in big Chinese cities like Beijing.

ACTIVITIES

1 Explain why the Three Gorges Dam is described as a 'multi-purpose dam'.

2 Give reasons why the Chinese government thought that it was essential to build it.

3 State one problem under each of the following headings caused by building the Three Gorges Dam: **(a)** social, **(b)** economic, and **(c)** environmental.

4 How sustainable is the Three Gorges Dam scheme? Explain your view.

5 Do a project about a dam in your country or world region.

   Refer to location, reasons for building it, uses, and problems/local issues.

Water pollution and its sources

Many of the world's people live close to rivers. The numbers of people and the scale of economic development both increased greatly during the second half of the twentieth century. It comes as no surprise, therefore, that human activities have a growing, and in some places, a dominant effect upon water quality.

Figure 4.21 illustrates ways in which river water quality can undergo major changes due to human activities. Both natural and man-made water stores are shown in the uplands. Along rivers which flow through well-populated areas, water can be taken from them several times and used for agricultural, domestic, and industrial purposes, before being returned back into the rivers.

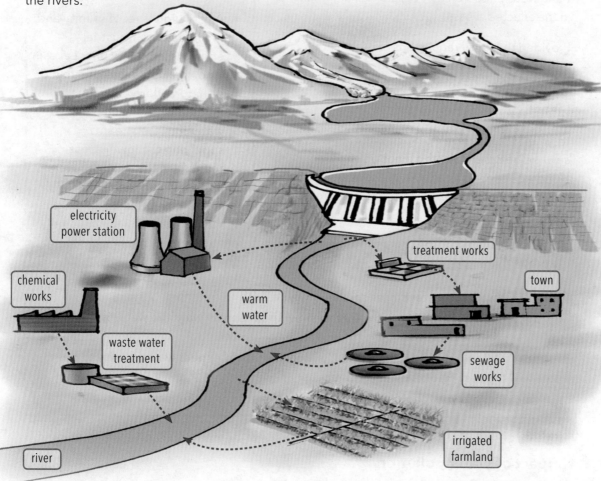

FIGURE 4.21   Water use and the possibilities for pollution

Main causes of water pollution

Agriculture is one. Surpluses of phosphorus and nitrogen not absorbed by the plants are washed from the land or percolate into the groundwater. On farms, animal manure, synthetic fertilizers, and chemical pesticides are the main sources. Amounts released into rivers have greatly increased as farmers have tried to increase crop yields and farm output (Chapter 3).

OXFORD
UNIVERSITY PRESS

Domestic waste is another cause. Human waste carries many pathogenic (disease-producing) micro-organisms, as well as adding to the quantities of nitrates and phosphates released. Domestic waste also includes detergents, metals, and many other manufactured products containing traces of toxic chemicals.

Industry is the third cause. Industrial processing of metal ores, metal-using industries, and the leaching of metals from waste heaps and dumps are responsible for the frequent presence of traces of a wide variety of metals in rivers. Among the metals detected, most are mercury, copper, manganese, nickel, chromium, lead, and arsenic (Chapter 1). The discharge of untreated industrial effluents into lakes and rivers, especially in developing countries, has dangerous effects on human, animal, and plant life in the affected areas.

Provided that local regulations exist and are enforced, domestic and industrial wastes should be treated before being released. Even in well-regulated countries, leaks of untreated toxic materials and metals into rivers occur from time to time. In many developing countries, however, sewage treatment plants cannot be afforded. Hundreds of millions of litres of raw sewage and toxic industrial wastes are emptied into rivers and seas every year.

INFORMATION BOX

■ A very high level of salinity and the release of industrial effluents into Manchhar Lake, in Sindh, Pakistan, has destroyed its natural flora and fauna. Release of this contaminated water into the streams supplying the lower areas resulted in the death of over 30 people in summer, 2004.

ACTIVITIES

1 (a) Name the water stores shown in Figure 4.21.
   (b) Draw a sketch of Figure 4.21 to show the different ways the water is being used.
   (c) On your sketch, label H and L where you would expect water quality to be highest (H) and lowest (L).
   (d) Explain your choices of locations.

Impact of water pollution

Water pollution has consequences for both people and the environment. How much human waste is discharged into rivers, lakes, and seas to cause this pollution is controlled by how well the waste is treated in sewage treatment works. The big variations in clean water supply between developed and developing countries, and between rural and urban areas within developing countries, have already been referred to (Figure 4.16). The same is true for sanitation and sewage treatment, but here the gap between developed and developing, and between urban and rural, is even wider (Figure 4.22). In other words, treating waste before it enters waterways is the exception rather than the rule in rural areas of developing countries, whereas it is the norm throughout most of the developed world.

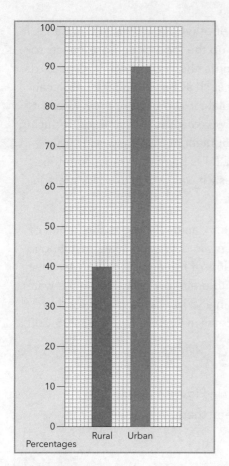

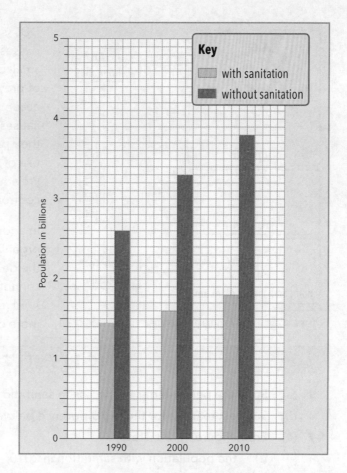

FIGURE 4.22

A Access to sanitation in rural and urban areas (world averages)

B Population with and without sanitation in developing countries

Pollutants carried in untreated sewage can cause infectious water-borne diseases such as typhoid, cholera (an intestinal infection), dysentery, and diarrhoea leading to dehydration and eventually death. Epidemics occur after natural disasters, such as earthquakes and floods, in poor areas of South America, Africa, Middle East, and Asia when piped water supplies are often disrupted and contaminated by contact with raw sewage. A major epidemic occurred in Haiti after the massive earthquake in 2010. Cases are still being reported in the capital, Port au Prince, one of the world's poorest cities, eight years later.

The harmful effects of water pollution on natural ecosystems were described in Chapter 3, pages 88–90 and Figure 3.20. Toxic substances from industry and agriculture entering lakes and rivers are poisonous. Some quickly break down in the environment into harmless substances, but others do not. Instead, they accumulate in the food chain. As they pass through the food chain, they affect and damage all the organisms in it, even the top predators. **Bioaccumulation** refers to the accumulation of such pesticides or other chemicals or metals in an organism. It occurs when an organism absorbs a toxic substance at a faster rate than it can be broken down or excreted. An example is shown in Figure 4.23 of how mercury can accumulate in the food chain. Until recently, mercury was used in many chemical industry products, including insecticides. Mercury damages the nervous and reproductive systems.

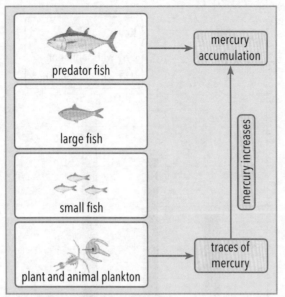

FIGURE 4.23 Bioaccumulation of mercury in a food chain

DDT is another persistent toxic material. It passes up the food chain from insects to small birds, then from small birds to birds of prey such as hawks and falcons. It can accumulate in the birds of prey, where it causes weaknesses in their eggs, reducing their populations. For this reason, the use of DDT is banned in most countries. Previously it was widely used for malaria control.

In addition, acid rain affects the health of organisms in rivers and lakes, resulting in the deaths of fish and plant life. Many fish cannot tolerate low pH values in the water. Acid rain and its effects are covered in more detail in Chapter 7 (pages 205-208).

ACTIVITIES

1 (a) State the percentages for access to sanitation in Figure 4.22A.

   (b) Suggest reasons for the big difference between them.

2 (a) From Figure 4.22B, state

     (i) the population with sanitation in 2010;

     (ii) the population without sanitation in 2010;

     (iii) the total population living in developing countries in 2010.

   (b) Calculate the percentage of the total without access to sanitation in 2010.

   (c) Does a study of Figure 4.22B suggest that the problem of lack of sanitation in the developing world is getting better? Explain your answer.

3 (a) State what is meant by bioaccumulation and describe how it works.

   (b) Draw a labelled diagram to show the bioaccumulation of DDT in a food chain.

   (c) Explain why the top predator is often the one most affected by bioaccumulation.

4 Investigate water pollution in a local river.

Managing pollution and improving water quality

Strategies for improving water quality are shown in the spider diagram in Figure 4.24. Some apply everywhere, such as improved sanitation, treatment of sewage, and pollution controls backed by legislation that are enforced. Clearly, the need for improvement is greater in developing countries. In many of these countries, the better provision of essential public services such as piped water supply and modern sewage treatment works is made more difficult because of lack of funds and weak administrations. High population growth and poor access to rural areas, where many people live, do not help. Passing laws to control pollution is a worthless exercise if the authorities do not have the interest or resources to enforce them.

Some strategies apply more widely. All countries, whether developed or not, can adopt water conservation measures and be more efficient in their water use. This is the same as persuading people and companies to reduce their energy use that was referred

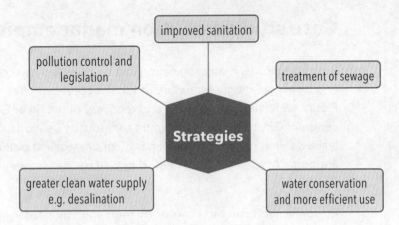

FIGURE 4.24 Strategies for improving water quantity

to in Chapter 2. It is making the Earth's limited natural resources last longer. Of course, the need to save on water use is most critical in desert and water-poor countries. Saving water in use is much cheaper than having to increase the supply. Building dams, reservoirs, and canal systems for water transfer is expensive. Farmers can use water efficient methods of irrigation such as **trickle drip irrigation** (Chapter 3, page 101).

As previously mentioned, some desert countries receive so little rain that **desalination** is the only way to satisfy increasing demand. The top five countries for desalination are listed in Table 4.2. Three are located in the Gulf, one in North Africa (desert climates), and one in Europe (Mediterranean climate). Spain is the driest of the European countries, but it has an enormous commercial agricultural sector for vegetables and fruit exports to other EU countries located further north with cooler climates.

TABLE 4.2   Desalinated water production – top 5 countries (2014)

Rank	Country	Amount (million cubic metres)	Total population (in millions)	Natural fresh water resources per head (cubic metres)
1	Saudi Arabia	9.17	28.7	118
2	UAE	8.38	8.1	58
3	Spain	3.78	46.8	2794
4	Kuwait	2.59	2.9	10
5	Algeria	2.36	36.5	460

ACTIVITIES

1 State briefly what is meant by each of the following terms:

   (i) water conservation, **(ii)** pollution control, **(iii)** improved sanitation, and **(iv)** sewage treatment.

2 **(a)** What is desalination and how does it work?

   (b) Identify two characteristics of the countries with high desalinated water production.

   (c) Why is desalination not a suitable strategy for additional water supply for all countries?

Case study: Pollution management in the River Clyde ■

Both pollution and eutrophication can be reversed by cutting off the sources of pollution and by allowing time for nature to take its course and repair the damage. The time line in Figure 4.25 charts the decline and recovery of the River Clyde, which flows through the centre of Glasgow, the main centre for industry in Scotland during the Industrial Revolution. It shows what can be done when regulations against pollution are passed and enforced, although the clean-up was helped as well by the decline in the amount of industry in Glasgow.

Eutrophication can be reversed by regulating industrial, agricultural, and domestic discharges of phosphorus and nitrogen. Simple measures, like replacing domestic detergents by soap, also help. Local people are often willing to cooperate when they are educated about conservation and the environment. However, water quality still needs constant monitoring to check that regulations about discharge into rivers are not being broken.

Time line for pollution on the River Clyde in Glasgow

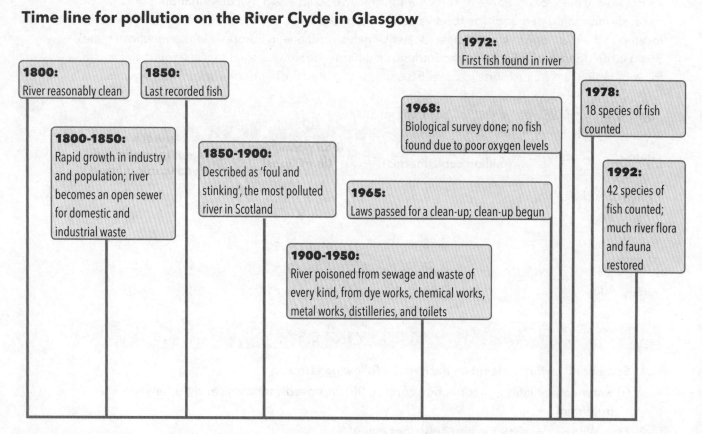

1800: River reasonably clean

1850: Last recorded fish

1972: First fish found in river

1978: 18 species of fish counted

1800-1850: Rapid growth in industry and population; river becomes an open sewer for domestic and industrial waste

1850-1900: Described as 'foul and stinking', the most polluted river in Scotland

1968: Biological survey done; no fish found due to poor oxygen levels

1965: Laws passed for a clean-up; clean-up begun

1992: 42 species of fish counted; much river flora and fauna restored

1900-1950: River poisoned from sewage and waste of every kind, from dye works, chemical works, metal works, distilleries, and toilets

FIGURE 4.25 Time line for pollution and it's management on the River Clyde in Glasgow

Providing clean water to rural areas in developing countries

International awareness of the importance of improving access to safe water for millions of people in developing countries has been increased by the work of charities such as Water Aid and by organizations like the United Nations. Raising finance is more difficult.

One example of a new policy initiative is 'Water For All', launched by the ADB (Asian Development Bank) in 2001 for the Asia-Pacific region. It recognizes how dire the region's water problems are. One in three Asians lacks access to safe drinking water within 200 metres of home; half the people living in Asia do not have access to basic sanitation. Until these needs are met, output, income, and health are at risk. The poor are the ones hardest hit by water scarcity, lack of access to safe water, and by pollution and flooding. The main aim is to focus on the real needs of people for water, so that sustainable improvements and development are achieved.

Example: Rural water supply to farming villages in the Punjab—before and after

Before

A tale from a village in the Punjab

'I spend between 3 and 6 hours a day carrying water from as far away as 6 kilometres. My children help me.

Sometimes we can take water from irrigation canals. These are closer to the village, but the water is muddy. It is bad water because the farmers spray chemicals on their crops in the fields around the canals.

Most of the time we use a stagnant rain water pond. Animals use the land around it. The water is so dirty. It is all we have got for drinking, bathing and washing clothes.

Often my children get sick with diarrhoea, and there is cholera in the village in the rainy season. We do not have any money to go to the doctor. Life is so bad that some families are leaving the village.'

FIGURE 4.26 A tale from a village in the Punjab in Pakistan

FIGURE 4.27 Water supply in a village in southern Pakistan—but how safe and clean is it?

Case Study

After

Success Story

ADB Review
January-February 2003

A rural water supply project in Pakistan is boosting family incomes and increasing women's confidence

The Punjab Rural Water Supply and Sanitation Sector Project provides simple, low cost water supply and drainage systems in 335 rural villages in Punjab Province for safe drinking water and sanitation facilities. It was the first ADB project in Punjab to employ a community-driven approach in which local people were involved in planning and overseeing the construction.

It was badly needed. Punjab is Pakistan's most densely populated province with a population of about 84 million. About 60 per cent of the population lives in rural areas and 36 per cent of these lives below the poverty line. Just over half the rural population has access to safe water; the remainder relies on water sources such as uncovered wells, rivers, rain-fed canals and ponds.

The project, financed with an ADB loan of US$46 million ran from 1995 to 2002 and constructed 305 pumping and 30 gravity systems to benefit about 800 000 rural dwellers, whose average monthly income is less than $63.

Spin-off benefits

The incidence of waterborne diseases has decreased by 90 per cent. Children are no longer required to fetch water and are instead sent to school. This has resulted in an 80 per cent increase in enrolment. Household income has increased by more than 20 per cent because women have more time to generate income. With clean water supply in homes more time is spent on productive activities. Life styles have changed. Efforts are now focused on promoting livelihood activities such as embroidery, poultry raising, milk production and marketing produce in urban centres. Because women now have more dignity and are feeling good, they are helping the men generate revenue. People who had migrated to the cities are coming back to the villages.

FIGURE 4.28   Extract from a report in the ADB Review (January - February 2003)

ACTIVITIES

1 **(a)** 'Until 1950, the River Clyde was in a similar state to many rivers flowing through big cities in developing countries today.' Explain this statement.

   (b) State two reasons why it was possible to reduce water pollution in the River Clyde.

   (c) How does the example of the River Clyde suggest that there is still hope for the world's other polluted rivers?

2 Explain as fully as you can why it is difficult for people living in rural areas like the Punjab to obtain clean water supplies.

3 Case study: Taking clean water supply to villages in the Punjab

   With reference to pages 131-132, write under these headings:

   A   Why a clean water supply was badly needed

   B   Details about the scheme

   C   Economic and social benefits

   D   What was done to try to make sure that it was a success

Managing water-related diseases

Many of the diseases that people suffer from in the Tropics are associated with water. There are three main types of environmental diseases related to water.

- Water-based—the carrier lives in water
- Water-borne—diseases spread by drinking contaminated water
- Water-bred—the carrier breeds in water and spreads disease by biting its victims

Malaria is a water-bred disease. The female *anopheles* mosquito is the vector (carrier) for malaria. Only the females drink blood; the males are vegetarians. Mosquitoes breed in stagnant fresh water in swamps, ponds, and lakes, which are plentiful in the wet season. The most likely time for the female mosquito to bite and suck blood is at night. To transfer the disease, the mosquito must bite a person whose blood already contains the malaria parasite called plasmodium. When the next person is bitten, the mosquito injects her saliva into the bloodstream and thousands of tiny parasites thread their way through the bloodstream to the human liver. Here they multiply. After about a fortnight, the victim begins to feel very feverish, cold, and very ill. The invaders continue to multiply until the victim is cured by drug treatment, develops some sort of immunity, or in some cases, dies. Malaria is a debilitating disease. Bouts of high fever keep coming back every 48–72 hours. All the victim can do is lie down or sit around until the fever passes its peak. People are left feeling very weak. Malaria stays with many people for the rest of their lives and they suffer from periodic bouts of fever.

Symptoms that are common for many of these water-related diseases include high temperature and fever, diarrhoea, dehydration (loss of body water and salts), and feeling very weak and unwell. Many people are too weak to undertake normal work.

Death from these diseases is most likely for those victims who are already weak as a result of suffering from another disease or from hunger. The young and the elderly are most at risk, particularly infants under one year old.

INFORMATION BOX

Malaria in 2016
The grim details
- Half the world's population lives in countries with a malaria risk.
- It is killing more than 1000 people every day.
- It still kills 400,000 people a year.

Signs of hope
- Sri Lanka declared itself a malaria-free country.
- Another 13 countries have reported no cases for a year.
- By 2020 another 20 countries could be free of the disease.

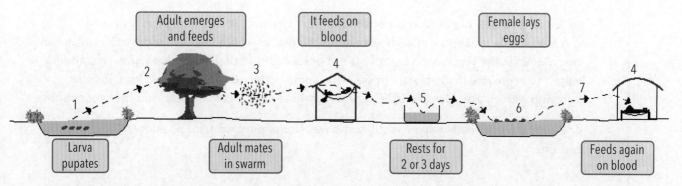

FIGURE 4.29   Stages in the life of a female anopheles mosquito

OXFORD
UNIVERSITY PRESS

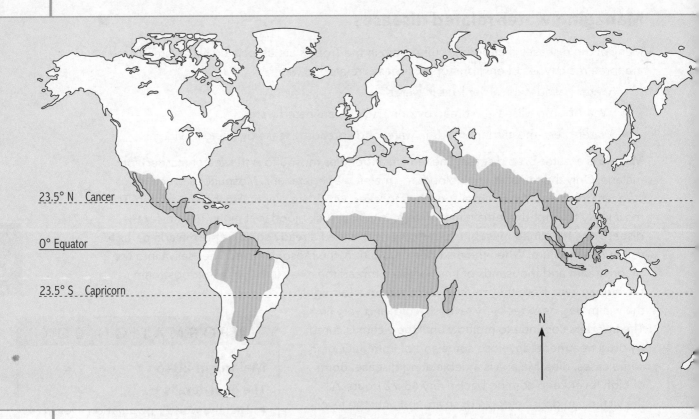

FIGURE 4.30 Malaria–main regions affected

Some areas clear of malaria today were badly affected in the past. These included the southern states in the USA and countries around the Mediterranean Sea. In these places, there was a concerted attack on the mosquito breeding grounds during the twentieth century. One policy was to drain the marshes; unfortunately, this took away many of the world's natural wetlands and resulted in the disappearance of diverse range of plants and animals. The second was to use DDT, a long-lasting pesticide; unfortunately, DDT killed much else too, including the insects upon which the birds fed. Its use is now banned in most developed countries but it is still used in some developing countries.

Strategies for control of malaria

As for all diseases, prevention is better than cure. One way is to destroy the breeding grounds. While draining wetlands eliminates the places where the carrier breeds, rainfall can be so great in the wet season that this is not practicable. Padi rice needs to grow in standing water, so in the rice lands of Asia this is not a commercial option. Other options, such as spraying with insecticides like DDT, destroy far more than just the larvae and the mosquitoes.

The battle to eradicate malaria is still some way from being won, for a variety of reasons.

- Prophylactic drugs, (drugs taken to prevent malaria being caught), such as chloroquine, no longer work in many places as the microbe mutates (changes) and the plasmodium parasite develops resistance. Newer drugs such as larium are stronger, but they come with more side effects for the people using them.

- Tourists and temporary visitors can afford the drugs, but many people in rural areas in Africa and Asia living on less than US$1 per day cannot.

- From time to time government and international health programmes target malaria, but any improvements made are lost once the campaigns end.

- Medical programmes collapse when political unrest or wars break out. This is a major factor in many African countries.

- Although most people know that the only way to keep out the malaria-carrier mosquito at night is by sleeping under a net, too many do not do so, even in high risk areas.

In 1998 the World Health Organization (WHO) launched its 'Roll Back Malaria' campaign. The target was to reduce by half deaths from malaria by 2010. However, with limited funds, and the global need to use resources to fight other diseases such as Aids / HIV, deaths increased for a time. With better funding since 2010, deaths have come down from more than a million per year in 2000 to 400,000 in 2016-still an awful lot of deaths, but a real improvement. In 2015, the UN and the Bill and Melinda Gates Foundation developed a plan to eradicate malaria worldwide by 2040. Everyone agrees that eradication is the only sustainable solution to malaria. Otherwise the research and investment into new drugs and insecticides will go on forever because of the great ability of both mosquito and parasite to develop resistance.

At one time the big hope was discovering a vaccine to boost people's own immune systems against malaria. Trials of new vaccines were frequently optimistic at first, but their effectiveness reduced over time. Also, they offered only low level protection.

Now the focus is on the approach that proved successful in Sri Lanka. Here the government was totally committed to eradication. It provided all the financial and human resources needed. Millions of mosquito nets were bought; large quantities of insecticides and a variety of different drugs were distributed to rural areas, where 80 per cent of the country's people live. Sri Lanka made good use of its effective public health system. This time the government was determined not to give up until no more malaria cases were reported. When it had eased back on an earlier eradication programme in the 1960s, cases of malaria rebounded as soon as control efforts were relaxed.

However, the task of eradicating malaria in some sub-Saharan African countries is going to be difficult. Fatal cases of the disease in just two countries, the Central African Republic and Nigeria, account for 40 per cent of all malaria deaths. Both have problems with terrorist groups and poor governance—exactly the opposite of what is essential for a systematic eradication programme to succeed.

ACTIVITIES

1 (a) Why is malaria described as a water-bred disease?

(b) Describe the life cycle of the malaria parasite.

(c) Suggest reasons why outbreaks of malaria are more likely (i) in the wet season than the dry season and (ii) in rural areas than urban areas.

2 Describe the methods which might be used to control or destroy malarial mosquitoes (a) at stages 1 and 6, and (b) stage 4 in Figure 4.29.

3 (a) State the information that shows that malaria is still a major killer, especially in sub-Saharan Africa.

(b) Describe how and why there are signs of hope for the future in the fight against malaria.

(c) Explain why some countries have been, and will be, more successful than others in eradicating malaria.

Cholera is a water-borne disease. It is caught from drinking unsafe water or by eating food contaminated with the bacterium *Vibrio cholerae*. This causes severe diarrhoea, which may lead to dehydration and eventually death. The short incubation period means that it can 'spread like wildfires' in densely populated places causing epidemics, and sometimes pandemics (millions affected). Cholera is endemic (ever present) in many developing countries. Places where people are most at risk of catching cholera are squatter settlements around big cities, war zones, refugee camps, and earthquake disaster zones, where the minimum requirements of clean water and sanitation are not, or just cannot be, met.

Short-term strategies to control cholera are instructing people to boil water before drinking it, and in some emergency situations, the distribution of bottled water or use of water tankers. The long-term strategy lies in economic development and universal access to safe drinking water and adequate sanitation. These are the keys to preventing both epidemic and endemic cholera.

INFORMATION BOX

Cholera—the grim details

- Number of cases per year: between 1.5 and 4.0 million

- Deaths per year: between 30,000 and 150,000

- Short incubation period: between 2 hours and 5 days

- Bacteria presence in human faeces: between 1 and 10 days causes acute diarrhoea and dehydration: can kill within hours if not treated

The good news

- Up to 80% of cases can be successfully treated with oral rehydration salts.

Actions which help to ensure these results include:

- water treatment facilities, e.g. adding chlorine (chlorination)
- piped water distribution systems
- in households, safe water storage containers and water filters
- boiling all water first when permanent supply source cannot be trusted
- construction of systems for sewage disposal, chemical latrines

What do all these actions have in common? They need funding and organization; they need long-term investment and infrastructure provision. And what do the world's least developed countries most lack? Money and efficient, non-corrupt administrations.

Unlike for malaria, there is a vaccine for cholera, which is reasonably effective, and is an additional way to control the disease during an outbreak. However, it is not widely used, even by tourists visiting countries where cholera is endemic.

ACTIVITIES

1 (a) Why is cholera described as a water-borne disease?

 (b) Describe the circumstances which lead to countries having cholera outbreaks.

2 Explain why cholera is described as a 'poor country disease'.

3 Are the chances of eradicating cholera from the world higher, the same, or lower than those for eradicating malaria? State and explain your view on this.

CHAPTER 5

Oceans and fisheries

OBJECTIVES

In this chapter you will learn about

- the resource potential of the oceans
- world fisheries and their exploitation
- exploitation of the oceans (overfishing) and its impact
- management of the harvesting of marine species

FIGURE 5.1 Traditional fishing boats in south-west Portugal

INTRODUCTION

Oceans occupy 70 per cent of the Earth's surface. Of all the water on Earth, 97 per cent is in the oceans. They exert a great influence over the planet's weather and climate. They stabilize temperatures on land. More importantly, they yield moisture back into the atmosphere through evaporation, which replaces the Earth's fresh water supplies in rivers and lakes so that all of us can use it. In the life-filled oceans, oxygen is generated and carbon dioxide absorbed. Without the oceans, Earth would be a lot like Mars—a place unsuitable for humans and the rest of life on Earth as we know it.

The primary producers, upon which all other ocean life depends, are the phytoplankton, simple single-celled organisms of the sea. They only exist in the upper layers of water because they depend upon sunlight for the production of organic matter through the process of photosynthesis. An example of a marine ecosystem is given in Figure 5.2. Work upwards through the four trophic levels. Of the 100 per cent of energy available from the phytoplankton level, only about 2 per cent is left by the third level, marine life, and potentially available for human use. The rest has been lost to respiration and waste.

INFORMATION BOX

Key feature of all ecosystems
Interdependence

- Each part of the system depends on the other.

- What would be the knock-on effects of a decrease in nutrient availability in one part of the ocean?

Trophic Level	Food Chain	Comment	Energy
4th	Carnivores 2 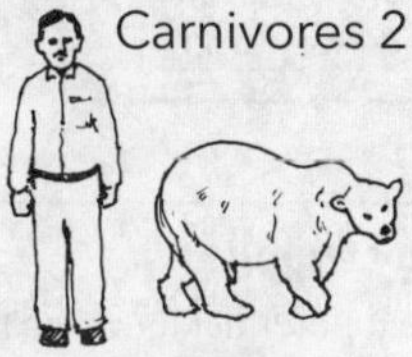	■ Top of the food chain ■ Depend on everything below	
3rd	Carnivores 1 	■ Eat the flesh of the herbivores	1-2 % of energy left
2nd	Herbivores 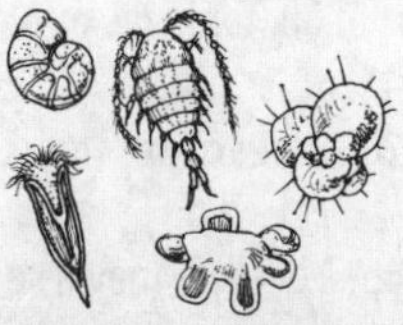	■ Zooplankton is the food supply for the 3rd level. ■ They are small organisms that graze on the phytoplankton.	Energy losses
1st	Primary Producers 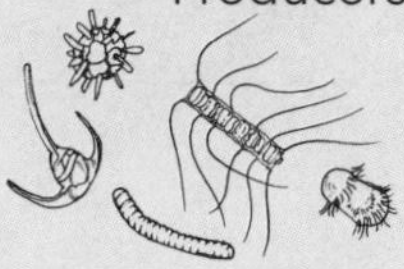	■ Phytoplankton is the food supply for the 2nd level. ■ They convert nutrients into organic compounds using energy and sunlight.	100% energy at start

FIGURE 5.2

A marine ecosystem

OXFORD
UNIVERSITY PRESS

Resource potential of oceans

Ocean resources are many and varied. Some have been exploited for centuries, notably fishing and transport. Fish feed coastal communities worldwide. They are a major source of protein, particularly in developing countries where diets are often plant-based. Many processing industries, such as canning, curing, and freezing for human food, and making animal feed and fertilizers for agricultural use, are dependent on fishing.

Travel by sea was always easier than travel over land. Only landlocked countries in Asia, Europe, Africa, and South America could not be reached by ocean travel, and to this day this has hindered their economic development. The world's major ocean shipping lanes are busy with bulk ore carriers, supertankers, and container ships linking exporting and importing countries.

For some resources, the great increase in importance has been more recent, such as tourism, offshore drilling, and desalination. Others, like wave energy, are still in the development stage.

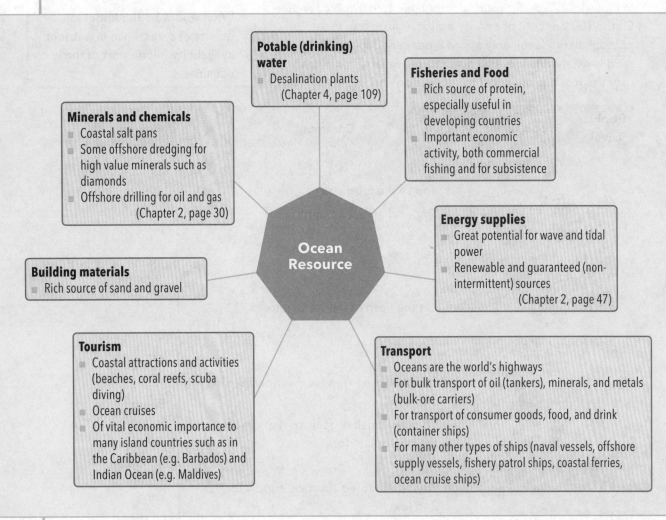

FIGURE 5.3   Ocean resources

Resources which people can use are concentrated along the coastal strip and on the **continental shelf**. This is the platform of level land, no more than 200 metres deep, which lies between the low tide mark and the continental slope (Figure 5.4). Beyond the shelf are the ocean deeps, about which much less is known because of problems of access.

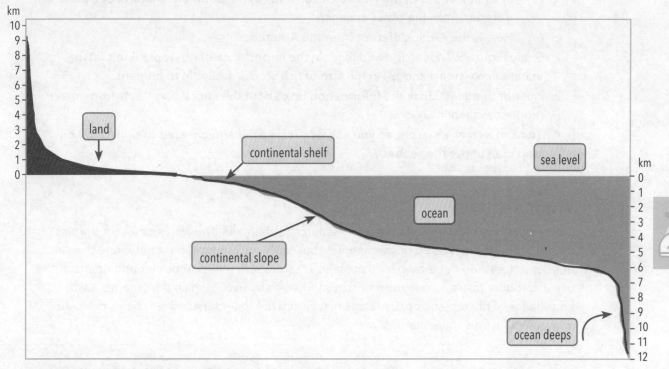

FIGURE 5.4   Cross profile of the oceans

The width of the continental shelf varies greatly from place to place. It tends to be widest along coasts fringing lowland areas. Examples include:

- off Western Europe (where it can be over 300km wide);
- off the north-eastern coast of North America;
- along the Arctic coast of Siberia (where it is up to 1200km wide).

Around other continents the shelf is much narrower. It is almost completely absent from coasts where fold mountains run parallel and close to the sea, as along the borders of the Eastern Pacific in both North and South America.

Certain areas of shallow water, such as the Arabian Gulf in the Middle East and the Gulf of Mexico in North America, have hundreds of drilling platforms and rigs. The size and value of the oil and gas resources located here mean that the extra costs of operating in the sea, compared with on land, can be recovered. Within tropical waters, coral reefs attract tourists because of their natural beauty and the teeming life of brightly coloured fish. Resorts in the Caribbean, around the Red Sea, on the islands of the Indian Ocean, and on the Great Barrier Reef in Australia attract visitors fascinated by the diving and snorkelling possibilities among the reefs.

ACTIVITIES

1 Look at a physical map of the world in an atlas.
   (a) On an outline map of the world, name the oceans and major seas.
   (b) In what way are (i) the Pacific Ocean and (ii) the Southern (Antarctic) Ocean different from the other oceans?
   (c) How is the Arctic different from the Antarctic?
2 Study Figure 5.2. Describe and explain the importance of phytoplankton (a) in marine ecosystems and (b) in the size of fish stocks available to humans.
3 Answer the question in the Information Box about the knock-on effects from lower nutrient availability.
4 Think of as many reasons as you can why it is easier and cheaper to drill for oil on land than under the seabed.

World fisheries

Fish remains the most important ocean resource for humans. The world's most important fishing grounds are located on continental shelves. More light can penetrate here than in deeper waters, and more oxygen is present. They are also the most nutrient-rich parts of the oceans. Nutrients are carried from nearby land areas by rivers, which encourages an abundance of phytoplankton. Look again at Figure 5.4 to understand why fish stocks are more plentiful on continental shelves.

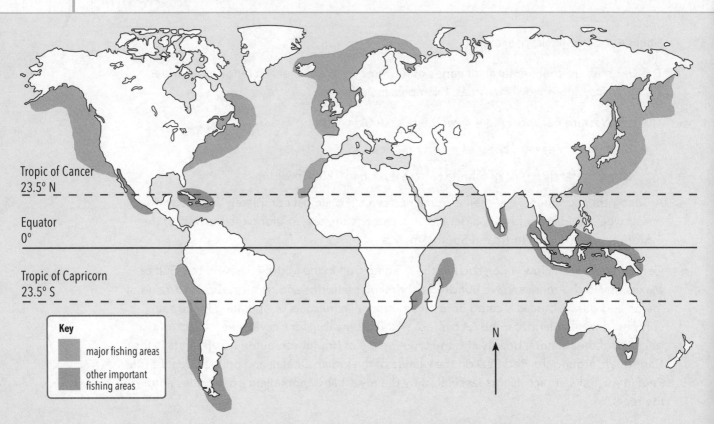

Tropic of Cancer 23.5° N
Equator 0°
Tropic of Capricorn 23.5° S

Key
major fishing areas
other important fishing areas

N

FIGURE 5.5 Major fishing grounds

OXFORD
UNIVERSITY PRESS

Major fishing grounds are located predominantly in the temperate zone of the Northern Hemisphere (Figure 5.5). This is mainly due to environmental (physical) factors, the main one of which is wide expanses of continental shelf off the east coasts of North America and Asia, and off the west coast of Europe. Although these areas are naturally rich in plankton because of their shallow waters, there is another factor: the presence of ocean currents (Figure 5.6).

Ocean currents carry nutrients. They are constantly being replenished to support great amounts of phytoplankton, the primary producers (Figure 5.2). This means that at a higher level in the ocean food chain large fish stocks can exist. Ecologically, the richest areas are in two types of location. One is where ocean currents meet, such as in the Grand Banks fishing grounds off Labrador in North America (Labrador and Gulf Stream currents). The other is where water from the ocean deeps wells up to the surface, such as off the coast of Peru (Peruvian current). Shoal fish like herring, mackerel, cod, and haddock prefer cooler temperate waters, while vast shoals of anchoveta thrive (Figure 5.6) in the cold waters of the Peruvian current off Peru.

> ## INFORMATION BOX
>
> ### Ocean Currents
> - **Cold** – carry water that is colder than surrounding waters
> - Move from the Poles towards the Equator e.g. Peruvian current
> - **Warm** – carry water that is warmer than surrounding waters
> - Move from the Equator towards the Poles e.g. Gulf Stream

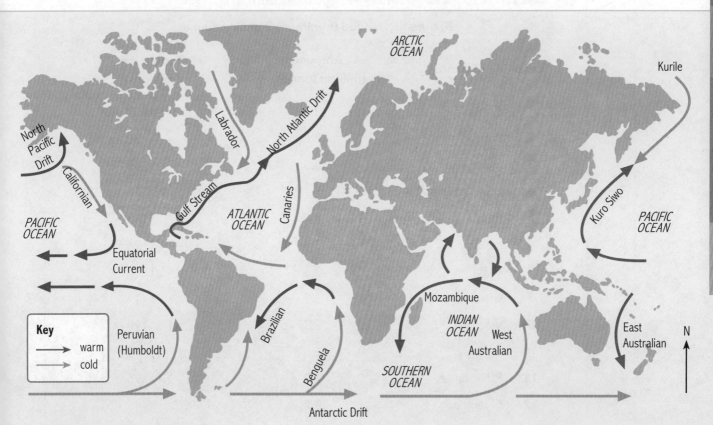

FIGURE 5.6 Major ocean currents

Human factors also help to explain the distribution of major fishing grounds shown in Figure 5.5. Many coastal regions in temperate areas are heavily populated. Fish has traditionally been an important part of the diet, especially in Japan, and in Scandinavian countries like Norway and Denmark. Many boats work in the tropical waters between and around the islands of Indonesia. Great quantities of fish are also eaten in many South-east Asian countries, although a lot of the fish eaten in this part of the world comes from fresh-water sources and fish farming.

During the last 30 years the demand for fish has increased well in excess of supply. This has encouraged the search for new fishing grounds in parts of the globe more remote from centres of population. The increasing size of fishing boats and the development of factory ships have allowed commercial fishing to be extended to the far south of the world. Many Russian and Japanese boats fish in the cold waters of the South Atlantic and Southern Oceans.

ACTIVITIES

1 Study Figure 5.5.

   (a) Describe the distribution of the world's major fishing grounds.

   (b) Explain the distribution by referring to (i) environmental factors and (ii) human factors.

2 **TABLE 5.1**   Major marine (sea and ocean) fishing countries (2011)

Marine fish landed (minimum 2 million tonnes)			
Rank	Country	Amount (million tonnes)	Population (millions)
1	China	13.5	1353
2	Peru	8.2	30
3	Indonesia	5.3	245
4	USA	5.1	316
5	Russia	4.0	143
6	Japan	3.7	126
7	India	3.3	1258
8	Chile	3.1	17
9	Vietnam	2.3	90
10	Norway	2.3	5
11	Philippines	2.2	96
12	Myanmar	2.2	49

(a)   On a world outline map of countries, shade and name the marine fishing countries listed in Table 5.1.

(b)   Draw a bar graph to show the amounts of fish landed by these 12 countries.

(c)   Use different colours or shading for the bars to show countries

    (i)   close to the fishing grounds in the temperate zone of the northern hemisphere;

    (ii)   next to the Peruvian current;

    (iii)   in warm tropical waters.

3   From Table 5.1, choose one country likely to export a lot of the fish landed, and another country unlikely to export much fish. Explain your choices.

Decline in fish stocks

During the last 100 years, as the total world population has increased massively (by about 6 billion people), not much thought was given to the world's oceans and seas. People have removed billions of tonnes of living creatures from the sea in the blind belief that this was an inexhaustible resource. In exchange, they have added billions of tonnes of toxic substances to the oceans. Fish and other living things are seen as commodities instead of important components of a living ecosystem. There needs to be more awareness of the need for healthy oceans for a generally healthy Earth.

While humans are definitely responsible for the overall decline in world fish stocks, there can also be natural causes. Fish stocks do go up and down according to variations in ocean temperature and changes in ocean current strength and direction. The best known example is simply referred to as El Niño, although the full title is El Niño Southern Oscillation (ENSO).

El Niño and its effects on fish stocks

Fishing is an important economic activity in Peru. Most years it stands first or second for the catch landed. The presence of the Peruvian (or Humboldt) current explains why its coastal waters are so fish-rich (Figure 5.6).

Movements of ocean currents are very complicated, but the change that occurs off the coast of Peru, between the Peruvian and Southern Equatorial currents, is the greatest of all. Its effects are worldwide, so that it is not confined to Peru and South America; however, it is Peru and its fisheries that feel the strongest impact. The worst El Niño event in living memory was in 1997-98 (pages 147-148); none of the events in the twenty years since have had such great effects.

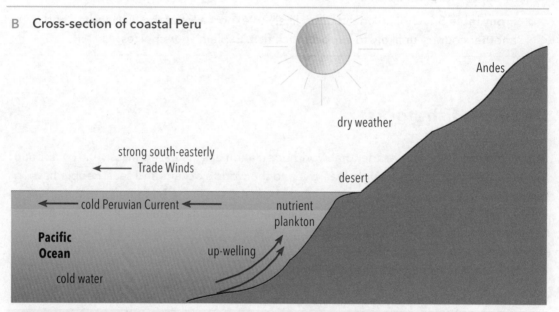

A **Ocean currents in the Pacific Ocean**

0°

Equator

Southern
Equatorial
Current

warm surface

Australia

cool
surface

Peruvian
Current

South
America

B **Cross-section of coastal Peru**

Andes

dry weather

strong south-easterly
Trade Winds

desert

cold Peruvian Current

nutrient
plankton

**Pacific
Ocean**

up-welling

cold water

FIGURE **5.7**   Fishing in Peru

C **Reasons for rich fishing grounds off the coast of Peru**

- The Peruvian Current is supplied by cold water from the Antarctic Drift.
- Up-welling of cold water to the ocean surface takes place next to the coast of Peru.
- Surface water off Peru is about 5°C cooler than expected.
- The current is rich in nitrates and nutrients.
- Higher up the food chain, great shoals of anchoveta fish are supported.
- Large flocks of sea birds feed on the fish.

D **Economic importance of fish to Peru**

- Anchoveta are processed into fishmeal in factories in the coastal ports.
- Fishmeal is exported for animal feed.
- Earnings account for about 15 per cent of Peru's exports by value.
- Many people work as fishermen and in the processing factories in the coastal towns.
- Since it is a desert coast, other types of work are scarce.
- Fish remains are crushed and bird droppings (guano) are collected for fertilizer.

An El Niño year in Peru

For reasons not fully understood, the South-east Trade Winds are weaker in some years. Warm water from Indonesia is allowed to drift eastwards across the Pacific. The usual pattern of flow of surface currents is reversed (Figure 5.9). This happens around Christmas off Peru, which is why Peruvian fishermen gave it the name 'El Niño', meaning the Christ Child. This happens every 3–8 years.

The sudden change in sea water temperature has a dramatic effect on life both in the sea and on the land. Warm ocean water kills plankton and fish because its currents are low in oxygen and nutrients. Beaches become littered with washed up dead fish and sea birds. The large fish shoals move further offshore into colder waters, out of range of fishermen with only small boats.

It has remarkable climatic effects. In one El Niño event, 380mm of rain fell in March in the port city of Trujillo compared with a normal total of 38mm for the month. Normally dried-up river channels become raging torrents of mud, boulders, and debris which sweep away bridges, destroy crops, and wash away whole villages (Figure 5.8). Irrigation works, essential for cultivation in normal years, are destroyed. Mosquitoes and insects multiply in the wet environment.

Effects of the 1997–98 El Niño event

This very strong El Niño devastated coastal Peru.

- Up to 350 people died.
- Up to 250,000 were made homeless by heavy rains.
- Peru's economy declined by 5 per cent.

It was also blamed for upsetting world patterns of rainfall and drought over a wide area of the world, in Asia and Africa as well as the Americas.

Although many areas suffered, a few benefited. Fewer hurricanes hit the Caribbean, and higher rainfall in Los Angeles helped to clear its famous smog.

FIGURE 5.8 The village of San Bartolome in Peru was destroyed by great floods in the 1982–83 El Niño event.

OXFORD
UNIVERSITY PRESS

A Ocean currents

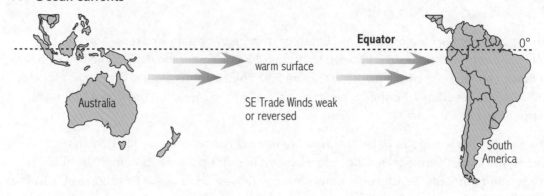

B Cross-section

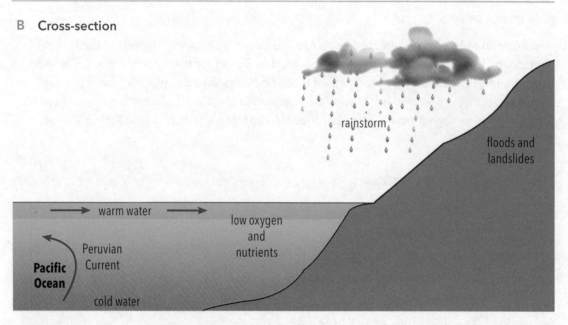

FIGURE 5.9 An 'El Niño' year in Peru and the Pacific

ACTIVITIES

1 Study Figure 5.9 and compare it with Figure 5.7 on page 146.

Describe the changes in an El Niño year using these headings:

Ocean currents, Life in the ocean, Climate on the coast of Peru.

2 The main occupations for people living in coastal Peru are fishing, farming, and factory work. Explain why all three occupations become more difficult, or even impossible, in an El Niño year.

3 Taking an overall view, do you consider the presence of the Peruvian Current to be good or bad for Peru? Explain your view.

Overfishing and its consequences

Every major fishing ground in the world is now considered to be at risk; some have collapsed. It is estimated that 70 per cent of all world fish stocks have reached the point where commercial fishing is no longer sustainable. When European settlers first arrived in what is now Canada, they heard rumours that there were so many fish in the sea you could almost walk on them. Today, on the Grand Banks off Newfoundland there are practically no fish. Overfishing has meant that there are insufficient fish left to carry on the reproductive cycle and raise stock levels to the point where large-scale commercial fishing can return.

What has now become clear is that the number of fish caught should not be determined by the number of fish available, but by the numbers that will be left to maintain future fish stocks. Making money has been more important than leaving sufficient fish to grow to full size that will allow maximum levels of reproduction to be achieved. Look at Table 5.2: what suggests that Peru's rich offshore fishing grounds were overfished during the 1960s?

TABLE 5.2   Total fish catches in Peru, 1970–2014 (million tonnes)

1970	12.5	1980	2.8	1990	6.9	2000	10.7	2010	4.2
1971	10.5	1981	2.8	1991	6.9	2001	7.1	2011	8.3
1972	4.7	1982	3.6	1992	7.5	2002	9.7	2012	4.7
1973	2.3	1983	1.6	1993	9.0	2003	5.4	2013	5.8
1974	4.2	1984	3.3	1994	1.2	2004	10.5	2014	2.2
1975	3.5	1985	4.1	1995	8.9	2005	10.2		
1976	4.4	1986	5.6	1996	9.5	2006	7.2		
1977	2.6	1987	4.6	1997	7.9	2007	7.8		
1978	3.5	1988	6.7	1998	4.3	2008	7.5		
1979	3.7	1989	6.9	1999	8.4	2009	6.9		

OXFORD
UNIVERSITY PRESS

Causes of overfishing

Few have doubts about the main cause—the use of new technology. In Table 5.3 a comparison is given between old and new boats and methods of fishing. Luck no longer plays any part in finding great shoals of fish. Instead, sophisticated fish-finding sonar and satellite navigation allow locations to be pinpointed with great accuracy (Figure 5.10). Once taken on board the modern factory ship, useful fish are sorted, gutted, filleted, and frozen; their remains, along with the fish considered non-commercially useful, are thrown back into the sea. Working close to the home port is no longer essential.

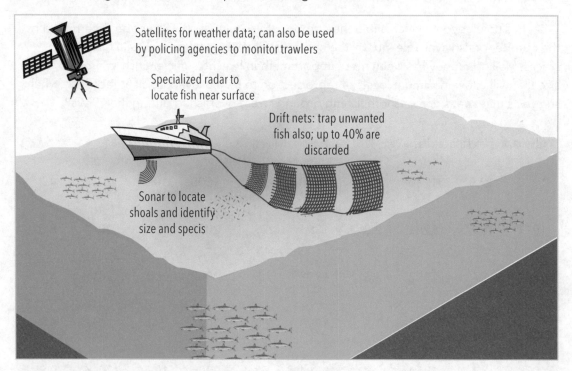

FIGURE 5.10   How high-tech fishing leads to a reduction in fish stocks

In summary, today's modern boats are larger, can travel further, detect the whereabouts of the big shoals of fish with precision, and use nets so large that they scoop up everything in the sea including small and immature fish.

Despite falling stocks, fishing continues. Demand for fish continues to rise as the world population increases; fish shortages mean good prices for everything that is caught. Having invested a lot of money in boats and equipment, it is easy to understand why fishermen are desperate to stay in business and preserve their livelihoods. This is why some boat owners continue to overexploit fish stocks and use nets with too small a mesh size that trap immature fish.

INFORMATION BOX

Definitions of key terms

- **Target species:** types of fish fishing boats want to catch
- **Bycatch:** fish caught that are of no value, usually discarded and wasted
- **Immature fish:** fish too young to breed and continue the species

Where a change in natural circumstances for the worse is combined with overfishing, the results are dire. Look again at Table 5.2 to see what happened to fish catches in Peru during the El Niño years of 1972–73.

TABLE 5.3　Fishing old and new

Factors	Old fishing boats	Modern fishing boats
Boat size	Under 20m long	Up to 100m long
Crew	Owner-skipper and 4 or 5 crewmen	As many as 100 people employed by a company
Range	Worked close to the home port due to limited fuel and refrigeration and perils of the weather	Away from port for weeks or months in every corner of the ocean
Finding fish	Experience of waters, fish instinct, and good luck	Radar and sonar to find fish, satellites for navigation and weather data
Nets	Covered at most 1 or 2 hectares of sea	Nets at least 1km wide are trailed that can scoop up 400 tonnes of fish in one gulp.

Consequences of overfishing

Fish stocks on some fishing grounds are now at such low levels that for many years they will not recover the numbers needed for commercial fishing to begin again. All wildlife populations have their good times and bad; huge surpluses of fish that build up in years when food supply is plentiful are needed to ensure sufficient breeding stock for the lean years which will certainly come. Humans have regarded such surpluses as a gift of nature just waiting to be extracted and are now paying the price.

Hundreds of thousands of jobs in fishing and related industries were lost in the 1990s. Fishing boats were left rusting in ports, worth less than what owners paid for them. Small port communities, in remote locations where fishing is the only source of employment, have been badly hit. The desperate search for new fish supplies is spreading the problem of overfishing to other parts of the world hitherto untouched, such as the Southern Ocean.

OXFORD
UNIVERSITY PRESS

ACTIVITIES

1   Total world marine fish catches (million tonnes) 1959–2009:

   1959: 30.0; 1964: 38.8; 1969: 47.2; 1974: 52.1; 1979: 55.0;
   1984: 63.6; 1989: 72.8; 1994: 73.5; 1999: 71.2; 2004: 67.0; 2009: 79.6

   (a)   Draw a line graph to show world catches, 1959–2009.

   (b)   Describe what your graph shows about world fish catches from 1959.

2   Draw labelled sketches to explain how the use of new technology leads to overfishing.

3   'Fish in the ocean is an unlimited and inexhaustible natural resource.' Explain why (a) people used to think this was true and (b) why we now know it is not true.

4   Investigation

   (a)   Use an Internet search engine to find the views of one conservation group, such as Greenpeace, about whaling.

   (b)   Do you agree with these views? Explain.

Fish farming

The big growth in fish farming since 2000 has been a response to increasing world demand for seafood and the decline in natural fisheries due to overfishing. Seventy-five per cent of world fisheries are either overfished or fully fished. It is estimated that over half of all seafood consumed by Americans comes from aquaculture of some kind.

INFORMATION BOX

Other names for fish farming
- **Pisciculture** – literally 'cultivating fish'
- **Aquaculture** – literally 'cultivation in water'

Fish farming is raising fish in tanks or enclosures for sale. Most fish farms are run by large companies who have the investment money needed. Only one type of fish is kept. Some are freshwater, for fish such as trout and carp, while others are marine, especially for salmon. In some Asian countries, however, fish are reared more for subsistence than for sale; here fish are bred for food in irrigation channels and ponds on a much smaller scale.

Case studies of fish farming

1 Example of marine fishery: Atlantic salmon fishery in southern Chile

Fish farms are located in many places in southern Chile, but the greatest concentration is south of the city of Puerto Montt, some 1000km south of the capital city Santiago. Open net fish farming is used, in which fish are kept in pens in the sea. The clean, non-polluted coastal waters of the Pacific, in the shelter of many islands, make for an ideal physical location. The fact that labour and energy costs were lower in Chile than in Norway attracted the big companies. The industry grew rapidly in the 1990s and Chile became the world's second largest salmon producer after Norway.

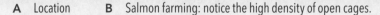

A Location   B Salmon farming: notice the high density of open cages.

FIGURE 5.11   Fish farming in southern Chile

Then between 2005 and 2010 there was a crisis. The farms were hit by an outbreak of a deadly disease, the infectious salmon anaemia, which halved the country's salmon stocks. In 2007 the industry nearly collapsed. Thousands of workers were laid off, fish farms were lying empty, and local waters were polluted.

The rapid spread of the disease was blamed on farms being packed together and the lack of strong regulation. Environmentalists, however, had concerns about disease and pollution before this crisis. From open net pens, waste is discharged directly into the sea, so that it spreads parasites and diseases. Also, Chile uses significantly more antibiotics in farming than anywhere else. These threaten other marine life.

Since 2010 farmers have adopted more sustainable practices. They use inoculation against diseases rather than medication with antibiotics. They have strengthened barriers between the farms and the ocean. There have only been a few small-scale outbreaks of disease since then. In other words, it took a disaster to bring the industry to its senses.

ACTIVITIES

1 Short answer questions about fish farming.
   (a) What is meant by fish farming?
   (b) Name the main fish farmed in (i) marine and (ii) freshwater farming.
   (c) Give three reasons for the worldwide growth of fish farming.
   (d) State two problems associated with fish farming.

2 Make brief notes for the case study of fish farming in Chile using these headings as a guide:
   (a) location;
   (b) advantages for fish farming;
   (c) problems and issues;
   (d) their management.

2 Example of farming of marine species: Norway

The main marine species farmed are Atlantic cod and halibut. Norwegian coastal waters provide an excellent natural environment for these two species of fish. Waters are clean and clear; the warm waters of the North Atlantic Drift (a continuation of the Gulf Stream in Figure 5.6) keep them ice-free in winter, as well as carrying plentiful supplies of plankton. In addition, Norway, with its long coastline and islands, has always been a fishing nation. Norwegian fishermen have great expertise.

Although marine species farming began in the 1980s, it has not been as successful as salmon fish farming. Cod production actually declined to 15,000 tonnes in 2011 and halibut output has remained low at about 3000 tonnes per year. Cod have a remarkable ability to escape from their cages (far more so than salmon). The Norwegian Environment Agency has concerns about the escaped cod—will they have an impact on local natural cod stocks, which are genetically distinct? Will it result in lower survival rates for coastal cod stocks, already under pressure, which have adapted to their natural habitat over a long period of time?

Otherwise, the environmental issues from keeping marine cod in cages are similar to those associated with salmon farming. These include:

- parasites and diseases that may spread to natural stocks;
- farming facilities can disturb the habitats and breeding grounds of other marine creatures.

A separate part of the industry specializes in farming shellfish such as mussels. Local species of wild mussels are allowed to attach themselves to ropes anchored out in the water, instead of being caged. Although healthier than cod farming, mussels are the main food for some sea birds like eider ducks. There is evidence of these birds moving away from their natural feeding grounds and causing significant losses on the fish farms.

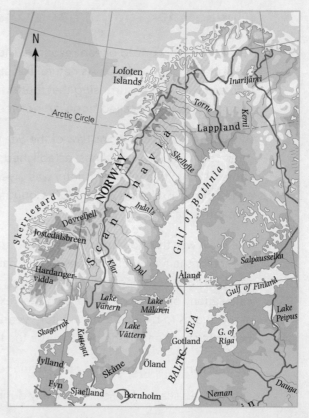

FIGURE 5.12   Norway, a maritime nation

ACTIVITIES

1   Make brief case study notes of marine fish farming in Norway for exam practice. Use these headings as a guide:

(a)   Types of fish farmed

(b)   Favourable factors for fish farming

(c)   Impact on the natural habitat

(d)   Other issues and problems

Management of the harvesting of world fisheries

Fish are a highly prized ocean resource. There are no national borders in the oceans; movement is international. As natural fish stocks decreased, and human demand for fish increased, it was not surprising that there were some heated clashes over fishing rights. One example was the so called 'cod war' between Iceland and the UK in the 1960s.

By 1982 the United Nations Law of the Sea Convention, agreed to by the governments of most countries with coastlines, established zones of 200 nautical miles (370km) around their shores. Within this zone, a country was given sole rights to natural resources. This is known as an Economic Exclusion Zone (EEZ). Countries are responsible for marine resources in their own territorial waters.

The main way that countries manage fish stocks in their EEZs is through quotas. Annual limits are set for the amount and types of fish that can be caught. Once the quota limit has been reached, further fishing is forbidden; boats have to remain in harbour. Provided that scientific calculations of fish stock size are correct, existing stocks should recover to levels that will allow quotas to be increased in future years. To be effective the limits need to be policed both out at sea and in the ports where the fish is landed.

Quotas can be supported by other management policies. These include:

- closed season for fishing, usually during the main breeding time during the year;
- restricted areas with no fishing allowed so that breeding can take place and stocks recover;
- limits on net types and sizes, so that young fish can swim through the nets, leaving them time to grow to maturity and reproduce.

Peru now manages its fishing grounds better than it used to do. Nets are inspected and there is a 2–3 month closed season. Patrols are used to enforce the exclusion zone to keep out foreign vessels, especially Japanese.

Iceland refused to join the EU (European Union) so that it could keep full control over the management of the rich marine resources within its exclusion zone. Fish account for about 15 per cent of Iceland's national income and up to 70 per cent by value of its exports. The quota to be caught by Icelandic fishermen each year is worked out as shown below.

- The Marine Research Institute, which is an independent scientific organization, estimates the size of the cod stock aged four years and above.
- Fishermen are allowed to catch 25 per cent.

Two of the most critical factors in managing fish stocks are net type and mesh size. Figure 5.13 shows two types of net used by large boats for commercial fishing. Of the two, the bottom trawl does the most damage, removing up to 25 per cent of seabed life. This is why the UN in 2002 recommended phasing it out, and it is now less used. The major issue with both nets is the large catch of unwanted, non-commercial species (the bycatch) among the species of fish being targeted. A large total amount of fish may be caught, but including only a small amount of the fish wanted for sale: a real waste, reducing marine life.

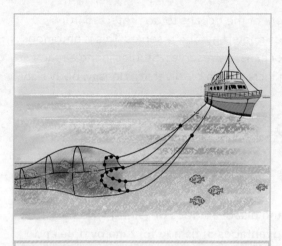

A   Bottom trawl net

▪ A large net, conical in shape, designed to be towed along the sea bottom; used to catch deep water fish such as cod, squid, and halibut.

B   Purse seine net

▪ A large net is used to surround fish, often a shoal of fish. The bottom of the net is then closed, like the mouth of a purse, by pulling a line threaded through the top.

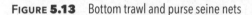

FIGURE 5.13   Bottom trawl and purse seine nets

Small mesh sizes increase the quantity of fish caught, but not the quality of the catch. If the mesh size is too small for young, immature fish to pass through it easily, high amounts of fish today will be at the expense of fish tomorrow. Large mesh sizes for the target species are essential to allow immature fish to breed and reach full size. This is essential to maintain healthy fish stocks.

One type of fishing much favoured by environmental groups such as Greenpeace is pole and line for tuna fishing. Tuna fishing is big business. It is the world's most popular fish. Most tuna are caught using large-scale industrial fishing methods and purse seine nets. These nets collect many other types of fish, as well as sharks and even turtles. In contrast, in the Maldives, a major exporter of

FIGURE 5.14   Pole and line tuna fishing in the Maldives

tuna, fishermen continue to use the traditional pole and line (Figure 5.14). This is selective, well-targeted fishing, with minimum bycatch. It supports local communities; people are living and working in balance with the oceans. Greenpeace is putting pressure on canning companies and large supermarket chains to ensure that their tuna is responsibly sourced as there has been an alarming decline in world tuna stocks.

Another Greenpeace target is for over 40 per cent of the oceans to be protected from commercial fishing or development by being designated marine reserves. This is ambitious because not much more than 1 per cent of the oceans are reserves. Studies in the already existing reserves have found benefits, including increases in biodiversity, density, body size, and reproductive potential.

ACTIVITIES

1 With the help of examples, name and describe three strategies used to manage fish stocks.

2 (a) Draw labelled diagrams to show (i) the disadvantages of fishing for tuna using purse seine nets and (ii) the advantages of fishing for tuna by pole and line.

   (b) How difficult is it going to be for Greenpeace to stop fishing for tuna using purse seine nets? State and explain your views on this.

Example of fisheries management – the European Union (EU)

The problems for implementing a successful international fisheries policy, when the national interests of more than one country are involved, can be seen in the EU. It operates a common fisheries policy between all its member countries, and sets quotas. After years of quotas, all the evidence pointed to a continuing decline in fish stocks in the North Sea (Figure 5.15). The obvious conclusion from looking at Figure 5.15 is that the quotas needed to be reduced further and bans on fishing be extended to allow fish stocks to recover.

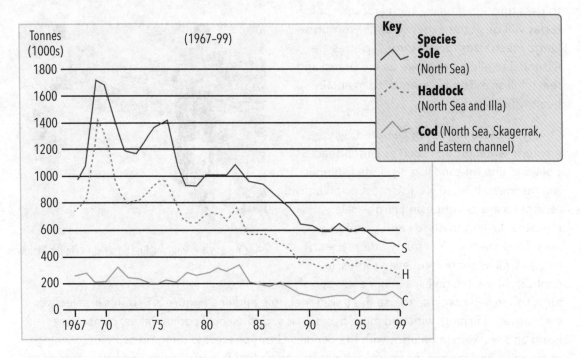

FIGURE **5.15** Landings of bottom dwelling fish for human consumption in the North Sea 1967 – 1999

The governments of the different member countries, under pressure from their own fishing communities, were reluctant to agree upon the size of cuts that scientific evidence suggested were needed. The EU, however, was attempting to do what it considered to be the best type of management for ocean resources—taking an overall view of all marine life over the whole area of the continental shelf. The underlying problem is that the national interests of too many different countries are involved.

The good news is that by 2015 there were real signs that stock levels for cod and haddock had reached the point of sustainability and were starting to increase again. Of course, this increased the pressure from fishermen and national governments for the EU to become more generous with its quotas.

Why have these strategies for sustainable harvesting had only limited success?

Many local fishermen do not believe that quotas and restrictions are necessary. They are not convinced that the scientific evidence is correct. Unless the regulations are strictly enforced by the authorities, many boat owners will engage in activities that are illegal, such as

- catching more than allowed by the quotas and not declaring the full amount caught;
- using nets with mesh sizes that are smaller than allowed;
- fishing in restricted areas or trespassing into fishing grounds belonging to another country.

Sometimes the regulations do not work in favour of sustainability, even when fishermen are sticking to the rules. When fish too small for the regulations are caught, or types of fish that are not allowed to be fished are brought up in the nets, the fishermen know that it is illegal for these to be landed in port and they are thrown back into the sea, usually dead. More than 25 per cent of the world fish catch consists of these rejected fish (called the by-catch).

One response is for fishing fleets to move from the protected fishing grounds near the coasts to sea areas just beyond the 200-mile limits. This means that overfishing in the same fishing ground is still taking place. Trying to obtain international agreements between governments about fishing and management of the open ocean beyond EEZ boundaries is difficult. Problems of overfishing are being transferred to other parts of the world where previously no problems existed, such as in the Southern Ocean.

ACTIVITIES

1 Draw a spider diagram to show the problems for implementing strategies for sustainable fishing.

2 (a) Describe what Figure 5.16 shows about fish stocks in the North Sea in the late 20th century.

    (b) What suggests that more management of fish stocks was essential?

    (c) Give reasons why successful management was difficult to achieve.

OXFORD
UNIVERSITY PRESS

CHAPTER **6**

Managing natural hazards

OBJECTIVES

In this chapter you will learn about

- five natural hazards and how they affect people
- tectonic hazards: earthquakes and volcanoes
- their causes, impacts, and management
- climatic hazards: tropical cyclones, flooding, and drought
- their causes, impacts, and management

The last time it erupted was in 1869. Scenic and peaceful today, there is no guarantee that it will remain like this. Several other volcanoes in the same region of Chile have erupted in recent years. Volcanoes like this one have both advantages and disadvantages for people living near to them.

FIGURE 6.1 Osorno volcano in central Chile, formed by tectonic activity

INTRODUCTION

The definition of a natural hazard is *'a short-term event that is a threat to life and property'*.

Natural hazards are caused by **natural events** such as earthquakes, volcanoes, tropical cyclones (including hurricanes and typhoons), flooding, and drought. Although areas where there is a risk of them happening are generally known, it cannot be predicted when and where they will actually happen, not how bad they can be. People and property are never safe when a naturally hazardous event takes place.

Of the five hazards above, **earthquakes** are the most unpredictable. No one, despite some claims to the contrary, can tell when they are going to happen. Sometimes there are warning signs that a **volcano** is about to erupt but these are unpredictable as well. No two volcanic eruptions are the same. The nature, length, and extent of a volcanic eruption cannot be known until it happens.

The formation and movement of **tropical cyclones** can be followed by satellite. Unlike earthquakes, their existence out at sea where they form is known before they reach land areas where many people live. Even so, they can change track at any time; some intensify and become stronger and cause mayhem, while others weaken or turn away harmlessly before reaching land.

The normal climate in many parts of the Tropics is a wet summer season and a dry winter. The monsoon climate of India is a good example. Farmers in the Indian Punjab rely upon heavy summer monsoon rains to make their crops grow and fill water stores, as they have done for centuries. Winters are dry. Some summer flooding is normal. **Flooding** only becomes a hazard when monsoon rains are much heavier, begin earlier, and finish later than in a normal year, so that there is deep water everywhere, threatening people and property.

Deserts (places where annual rainfall is less than 250mm) do not suffer from drought as a natural hazard. This is because they are expected to be dry places. Dry weather is the norm not the exception. Areas around the edges of deserts can be affected by **drought**. Here a wet season is expected. In years when the expected summer rains do not arrive, these areas start to suffer from drought. When the rains fail for several years in a row, the drought becomes severe and people suffer greatly.

FIGURE 6.2   Thunderstorm clouds in the Mid-West, USA

OXFORD
UNIVERSITY PRESS

Plate tectonics, earthquakes, and volcanoes

The structure of the Earth, composed of **crust**, **mantle**, and **core**, was shown and described in the Introduction to Chapter 1 (page 2). The thin crust of the Earth (Figure 1.2) is not one continuous unbroken layer. Instead, it is divided up into seven major **plates** and many smaller ones; the Nazca and Philippine plates are named examples of smaller plates. In studying Figure 6.3, your eyes need to focus on the **plate boundaries**. It is here, and not in the middle of the plates, that the main tectonic activity is occurring. Plate boundaries are zones of movement and great crustal activity, leading to earthquakes and volcanoes.

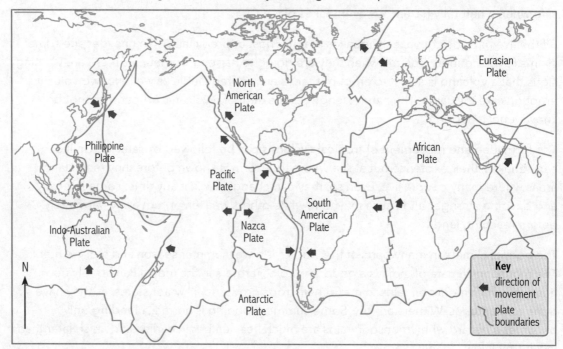

FIGURE 6.3 The Earth's main tectonic plates

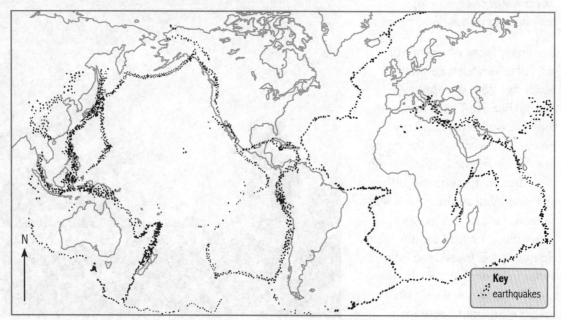

FIGURE 6.4 World distribution of earthquakes

1   Constructive or divergent

Two plates are moving apart from each other.

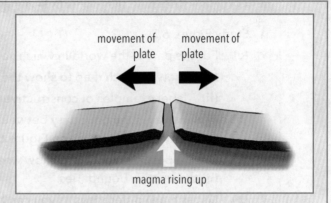

- New magma from the mantle rises to the surface to fill the gap between the moving plates.

- It is runny lava, which pours out almost continuously in a non-violent way, and cools to form basalt.

- This lava forms volcanoes with wide bases and gentle sides.

- Rift valleys are formed along faults caused by the crust splitting as the two plates move apart.

2   Destructive or convergent

Two plates are moving towards each other.

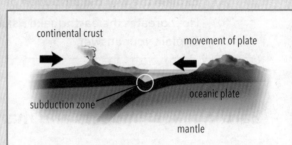

- One plate, usually the oceanic plate, sinks below the other.

- It is destroyed in the subduction zone.

- Sediments on the sea bed between the two plates are compressed and folded up to form the world's high mountain ranges (e.g. the Himalayas, Andes, Rockies, and Alps).

- The friction from plate movement in the subduction zone makes the rocks melt.

- This produces magma from which volcanoes are formed.

- These volcanic eruptions can be violent as the lava is shattered into many pieces by explosions and thrown out as rocks, ash, and other volcanic debris.

- Tall, steep-sided cones, like the one shown on page 160, are built up.

- Earthquakes are frequent; the ground shakes from the forced movement of rock against rock.

3   Conservative

Two plates move against each other.

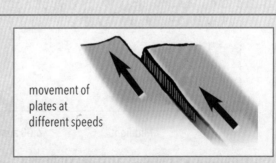

- They may be moving in the same direction but at different speeds.

- Stresses built up are released by occasional sudden plate movements.

- Friction caused by rock rubbing against rock forms earthquakes.

FIGURE 6.5   The three types of plate boundaries and movements

OXFORD
UNIVERSITY PRESS

ACTIVITIES

1 Study Figure 6.3.

   (a) For the part of the world in which you live

      (i)   draw a sketch map to show the plates and plate boundaries;

      (ii) label examples of constructive and destructive boundaries.

   (b) In what way is the boundary between the Pacific and North American plates different from the others on Figure 6.3?

2 **(a)** Draw labelled diagrams to show what is happening at **(i)** constructive and **(ii)** destructive boundaries.

   (b) List as many differences as you can between constructive and destructive plate boundaries.

3 **(a)** From Figure 6.3 make a tracing of the main plate boundaries.

   (b) Lay the tracing over Figure 6.4. Describe how they are similar.

   (c) Explain the world distribution of earthquakes.

   (d) How great is the earthquake risk in the part of the world where you live? Explain your answer.

Earthquakes: impacts and management

During an earthquake the ground shakes and vibrates rapidly. The waves caused by earthquake shocks are recorded on sensitive instruments called seismographs (Figure 6.6). The strength (or magnitude) of an earthquake is measured on the Richter scale (Table 6.1). When an earthquake is above 4, everyone in the area feels it. Above 5 and some damage is likely to be caused and loss of life becomes possible. When earthquakes exceed 6, much damage and destruction, accompanied by great loss of life, becomes more likely. Note also from Table 6.1 just how common small earthquakes are.

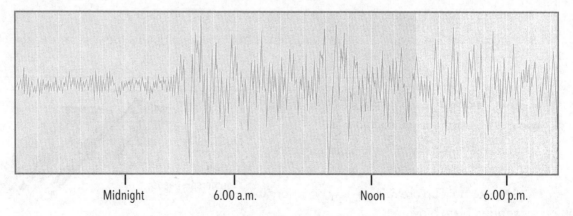

Midnight   6.00 a.m.   Noon   6.00 p.m.

FIGURE 6.6 Seismograph record for the Turkish earthquake in 1999

At what time did the first large earthquake shock occur? Why was this a bad time for people living in poor housing areas where building regulations had been ignored?

OXFORD
UNIVERSITY PRESS

TABLE 6.1 Earthquakes–Richter scale, possible effects and numbers

Richter scale	Possible effects	Number per year (approximately)
Less than 3.5	rarely felt by people	1,000,000
3.6–4.9	often felt but rarely cause damage	100,000
5.0–5.9	damage and loss of life become possible	1000
6.0–6.9	strong earthquakes, which can be destructive over areas up to 100km; much damage and considerable loss of life are possible	200
7.0 and above	major earthquakes, which can cause great loss of life and serious damage and destruction over a wide area	20

Although earthquakes occur along every type of plate boundary, nine out of ten strong earthquakes (above 6.0) occur at destructive boundaries. However, strong earthquakes also occur along the conservative plate margin between the North American and Pacific plates; the earthquake risk in California is well known. The point of origin of the shock underground is known as the focus; where it reaches the surface is known as the epicentre (Figure 6.7). The earthquake is strongest at the epicentre. Shock waves fan out from the centre and affect surrounding areas, decreasing in strength as the distance from the epicentre increases. It is like the ripple effect when a stone is thrown into a pool of water.

INFORMATION BOX

Richter scale

- It measures earthquake magnitude on a scale of 1–10.
- It is a logarithmic scale.
- An earthquake measured at 7 on the Richter scale
  - is 10 times stronger than measured at 6,
  - is 100 times stronger than one at 5,
  - is 1000 times stronger than one at 4.

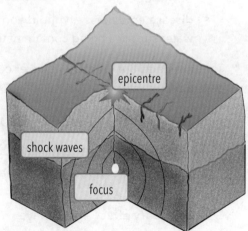

FIGURE 6.7 Earthquake: focus, epicentre, and area affected by shock waves

The **impact of earthquakes** on people is entirely **negative.** Figure 6.8 overleaf shows a scene that is all too familiar to people who have lived through a strong earthquake. The shock waves have damaged buildings to varying degrees—some have been totally destroyed, some are tilting, while others have lost no more than bricks and glass. Pillars supporting bridges and roads can collapse. People are killed in their homes, places of work, and vehicles. Many more are injured or trapped. These are the **primary effects** of an earthquake.

OXFORD
UNIVERSITY PRESS

Secondary effects of earthquakes are those that happen in the minutes, hours, and days after the earthquake. In towns and cities **fire** is the most dangerous secondary effect. Broken gas pipes can cause explosions, and sparks from damaged electricity cables can cause fires. Water to fight the fires is not available because the water pipes will also have been broken by the earthquake. In the Kobe earthquake in Japan in 1995, fires caused more damage than the earthquake shocks themselves.

FIGURE 6.8   Earthquake damage in Japan

Why are some buildings still standing while others have collapsed?

Other secondary effects include:

- **tsunamis** – giant sea waves caused by earthquakes on the sea floor; these are really dangerous for people living in low-lying coastal areas (see Information Box).
- **landslides** – mass movements of soil and rocks on steep slopes which can destroy whole villages as well as farms and farmland; the earthquake shock triggers the flow downslope.
- **disease** epidemics – typhoid and cholera spread easily when burst pipes lead to fresh water supplies being contaminated by sewage.

These impacts are greater in poorer countries because of inadequate measures to deal with earthquake damage.

INFORMATION BOX

Asian tsunami, December 2004

- **Cause** – 8.9 earthquake in the sea off Indonesia
- **Secondary effect** – giant wave
- **Countries most affected** – Indonesia, Thailand, Sri Lanka, India

■ Highest recorded wave	34m
■ Wave speed	500km/h
■ Distance travelled from epicentre	4000km
■ People dead or missing	220,000+
■ People displaced	about 2 million
■ Houses destroyed	over 500,000

Is it possible to find anything good to say about earthquakes? The answer has to be 'no'. Earthquakes are great killers and cause great human suffering and distress (trauma). The local economy can be shattered. Although people living near to plate boundaries may know they live in high-risk zones, when and if an earthquake actually happens is totally unpredictable. What people can do is make advance preparations so that if the worst happens, the effects will be less.

ACTIVITIES

1 Look at Figure 6.6. How does the record show that
   (a) the main earthquake occurred around 3 o'clock in the morning?
   (b) aftershocks occurred later in the day?
2 (a) What can be expected to happen in areas hit by earthquakes of magnitudes 4.5, 6.5, and 8.5?
   (b) (i) Describe the earthquake damage shown in Figure 6.8.
       (ii) This earthquake recorded 7.8 on the Richter scale. Is the damage shown what would have been expected? Explain your answer.

Good **earthquake management** saves lives. Table 6.1 shows that earthquake strength does affect the amount of destruction and number of casualties. However, there are more important factors such as

- number of people living close to the epicentre;
- quality of building construction;
- how well prepared people and emergency services are.

Two of the five strongest earthquakes between 2010 and 2014 led to no loss of life (Figure 6.10). Both were centred out at sea. However, the strongest did lead to a great loss of life. This was not due to primary effects since the earthquake epicentre was off the coast; it was the huge tsunami wave which hit a densely populated coastal lowland near Fukushima that led to more than 20,000 deaths (a secondary effect). The same wave caused the Fukushima nuclear disaster (Chapter 2, pages 38–39).

FIGURE 6.9 Aftermath of the Japan 2011 earthquake and tsunami

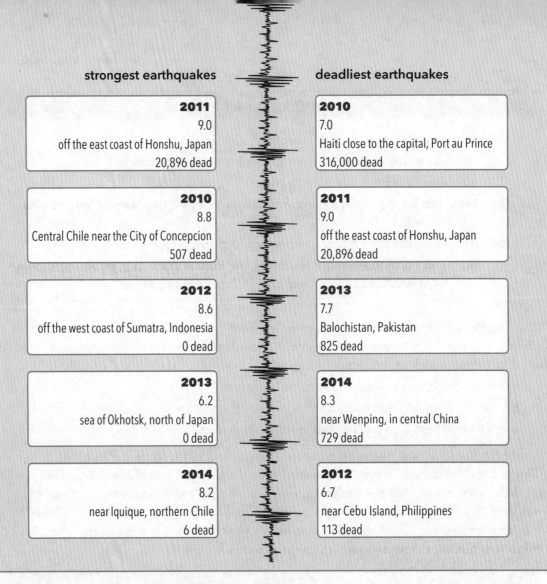

strongest earthquakes | deadliest earthquakes

2011
9.0
off the east coast of Honshu, Japan
20,896 dead

2010
7.0
Haiti close to the capital, Port au Prince
316,000 dead

2010
8.8
Central Chile near the City of Concepcion
507 dead

2011
9.0
off the east coast of Honshu, Japan
20,896 dead

2012
8.6
off the west coast of Sumatra, Indonesia
0 dead

2013
7.7
Balochistan, Pakistan
825 dead

2013
6.2
sea of Okhotsk, north of Japan
0 dead

2014
8.3
near Wenping, in central China
729 dead

2014
8.2
near Iquique, northern Chile
6 dead

2012
6.7
near Cebu Island, Philippines
113 dead

FIGURE 6.10 The strongest and most deadly earthquakes, 2010–2014

Measured on the Richter scale, 1=lowest 10=highest

The earthquake which caused the greatest loss of life was in Haiti. Although the Japan earthquake was 100 times stronger, the epicentre of the Haiti quake was close to its densely populated capital city, Port au Prince, where most buildings were too weakly constructed to withstand earthquake shocks of this magnitude. Deaths continued in the weeks and months after the event from a cholera epidemic, which spread rapidly due to continued disruption of water supply and sanitation. Haiti is too poor a country to be well prepared for earthquakes.

There is no doubt that the best strategy to prevent loss of life in earthquakes is by constructing buildings that can resist earthquakes. Some methods of doing this are illustrated in Figure 6.11. Unfortunately, in developing countries earthquake-resistant buildings are often considered to be too expensive to build. Building regulations that exist are often ignored because builders want to make more money and people can only afford cheap housing.

Planners can also help by ensuring that factories are not located next to houses. Oil tanks can explode and chemical works can catch fire; they need to be away from housing areas for safety. This is called 'land use zoning'.

Other strategies include educating people about what to do in an earthquake. People should know what is expected from them—get out of doors into an open space as soon as possible. If this is not possible, stay under a door frame or hide under a hard object like a table. In offices, use the stairs not the lifts. Teams of emergency workers should also be trained in advance— how to find and rescue people who are trapped, and how to give first aid. The authorities need to have emergency supplies of clean water, food, and medicines in store.

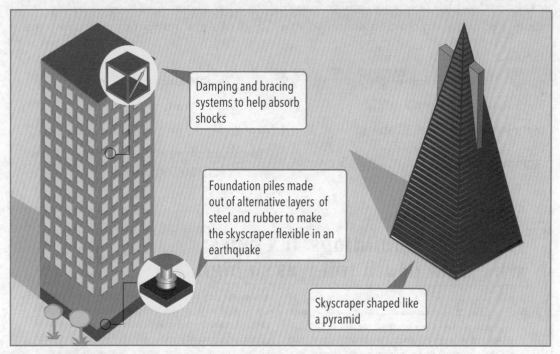

Damping and bracing systems to help absorb shocks

Foundation piles made out of alternative layers of steel and rubber to make the skyscraper flexible in an earthquake

Skyscraper shaped like a pyramid

FIGURE 6.11   How to make buildings earthquake resistant

The one good thing to come out of the horrendous Asian tsunami of 2004 has been the setting up of an international warning system for tsunamis. Previously, none existed. Warning notices about the tsunami risk and tsunami evacuation routes are now everywhere in Asian tourist resorts and coastal fishing communities. When another big earthquake occurred in the sea off Indonesia in September 2007, the authorities as far away as Kenya evacuated tourists from the coastal resort of Mombasa and warned local fishermen not to go out to sea.

ACTIVITIES

1 (a)   State **(i)** three primary and **(ii)** three secondary effects of earthquakes.

   (b)   Why are the primary effects of an earthquake usually more serious for people than the secondary effects?

   (c)   When and why can the secondary effects of an earthquake be greater?

2 Draw a labelled sketch or sketches to show how skyscrapers can be built to resist earthquakes.

3 Design a notice advising hotel guests about what they should do in the event of an earthquake.

Case study: Differences in earthquake management between California (USA) and Bam (Iran)

In December 2003 two earthquakes happened, only four days apart, both of the same magnitude: one in the wealthy USA, the other in much less economically developed Iran. The contrast in impacts could hardly have been greater (Table 6.2). The newspaper report from the time helps to explain why there were so many deaths in Iran. Figure 6.13 shows a poorly constructed and flimsy building which had little chance of withstanding the earthquake's shaking.

TABLE 6.2 A tale of two earthquakes

22 December 2003	26 December 2003
Earthquake in California	Earthquake in Iran
Magnitude: 6.5 on the Richter scale	Magnitude: 6.5 on the Richter scale
A clock tower was toppled, killing 3 people.	A large part of the city was flattened, killing an estimated 30,000 people.

Dangerous buildings, lax rules: why Bam death toll was so high

News report
27 December 2003

An expert on the devastated city of Bam said that many of those killed by the earthquake died only because of poor building methods and a lack of proper regulation.

In Iran, as in many developing countries, tremors that should have been survivable brought human tragedy on a vast scale because buildings collapsed on top of people. Thanks to safer construction methods, only three people died in an earthquake of similar strength in California four days earlier.

Efforts to encourage industrial growth in a backward agricultural area had caused fast population growth in Bam. This led to a shortage of housing, which local builders tried to meet by building cheap new houses, or by adding extra floors to existing houses. Building regulations existed, but they were only enforced for high-rise buildings. People were desperately in need of housing so that the authorities overlooked the code of building for earthquakes.

In Bam, much of the building work is done by property owners themselves, using untrained local labour. Typical houses are built from burnt brick with mud and lime for bonding. 'On my last trip to Iran I knocked two bricks

together and they became like powder. The cost of cement is very high, so they don't use much,' said the expert. 'Ideally houses in earthquake-prone regions should have lightweight, pitched roofs, closely bonded together.' But builders in Bam had largely abandoned the use of corrugated metal, because of short supplies and a belief that it does not last long. Instead many roofs are supported by metal beams between traditional brick arches. On top they put a layer of concrete and water-proofing. Roofs and ceilings were heavy. 'Ends of beams sit freely on the walls, so with any shake, if one goes, the whole roof collapses,' the expert added.

Despite the lack of safety precautions, the authorities in Iran are used to dealing with the aftermath of earthquakes. Their response was quick, although hampered by the loss of telephone connections with the city. The more serious problem is the lack of sustained efforts to prevent future tragedies. The expert finished the interview by saying, 'They may create a policy after a disaster, but it is never implemented. Six months after a disaster the authorities forget about it.'

FIGURE 6.12 Newspaper report, 27 December 2003

Both California and Iran are well used to earthquake shocks. California has the San Andreas fault passing through it, part of the conservative plate boundary, where the North American and Pacific plates are rubbing and moving against each other. Iran is located on a destructive boundary, near to where three major plates meet and push into each other (African, Indo-Australian, and Eurasian). It is one of the most seismically active places in the world. Look back to Figures 6.3 and 6.4.

Not only does California have some of the world's strongest building regulations for earthquake resistance, but they are rigidly enforced. Only recently have building height restrictions in San Francisco been relaxed, reflecting confidence in modern building technology. San Francisco suffered the disastrous 1906 earthquake. People keep talking of the 'Big One' that is due in California. The government is constantly educating companies and people about the earthquake risk, with booklets, on the net, and practice drills—what to do in advance and what to do during and after the earthquake. Over 20 million people took part in Great ShakeOut Earthquake Drills in 2015.

As early as 1991 Iran launched a hazard reduction programme. Over the years its effectiveness has been limited by
- lack of adequate central funding,
- poor coordination between different organizations,
- uncontrolled urbanization and growth of unplanned housing areas,
- persistence of widespread rural and urban poverty.

As was highlighted in the Bam newspaper report, earthquake management has focused more on emergency responses than preparation in advance. Earthquake drills do take place, but mainly in the wealthier neighbourhoods of the capital city, Tehran. It was last hit in 1830 by a 7.2 earthquake—is another big one due in Iran's capital city?

ACTIVITIES

1 (a) State one similarity and one difference between the 2003 earthquakes in California and Bam.

   (b) Explain why the loss of life was so great in Bam.

   (c) Is it likely that the next big earthquake in Iran will cause as much loss of life? Explain your view about this.

2 27 December 2003: List of relief supplies needed in Bam
   - 20,000 family tents
   - 30,000 plastic sheets
   - 200,000 kerosene heaters
   - 40,000 kitchen sets
   - 30 generators
   - 200,000 blankets
   - 400,000 water purification tablets

   These are the types of relief supplies needed after all destructive earthquakes.

   Choose any three of these supplies and explain why each one was needed.

3 'The stronger the earthquake, the greater the loss of life'.

   Do you agree with this statement?

   Explain your answer making use of information from the text, figures, and tables in this section about earthquakes.

FIGURE 6.13 Earthquake damage in Bam

Volcanoes: impacts and management

A volcanic eruption occurs when magma rises to the Earth's surface. Lava pours out of a crater and, with time, builds up a cone-shaped mountain. This happens at both constructive and destructive plate boundaries. The world distribution of active volcanoes is shown in Figure 6.14. Look back to Figure 6.3 and compare the two maps.

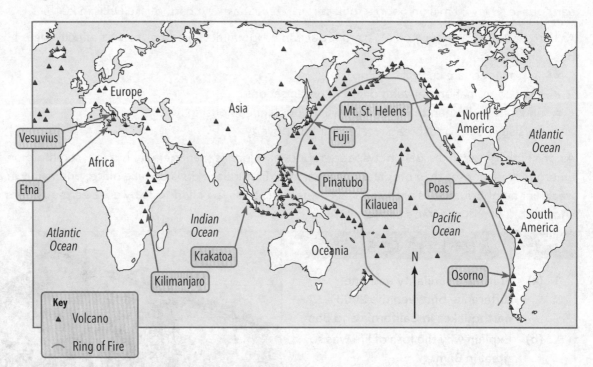

FIGURE **6.14**   World distribution of active volcanoes

No one usually lives near the top of a volcano. Take a look into the crater of the volcano Poas in Costa Rica in Central America in Figure 6.15 and you can see why not. It is a wasteland of bare ground from previous eruptions, the last major one being in 1995. The bubbling crater lake shows that the volcano is still active and not safe for people to enter. The photograph in Figure 6.16 was taken on the lower slopes of the same volcano. Note the difference! It shows a rich farming region. Old lava flows from hundreds and thousands of years ago have weathered to form deep fertile soils here. Volcanic soils are some of the world's most fertile, because they are rich in minerals of many different types, as well as being well drained and easy to work.

Not all the impacts of volcanoes are good. During a major volcanic eruption, nature is seen at its most powerful and most violent, especially in volcanoes located along destructive plate boundaries. People living on the volcano's slopes can be in great danger. Most dangerous of all are volcanoes that erupt suddenly without warning, having been dormant for hundreds of years.

FIGURE 6.15   Crater of volcano Poas in Costa Rica–a hot wasteland

FIGURE 6.16   Lower slopes of the same volcano–coffee is the main crop here, but elsewhere maize and many different fruits and vegetables are grown.

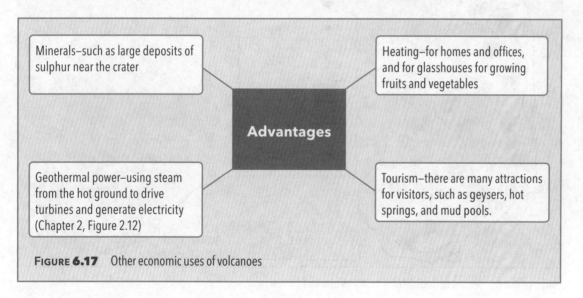

Minerals–such as large deposits of sulphur near the crater

Heating–for homes and offices, and for glasshouses for growing fruits and vegetables

Advantages

Geothermal power–using steam from the hot ground to drive turbines and generate electricity (Chapter 2, Figure 2.12)

Tourism–there are many attractions for visitors, such as geysers, hot springs, and mud pools.

FIGURE 6.17   Other economic uses of volcanoes

People are killed in volcanic eruptions in several different ways.

- Rocks, volcanic bombs, and ash may rain down on top of them.
- Lava flows can be so fast that people do not have time to move out of their path.
- Poisonous gases and fumes may drift over populated areas before people realize what is happening.
- Heat may melt snow on mountain tops, which sets off mud flows that sweep houses and people away.

However, far fewer people are killed by volcanoes than by earthquakes. Unlike earthquakes, there are sometimes warning signs of a new eruption, so that people have more time to

environmental management

prepare and, if necessary, be evacuated from the danger area. New activity is often confined to the top of the mountain, where no one lives. However, if a volcano keeps on erupting for weeks, months, or even years, the destruction in a wide area around the volcano can be total: houses, crops, animals, wildlife, trees, and plants can all be covered by heavy layers of lava, ash, and dust. The Soufrière Hills Volcano has done just this to more than half of the land area of the island of Montserrat in the West Indies since 1995 (Figure 6.18). It had not erupted for 350 years. There was still some activity in 2015, twenty years after the first big eruption. Check to see whether it is still erupting by visiting the website http://www.mvo.ms!

Impact

EXAM TIP

For questions which ask for impacts of a hazard

- make sure that you look for both positive and negative impacts i.e. good and bad;

- if there are no positive and only negative impacts, then state this in your answer.

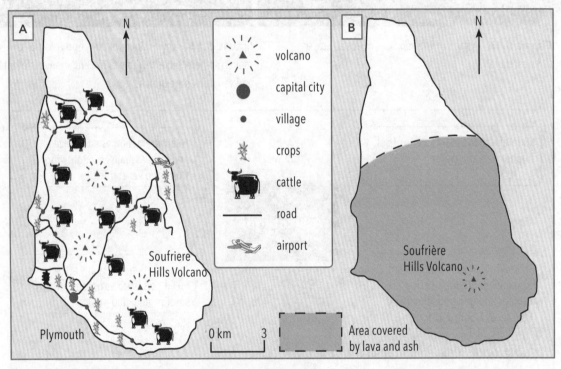

FIGURE **6.18**   Impact of the Soufrière Hills Volcano on Montserrat

A   Before the eruption

B   After the eruption

ACTIVITIES

1 **(a)** Describe the world distribution of active volcanoes shown in Figure 6.14.

(b) Name a place where **(i)** volcanoes are found along a constructive boundary and **(ii)** the two plates are moving apart. (See Figure 6.3)

(c) Name a place where **(i)** volcanoes are found along a destructive boundary and **(ii)** the two plates which are moving together. (See Figure 6.3)

(d) Explain briefly why volcanoes form along constructive and destructive plate boundaries.

2 It is estimated that 500 million people live in areas at risk from volcanic activity. Give as many reasons as you can why so many people live near volcanoes despite the risk from eruptions.

3 Explain why volcanoes

(a) can be dangerous to people living nearby.

(b) kill far fewer people in the world than earthquakes.

4 Look at Figure 6.18.

(a) Describe what Montserrat was like before the eruption. Refer to where most people lived, land uses, and economic activities.

(b) Describe what has happened after the eruption. Use these headings—loss of life, damage caused, population movement, and economic dislocation (lost sources of income).

5 Two opinions of people living in Montserrat:

'It is time to give up living here and go to another Caribbean island.'

'I was born in Montserrat. Montserrat is my home. I don't want to leave.'

Suggest reasons why some people are more willing than others to leave Montserrat.

Strategies for managing the risks from volcanoes are different from those for earthquakes. Earthquakes occur without warning, whereas volcanoes often give out some warning signs that an eruption is likely, such as

- temperature increases in and around the crater;
- increased amounts of steam and gases seen coming from the crater;
- small earthquake shocks felt in surrounding areas.

Even so, it is impossible to predict exactly when a volcano will become active again and how violent the eruption will be. Every volcano behaves differently. One strategy is to employ scientists to monitor the volcano. Mount Etna in Italy is an example of a volcano under constant watch. Scientists in their monitoring station at the top look out for any significant increases in the volcano's temperature. New technology is helping; satellites can be used to monitor heat changes, which is useful for volcanoes in remote locations and in developing countries without ground stations. Another strategy is to train and educate local people in emergency procedures. Once a volcano starts to erupt, there is usually little people can do except to move out of the way.

A seismograph making a continuous record

A scientist's view from the observatory

FIGURE 6.19 Volcano watch in Montserrat

The strategies in place in Montserrat have largely been successful in terms of preventing loss of life. In 1995 and 1996 the government evacuated 5000 people from the capital, Plymouth, and 6000 people from villages in the centre and east of this island to the safe zone in the north. Only 23 have been killed; this only happened because a much larger eruption in 1997 came without warning and killed people working in fields some distance away from the volcano.

FIGURE 6.20 An exclusion zone has been created by the government to keep people out of the danger area. This has now been in place for more than 20 years.

ACTIVITIES

1 Name and describe three strategies for managing the possible impacts of a volcanic eruption.

2 With earthquakes the management focus is on disaster preparation; with volcanoes the focus is on monitoring and warning.

   (i) Describe what this statement means.

   (ii) Explain why the management focus is different between earthquakes and volcanoes.

Climatic hazard: tropical cyclones

Tropical cyclones are storms which form in the deep (over 60 metres), warm (at least 27°C) tropical oceans, and cause very strong winds and heavy rain. Their visits to coastal locations may last only 24–48 hours, but destruction can be total. Figure 6.21 shows source areas and tracks followed. It suggests which coastal regions and island are most at risk during the cyclone season. Notice how the direction of movement of the cyclones changes as they move away from their ocean source regions between 5 and 20 degrees north and south of the Equator; this is caused by the Earth's rotation from west to east.

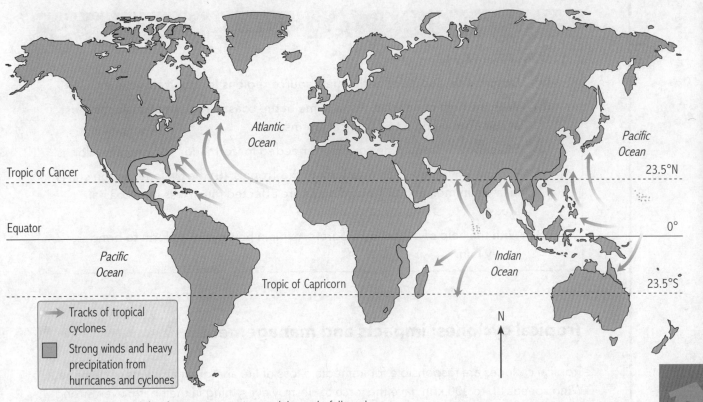

FIGURE 6.21   Tropical cyclones: source regions and the tracks followed

Cyclone is the name for the tropical storms which form in the Indian Ocean. Hurricanes in the Caribbean and typhoons in the South China Sea are the same phenomena but with different names. Cyclones are formed when the sea water is at its hottest (27°C or more). Air above the sea surface is heated and the warm moist air starts to rise. As it does so, a deep centre of low pressure develops, which sucks up even more air from the surface. Wind speeds around the centre of the cyclone increase to 150–200 kph in a huge circular swirl of cloud which may be up to 600km across. Torrential rain falls from towering cumulo-nimbus clouds, except in the 'eye' in the very centre where the weather is calm and dry (Figure 6.22).

The worst effects of cyclones are felt in coastal areas; because they feed off warm sea surfaces, cyclones lose their power source once they start to cross land. The low pressure centre is gradually 'filled in' and they become less dangerous.

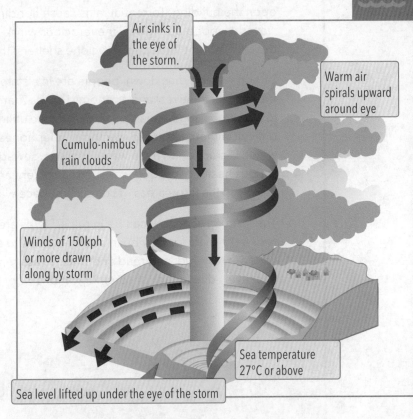

FIGURE 6.22   What happens in a cyclone

ACTIVITIES

1 Study Figure 6.21.

(a) Describe the locations of the main source regions for tropical cyclones.

(b) With the help of an atlas, name some of the coastal regions and islands most at risk from being hit by tropical storms.

2 (a) Describe the favourable conditions needed for formation of tropical cyclones.

(b) Explain why (i) they can only form in the Tropics, (ii) the cyclone season starts in late summer, and (iii) inland areas are affected much less than coastal areas.

(c) With the help of a labelled diagram, explain how cyclones form to bring heavy rain.

Tropical cyclones: impacts and management

Tropical cyclones are responsible for immediate loss of life and great amounts of damage. Wind speeds up to 300 kph have the force to destroy everything in their path; even strong buildings can be flattened by the strength and swirl of the winds once they have ripped open the building. Torrential rains cause flooding, made worse in coastal regions by tidal waves whipped up high by the ferocious winds. Without the pre-evacuation of people or their movement into special cyclone shelters, the lives of thousands are in great danger.

After the storm dies down, people are in a state of shock from social losses (deaths of good friends and relatives) and economic losses (damage to homes, possessions, and businesses, loss of crops and animals on farms). Public utilities are badly disrupted; life can be very difficult without access to electricity, telephones, transport, and supplies of clean drinking water. Disruption to fresh water supplies, sewage treatment, and waste disposal can have serious health consequences such as cholera and typhoid epidemics. Mosquitoes multiply rapidly in the large areas of standing surface water, greatly increasing the risk of malaria.

The farming economy can be in ruins. Fields are under water and livestock are dead. It will take 5-10 years for new bush and tree crops to start bearing fruit. Until power and telephone lines are restored, and road and bridges are repaired, offices and businesses cannot operate effectively due to lack of communications with the outside world. This can take weeks.

Strategies to reduce negative impacts of cyclones

Hurricanes which regularly strike the south-east corner of the USA usually lead to little direct loss of life. Hurricanes are notoriously unpredictable, suddenly changing course and becoming stronger, but meteorologists can now watch them continuously thanks to weather satellites in the sky. Warnings can be given in sufficient time for property to be boarded up and for people to be evacuated inland. Police, fire, and ambulance services practise emergency drills, and people are educated in advance about the emergency procedures to adopt after a weather office warning.

TABLE 6.3 A tale of two hurricanes – how the rich escape the ravages of nature and the poor suffer.

Rich world	Poor world
■ Hurricane Floyd, North Carolina, USA (1999)	■ Hurricane Mitch, Honduras and Nicaragua (1998)
■ Wind speed up to 250kph	■ Wind speed up to 280kph
■ 3 million people affected; around 7 dead	■ 4 million people affected; 18,000 dead or missing
■ Damage–scores of houses destroyed and roads washed away	■ Damage: over a million homeless and severe flooding triggered landslides
■ Losses estimated at US$16 billion	■ Losses estimated at US$7 billion
■ Losses covered by insurance: 75 per cent	■ Losses covered by insurance: 2 per cent

The USA is something of an exception, however, the majority of countries at risk from tropical cyclones are developing countries. If the cyclone comes ashore in a densely populated location in a developing country, loss of life can be enormous, as it was in the Orissa cyclone in 1999. In developing countries there is less chance of preparation in advance and of detailed warnings about its arrival. Therefore, building cyclone shelters containing emergency supplies of food and drinking water, close to villages is one strategy that could be used more widely in areas with a high cyclone risk. Cyclone shelters are used in Bangladesh (page 186), but there are not enough of them.

OXFORD
UNIVERSITY PRESS

Case study: Managing the impacts of a tropical cyclone

Cyclones in Orissa (India) in 1999 and 2013

The Indian state of Orissa is on the Indian Ocean cyclone track. It takes regular hits. The largest in living memory was the 'super-cyclone' of 1999. Winds reached 270km/h and drove a tidal wave over 10 metres high over coastal lowlands and villages. The results of 36 hours of mayhem are summarized in Table 6.4. Most shocking of all was the death toll, officially more than 10,000, but estimated by many to have been three or four times higher.

FIGURE 6.23 Location of Orissa

In 1999 the government and state authorities were heavily criticized for their poor preparation and slow relief efforts (Figure 6.24). The race against time to restore power lines and irrigation works and provide new seeds for a January planting was lost. This meant that upto five million people had to depend on food aid for at least seven months. Many of the survivors were so traumatized by their losses that they could hardly work out how to re-start their lives.

Views from the subcontinent

A Editorial in the Hindustan Times, New Delhi, 2 November 1999

What is already evident is the unpreparedness of both the state and central governments for the disaster. What is unpardonable is that it is not something that could have caught the authorities by surprise, like an earthquake … However, it may not be fair to blame the authorities alone because the local people often show a curious reluctance to move to safer places inland. At a time when transistors are found in the remotest of villages, surely they cannot claim to have been caught unawares. Since the cyclones are a regular feature of the region, the local people must be aware of what lies in store if they do not take precautionary measures.

B Editorial in The Times of Delhi, New Delhi, 2 November 1999

With wind speeds up to 300kph and tidal waves over 10m, buildings and other structures common in rural India can hardly be expected to remain intact. But the enormous loss of lives is due to social and economic constraints in India. For the poor farmer, no amount of early warnings of impending destruction are enough to make him abandon his only source of livelihood… Even if he wished to go, he is not likely to find suitable means of transport to put himself and his family out of harm's way … Once again the cyclone and its aftermath reveal the critical importance of information. Access to telecommunications should no longer be considered a luxury but a necessity.

FIGURE 6.24 What the papers said

TABLE 6.4 A tale of two cyclones in Orissa

	1999 Super-cyclone	2013 Typhoon Phailin
Maximum wind speed	270km/h	260km/h
Death toll	10,000+	under 100
Damage	destruction of homes, schools, roads, and power lines	destruction of homes, schools, roads, and power lines
Effects on agriculture (main economic activity)	annual padi rice crop ruined, irrigation works destroyed, half a million draught animals dead, 90 million trees uprooted (mainly privately owned coconut, cashew, and betel nut trees, a source of extra income)	loss of an estimated 5000 square miles of padi rice crops, loss valued at US$320m, coastal trees uprooted

The super-cyclone taught the Indian authorities a lesson. When weather forecasters were predicting the arrival of another super-cyclone, named Phailin, in 2013, the authorities acted by ordering and arranging a mass evacuation from coastal areas. Those who remembered the 1999 cyclone were more willing to move this time. Over half a million people were moved; many were placed in 500 specifically built cyclone camps. Each could take up to 1500 people and there were spaces on the ground floor for their draught animals. The government had stockpiled emergency supplies of water and food. Train and air services were stopped. However, no one could stop the total devastation of farmland and property along the coastal strip, hit by the cyclone at its peak. The natural ecosystem was equally badly affected as mangrove trees were uprooted. What was stopped was the horrendous loss of life seen in 1999.

ACTIVITIES

1 (a) Describe what Table 6.3 shows about the effects of tropical cyclones on rich and poor countries.

   (b) Describe the management strategies that can be used to reduce the impact of tropical cyclones.

   (c) Explain why strategies for preventing loss of life in cyclones are more successful in developed than developing countries.

2 Study Table 6.4.

   (a) What were the similarities between the cyclones which hit Orissa in 1999 and 2013?

   (b) What was the big difference?

   (c) Using all the case study information, explain the reasons for this big difference.

environmental management

Climatic hazard: Flooding

Most flooding is caused by rivers breaking their banks after heavy rainfall, or prolonged periods of rain, or rapid snow melt. The ground becomes saturated and cannot absorb any more water. Most rivers flood at least once a year. Flat land next to the river is known as the flood plain, because it is the first area to be flooded once river water overflows the banks.

On most occasions the cause is heavy rainfall, much more than usual. Persistent rain day after day, or a torrential downpour, or a combination of both, causes an increase in surface run-off to the point where the channels of rivers and streams cannot cope with all the water flowing into them. The same happens to rivers in high mountain areas when snow melts during hot weather in summer.

In water cycle terms, the percentage for run-off increases at the expense of the percentages for interception and infiltration.

- The interception percentage decreases because after days of rain the trees and leaves can hold no more moisture. Thundery rain hits the ground faster than light rain because it is less easy to stop.

- The infiltration percentage decreases because after days of rain all the soil spaces are already full of water. Heavy rain is less easily absorbed; more of it bounces off the surface.

Human activity can increase the risk of flooding and make it worse. For example, clearing forests and replacing them with urban areas is responsible for the increased flood risk in many towns and cities located in valleys (Figure 6.25 A,B).

Additionally, there is coastal flooding. Tropical cyclones are most responsible because they can dump up to 500mm of rain in 36 hours. The water from such heavy and persistent rain has nowhere to go. It can only stay on the surface, becoming deeper, until the rains stop and the processes of evaporation, infiltration, and run-off can work to return the surface back to its normal dry state. Also, strong winds blowing onshore during cyclones cause huge waves or storm surges, leading to widespread flooding in coastal lowlands. In some places, the flooding is made worse by the surges blocking river water from emptying into the sea. In this time of climate change, global warming, and rising sea levels, the risk of coastal flooding along low-lying coastlines can only increase. The Maldives are worried (Chapter 7, page 215); so too is Bangladesh.

ACTIVITIES

1 State and explain the natural causes of flooding **(a)** on river floodplains and **(b)** on coastal lowlands.

2 Explain how human activities may be increasing the risk of flooding **(a)** on the sides of rivers and **(b)** in low-lying island countries.

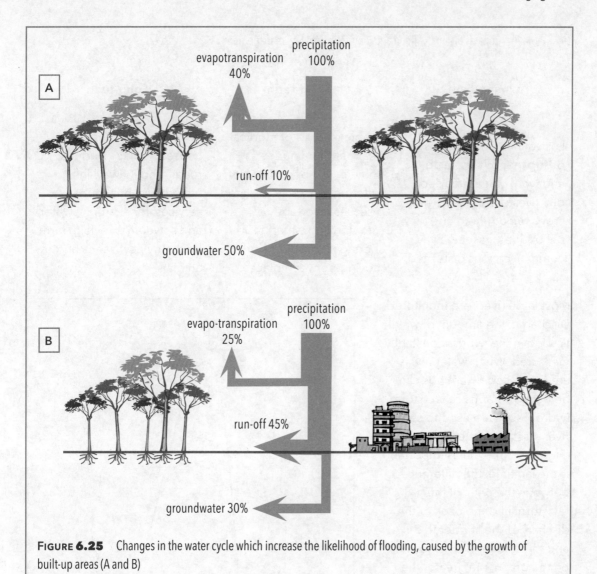

FIGURE 6.25 Changes in the water cycle which increase the likelihood of flooding, caused by the growth of built-up areas (A and B)

Flooding: impacts and management

As with all natural disasters, the consequences of a major flood can be split into immediate, short-term, and long-term effects (Table 6.5). The immediate effects happen so quickly that, when the flood is at its peak, people can do little about them and survival is the main aim. Only when water levels begin to go down can people seek and be given emergency help and aid to make the short-term effects (human suffering and damage to the local economy) easier to bear. Money is the key need for long-term recovery. Rich countries and rich people have the resources to enable them to recover faster. Poor countries must rely upon aid from overseas, which takes time to arrive (if ever).

TABLE 6.5 Impacts of a major flood and long-term recovery management

Immediate	Short-term	Long-term
Loss of human life; houses destroyed; offices, factories, and work places flooded out; livestock carried away; crops ruined; road and rail bridges washed away; communications disrupted.	People in need of medical treatment for injuries; homeless people; people suffering from water-related diseases; shortage of safe drinking water; food shortages; problems of moving between places.	Repair and build new houses; replace bridges, roads, and railway lines; restore essential public services, for example, water and sewerage; reclaim farm land; buy new seeds and animals.

Most large rivers are monitored. Discharge, the amount of water flowing in the river, is constantly measured. When water levels are rising, flood warnings can be issued. Graphs called storm hydrographs are used to show river discharge after a storm (Figure 6.26). What is important is the lag time, the difference between the peak of the rainstorm and the peak of the discharge. The shorter this is, and the steeper the rising line on the graph, the greater the risk of flooding and the more urgent the need to issue flood warnings. A steep rising line, like the one shown in Figure 6.26, shows heavy rainfall and high rates of surface run-off with little chance for underground flow by through-flow or ground water flow. Urgent action is needed. People should be advised to move to flood shelters built on higher ground.

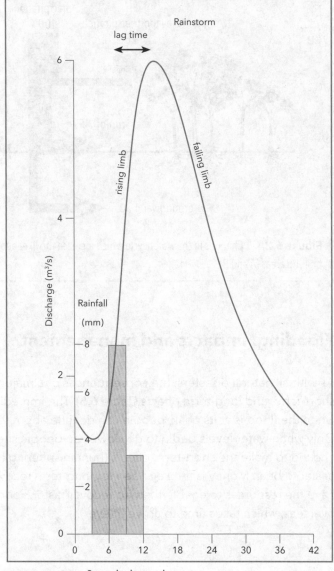

FIGURE 6.26 Storm hydrograph

Some big rivers are managed rivers, for example, those with large dams. Water can be held back in times of high rainfall and surface run-off to prevent flooding downstream. This was one of the many reasons for building the Three Gorges Dam (page 123). Banks along the sides of rivers can be increased in size and strengthened. These are examples of hard engineering management techniques; they can be effective, but also have disadvantages. They are expensive to build and costly to maintain. A more natural way to reduce the flood risk is to stop deforestation on valley sides and plant new trees. Table 6.6 shows how important the role of trees can be in flood prevention and reducing damage.

TABLE 6.6 How the clearing of trees in an area affected run-off

	Evapo-transpiration	Groundwater	Run-off
All trees	50%	40%	10%
Half trees, half the area cleared for buildings	25%	30%	45%

There is a good side to river flooding. Every time a river floods, it leaves behind covering of silt. Silt is a fine grained deposit, light and easy to work, and rich in minerals. It makes an excellent soil for farming. It is no accident that many of the world's most densely populated regions are in large river valleys, especially those in Asia (Chapter 8). Many people can be fed from farming on the fertile floodplains of rivers such as the Ganges, Mekong, and Yangtze. The great fertility of the Ganges Delta helps to explain why repeated flooding in Bangladesh is such a major issue.

ACTIVITIES

1 (a) Looking at the storm hydrograph in Figure 6.26, what shows that the flood risk is high?

   (b) Describe what people living near the river further downstream can do after a warning that water levels are rising and a flood event is likely.

2 (a) Draw two pie graphs to show the percentages in Table 6.6.

   (b) What important message about flood prevention do these percentages give?

186

Case study: Flooding in Bangladesh

Causes of flooding

The flood risk in Bangladesh is one of the highest in the world. This is because a variety of physical factors favourable for flooding come together in Bangladesh.

1 Tropical monsoon climate

From June to September rainfall is heavy and frequent, ideal for surface run-off (Figure 6.28). Rainfall totals are high; most places receive between 1500 and 2000mm of rain a year.

2 Tropical cyclones

In the period September to November, severe storms develop in the Bay of Bengal. Sometimes they move north to affect Bangladesh as violent tropical cyclones which bring torrential downpours. Water courses are already full from the monsoon rains. Even worse are the storm waves and sea surges that are driven onshore by the violent winds; these raise the water levels along the coast, causing widespread flooding.

3 Relief

About two thirds of the country lies less than one metre above sea level. It is on the flood plains and delta of two great rivers, the Ganges and Brahmaputra. These are the first places to flood after heavy rains.

FIGURE 6.27 Relief map of Bangladesh

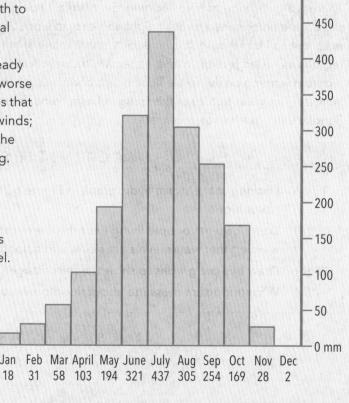

	Jan	Feb	Mar	April	May	June	July	Aug	Sep	Oct	Nov	Dec
	18	31	58	103	194	321	437	305	254	169	28	2

FIGURE 6.28 Precipitation in Dhaka, the capital city of Bangladesh

4 Drainage

Rivers, lakes, and swamps cover 10 per cent of the land area even when there is no flooding. At the same time as the River Ganges is swollen by heavy monsoon rains in India, it is carrying extra water from snow melt in the Himalayas.

Human actions make the flooding worse. Large areas of forest have been cleared in Tibet and Nepal, where the Ganges and Brahmaputra have their sources. Because there are fewer trees to absorb water, bind the soil together, and reduce the impact of rain droplets on the ground, rates of overland flow and run-off during times of heavy rain have greatly increased.

FIGURE 6.29 Flooding in Bangladesh

Effects of flooding

One of the worst floods in recent history occurred in summer, 2004. This affected around 30 million Bangladeshis and caused US$7 billion worth of damage. Forty per cent of Dhaka was underwater, and 41 of the country's 64 districts were severely affected. A million acres of crops were destroyed, hundreds of people lost their lives, and millions were made homeless. Rail, road, and air links were disrupted as 2-3 metres of water covered the land.

Case Study

Can anything be done to stop the flooding?

An action plan drawn up in 1987 emphasized what are known as 'hard engineering' solutions—constructing seven huge dams to store water, building a coastal embankment to keep the sea water out, increasing the height of embankments running along the sides of rivers, and using embankments to create basins to store and hold back flood water. Not only are all these ideas expensive, but there is no guarantee that they would work to prevent all the flooding. Moreover, Bangladesh is one of the countries most at risk from any rises in sea level due to global warming.

Others have suggested alternatives such as better flood forecasting, improved warning systems, more flood shelters, and better-prepared emergency services. They are all cheaper solutions: more use should be made of the knowledge and skills of local people, instead of so much emphasis on engineering and technology. Environmental disturbance would be less severe because of reduced interference with the delicate natural ecosystems of the delta.

ACTIVITIES

1 (a) Make a table to show the physical and human causes of flooding in Bangladesh.

   (b) Draw a sketch map of Bangladesh and add labels to explain why flooding occurs frequently.

2 (a) What is meant by 'hard engineering'?

   (b) Explain why it is not always the best solution to a problem such as flooding.

3 Do a research project about a river flood in your home country. Use the same headings as in this case study.

4 Flooding is a natural event, but it may be increased or reduced by the actions of humans.

   Explain this statement.

Climatic hazard: Drought

The definition of drought is a 'period of dry weather longer or worse than normally expected'. It occurs when wind and air pressure patterns are different from normal, so that expected rains do not fall.

This happens most in the Tropics in regions with climates that have a wet season and a dry season, such as savanna and monsoon. The area shaded in Africa (Figure 6.30) has been the most drought-affected part of the world since 1970. In some countries within the Sahel, rainfall amounts have been below the long-term average in more than 20 out of the last 30 years. India is no stranger to drought. During a 100–year period, 18 years of extreme drought were recorded, during which more than 25 per cent of India was affected. In drought years, the wet south-west monsoon does not blow with sufficient force to reach inland locations, where high pressure and sinking air continue to give dry weather.

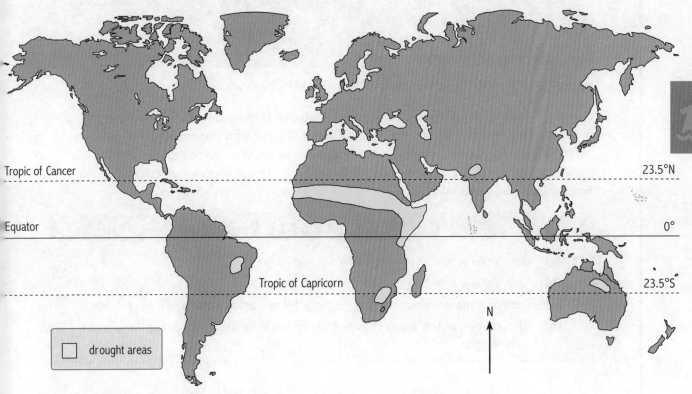

Tropic of Cancer — 23.5°N
Equator — 0°
Tropic of Capricorn — 23.5°S

N

☐ drought areas

FIGURE 6.30   Areas most at risk from drought

The persistence of high pressure and dry weather during what is expected to be the wet season dominated by low pressure is the most frequent cause of drought in the areas marked on Figure 6.30. The El Niño effect (Chapter 7) can cause droughts in areas where the climate is normally wet. The warming of ocean surface waters in the Pacific Ocean every 3 to 8 years replaces the cold ocean waters usually associated with the Peruvian currents. For reasons not fully understood, this changes world patterns of rainfall over much wider areas of the world, in Asia, Africa, Australia, and the Americas. Look at what happened around the world during the 1997–98 El Niño event, the strongest in recent times. There are examples of severe drought from all over the world during this period. At the same time, other places were flooded.

OXFORD
UNIVERSITY PRESS

INDONESIA	China	Tanzania	Argentina
■ Worst drought for half a century ■ Forest fires burnt out of control ■ Fire haze spread over neighbouring countries ■ No monsoon rains to put the fires out	■ Hit by worst drought for 20 years	■ Nationwide crop failure due to drought ■ 3 million suffered extreme food shortages	■ Heavy rains delayed planting of crops on the Pampas
Ethiopia	Jamaica	Venezuela	Papua New Guinea
■ Drought threatened food supplies of 4 million people	■ Worst drought for 40 years ■ Water rationing ■ Higher food prices	■ Yields of most crops reduced by flooding	■ About 30 000 starved as a result of drought

FIGURE **6.31**   Some of the worldwide effects of El Niño, 1997-98, on the climate

Climate change is being blamed for the persistence of some droughts. This is more difficult to prove, but it seems possible. Farmers in interior Queensland (Australia) know that in some years, rain-bearing winds from the sea do not reach them. In ten of the fourteen years between 2002 and 2016 there was no worthwhile rain; so many dry years, one following another, was unprecedented.

ACTIVITIES

1 (a) Give a definition of drought as a natural hazard.
   (b) Name three possible causes of drought.
2 (a) Describe the distribution of drought-affected areas shown in Figure 6.30.
   (b) Choose one of the areas shown and explain why droughts occur there from time to time.

Drought: impacts and management

In a drought, the flow in surface water courses becomes intermittent and then they dry up. The natural vegetation of grasses, bushes, and shrubs withers, turns brown, and dies out. This increases the risk of wildfires, and the smoke from these reduces air quality.

The worst effects of drought are felt in rural areas, where dependence upon water for survival and income is greater. Lack of water in farming areas causes many problems. Even if crops do not wither and die, yields are greatly reduced. Livestock lose condition and may die due to the shortage of grazing. People in rural areas typically have large families to support. Without outside aid, lack of food leads to malnutrition, famine, and death. Infants and young children are most vulnerable. Continuing the effort to try to grow crops and keep animals during a drought increases the risks of soil erosion and desertification (Chapter 3, page 94), which can result in permanent environmental damage. As water levels fall in surface reservoirs, people in both urban and rural areas turn to underground sources. Overuse leads to falling water levels and dry wells for many years to follow.

Droughts are responsible for more deaths than any of the other natural hazards (Figure 6.32). Sometimes millions of people are affected and hundreds of thousands die. This is because drought, unlike the other climatic hazards such as floods and cyclones, can last for a long time—months or even years. If the same area is affected for two consecutive years, the situation often becomes desperate for villagers because they have had no time to build up food stocks again. When malnourished and underfed, people are less able to resist diseases. The very young, sick, and elderly die first.

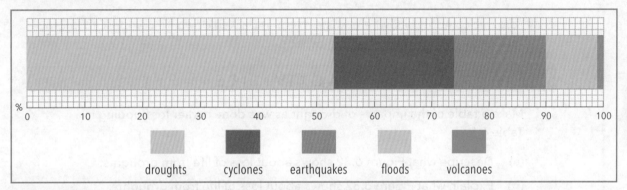

FIGURE 6.32 Percentage of loss of life from five natural hazards over a 10-year period

If food aid does not arrive quickly to a drought-stricken zone (and it often does not because of difficult communications), migration out of the area is the only option. Most people end up in temporary refugee camps, to which food aid is usually supplied by charities and international relief agencies. Despite the overcrowding and ensuing risks from the spread of diseases, food aid greatly increases their chances of survival. When the rains return, the majority move back to their own villages and farms.

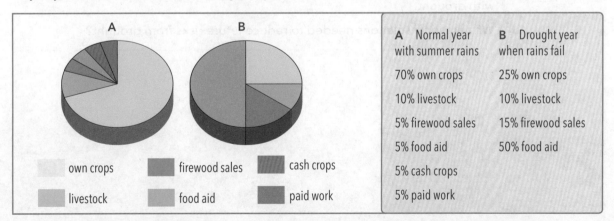

A Normal year with summer rains	B Drought year when rains fail
70% own crops	25% own crops
10% livestock	10% livestock
5% firewood sales	15% firewood sales
5% food aid	50% food aid
5% cash crops	
5% paid work	

FIGURE 6.33 How people in an Ethiopian village survived in a normal year and in a drought year

OXFORD
UNIVERSITY PRESS

International food aid cannot be anything more than a temporary solution. For the long-term, international development aid to give people help and guidance to increase food production in their village is better. Sometimes governments can help by increasing water availability, such as by water transfers from dams located elsewhere, or perhaps by desalination if the country is oil-rich. Much better, however, is the use of local solutions, at an appropriate level of technology for rural communities. NGOs (Non-Government Organizations), often charities like Water Aid, are much better at giving this type of international aid. Examples of successful local, community-based solutions include:

- water conservation and storage, such as building small stone or earth dams to hold back water flowing down valley sides;

- rainwater harvesting, collecting more of the rain falling in wet seasons for use in dry periods;

- tree planting on valley sides to stop run-off and soil erosion;

- organic compost pits, where waste matter is packed down for compost, to improve soil fertility and its water-holding capacity.

ACTIVITIES

1 Make a table of the impacts of drought as was done earlier for flooding in Table 6.5.

2 (a) Describe what Figure 6.32 shows about loss of life from droughts.

   (b) Explain what Figure 6.32 shows about loss of life from droughts.

3 Study Figure 6.33.

   (a) Make a list of the differences between a normal year and a drought year.

   (b) Which one is the most significant difference and why?

   (c) Why is environmental damage more likely in drought years?

4 (a) State the advantages and disadvantages of food aid as a strategy for dealing with drought.

   (b) Why are local solutions needed to reduce future risks from drought?

Case study: Drought in Niger

Niger, a country of about 19.2 m people, is located in the middle of the Sahel, Africa's main zone of drought (Figure 6.30). It is one of the world's poorest countries. It has the highest birth rate, just under 44.2 per 1000, and highest fertility rate, 7.6 children per woman (Chapter 8). Together they mean fast population growth. The rains failed in 2004, 2010, and again in 2012, and were not always good in intervening years. Drought in 2004 led to famine in 2005, with up to 3 million people desperate for food aid. The worst affected were the Fulani and other nomadic herders; up to 70 per cent of their livestock died due to lack of fodder. At first, food aid was slow to reach people. Only when the famine became so bad that the international news media covered the story did delivery speed up.

In 2012, crops failed due to the exceptional heat (a sign of global warming?). As vegetation dried out, swarms of locusts moved south into Niger and devoured what little was left. By 2014 the WFP (World Food Programme) was helping 3 million in Niger; but another 3 million needing food aid were not included. Deaths were highest among children; famine and malnutrition led to the spread of diseases such as diarrhoea.

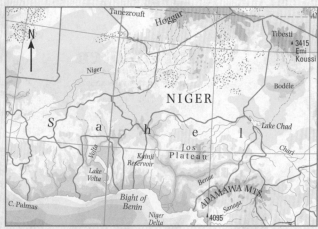

FIGURE 6.34 Location of Niger–in the Sahel, and a politically unstable zone

FIGURE 6.35 Niger: Muslim children seeking protection from the extreme heat under a tree

Case Study

What about the future? Food aid cannot reach everyone. The resources of the WFP are so stretched that aid reaches fewer than half the people who need it. World food prices are increasing. What is really needed is a massive injection of long-term development aid to replace short-term food aid. This is the only way to build up surpluses in wet years to tide people through the drought years. This is the Sahel, an area noted for unreliable rain. Many things are stopping this solution from happening. Governments keep changing; terrorist groups operate in neighbouring countries; the country is landlocked and not easy to reach; and the government has no population policy (Chapter 8).

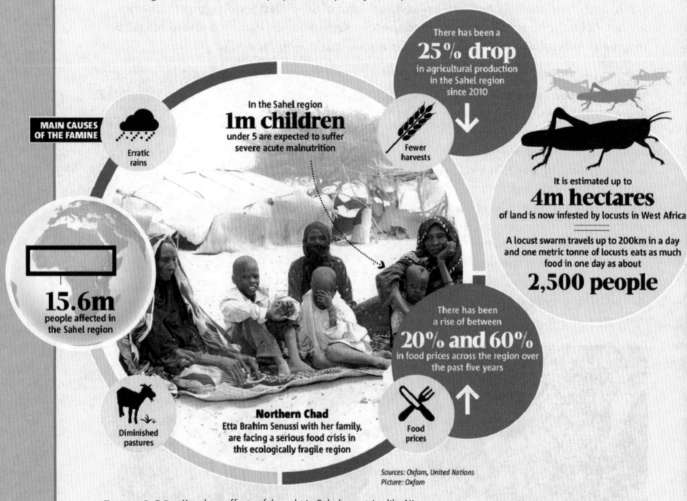

There has been a **25% drop** in agricultural production in the Sahel region since 2010

MAIN CAUSES OF THE FAMINE

Erratic rains

In the Sahel region **1m children** under 5 are expected to suffer severe acute malnutrition

Fewer harvests

It is estimated up to **4m hectares** of land is now infested by locusts in West Africa

A locust swarm travels up to 200km in a day and one metric tonne of locusts eats as much food in one day as about **2,500 people**

15.6m people affected in the Sahel region

There has been a rise of between **20% and 60%** in food prices across the region over the past five years

Diminished pastures

Northern Chad
Etta Brahim Senussi with her family, are facing a serious food crisis in this ecologically fragile region

Food prices

Sources: Oxfam, United Nations
Picture: Oxfam

FIGURE 6.36 Knock-on effects of drought in Sahel countries like Niger

---

ACTIVITY

Use the information about Niger to make brief notes for a drought case study under the following headings. (Note that these are the headings most likely to be used in examination questions, because they are syllabus terms as well.)

- Causes (both natural and human)
- Impacts (on people and the environment)
- Management (before, during, and after droughts)

ACTIVITIES – ALL NATURAL HAZARDS

1 (a)   Draw two pie or divided bar graphs to show these two data sets (A and B).

A Distribution of natural hazards		B Distribution of people killed by natural hazards	
Europe	14%	High economic development countries	2%
Americas	20%		
Africa	21%	Medium economic development countries	32%
Asia	42%	Low economic development countries	66%
Oceania	3%		

(b)   With the help of examples, explain why natural hazards have different impacts according to levels of economic development.

2   Refer back to Figure 6.32.

(a)   State the total percentages for deaths from (i) tectonic and (ii) climatic hazards.

(b)   Suggest reasons why the two percentages are so different.

3 (a)   Of the five natural hazards studied, which two offer positive opportunities for human economic activities?

(b)   Describe what these opportunities are.

(c)   Explain why the impacts from the other three hazards are almost entirely negative.

CHAPTER 7

The atmosphere and human activities

OBJECTIVES

In this chapter you will learn about

- the structure and composition of the atmosphere
- atmospheric pollution, its causes, and impacts
- smog, acid rain, ozone layer depletion, and enhanced greenhouse effect
- causes, impacts, and strategies for their reduction
- strategies for managing atmospheric pollution

FIGURE 7.1 Antarctica–penguins on a nesting site in the Antarctic. Despite the lack of permanent inhabitation, how have human activities affected the clear blue sky above and the ocean waters surrounding Antarctica? These Gentoo penguins feed on krill: how secure are the supplies of krill on which they depend?

INTRODUCTION

The Earth and its atmosphere is the greatest natural system (Figure 7.2). Solar energy is the input which drives the system. This energy is used, stored, and transferred between the Earth and its atmosphere. The output from the system is the energy radiated and lost into space.

The atmosphere is an envelope of gases wrapped around the Earth. Its relation to the size of the Earth is similar to that of the skin on an apple. The gases are transparent (allow light and view to pass through them) and odourless (without smell). The gravitational pull of the Earth keeps the atmosphere attached to it, although the atmosphere itself is in constant motion.

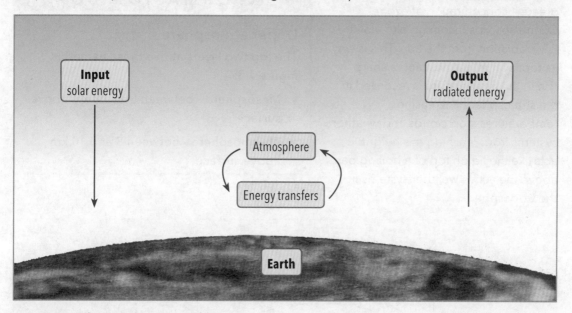

FIGURE 7.2   The atmospheric system of the Earth

Structure and composition of the atmosphere

Structure

Although it extends up to 10,000 km above the Earth, 97 per cent of the atmospheric mass is within 30km of the surface. Atmospheric pressure decreases rapidly with height. The different layers, which are identified mainly by temperature characteristics, have their own names. The two that are important for us and for life on Earth, namely, the troposphere and stratosphere (Figure 3.3), will be covered in more detail.

The troposphere is the lowest layer, which touches the surface of the Earth. The base of the atmosphere is warmed by conduction from the Earth's surface so that the temperature falls with increasing height above the ground. The tropopause, (the divide between troposphere and stratosphere), is reached at -50°C. It is higher in the Tropics (17,000m) than at the Poles (8000m). Above this, in the stratosphere, temperatures begin to rise.

OXFORD
UNIVERSITY PRESS

Some of the important characteristics of the troposphere are listed below.

- Percentages of both water vapour and carbon dioxide are higher than in other parts of the atmosphere.

- The Earth's cloud and weather systems are concentrated here.

- It contains most of the atmosphere's water vapour, cloud, dust, and pollution.

In contrast, the stratosphere above is dust-free and cloudless. Little carbon dioxide and water vapour are present. The air is dry. What this layer does have is the greatest concentration of ozone. Ozone absorbs incoming ultraviolet (UV) radiation from the Sun. This is why its top layer is warmest and a sharp rise in the temperature is recorded in the stratosphere. Increasing temperatures stop clouds and weather systems from reaching this height: it acts like the lid on top of a boiling pan above the active weather systems in the troposphere.

INFORMATION BOX

Upper atmosphere

The top two layers above those named in Figure 7.3:

- Mesosphere – between 5 and 8 km above surface

- Thermosphere – between 8 and 10 km above surface

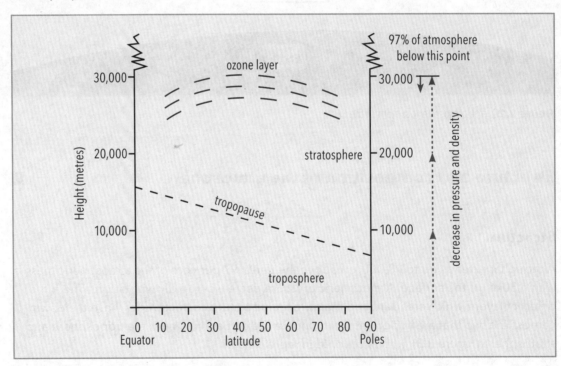

FIGURE **7.3** Structure of the lower atmosphere

Composition

Dry surface air is dominated by only two gases, nitrogen and oxygen, which make up 99 per cent of the atmosphere by volume. Both are needed for plant growth. Oxygen is produced by plants during photosynthesis and is used by other forms of life on Earth.

TABLE 7.1 Composition of the atmosphere

	% by volume
Nitrogen	78.09
Oxygen	20.95
Argon (inert gas)	0.93
Carbon dioxide	0.03

INFORMATION BOX

Other atmospheric ingredients

- other inert gases (e.g. helium)

- traces of dust, salt, smoke, and other pollutants (e.g. sulphur dioxide, nitrogen oxide, and methane)

- varying amounts of water vapour

The percentage of carbon dioxide is tiny, but its importance is enormous. First, it is soaked up by plants for photosynthesis. Secondly, it absorbs long-wave heat radiation from the surface. Nitrogen and oxygen that make up 99 per cent of the atmosphere retain little heat; without carbon dioxide the Earth would be about 30°C colder, which would make it frozen and lifeless. This is the natural greenhouse effect.

The amount of ozone in the atmosphere is a minute 0.00006 per cent, yet it plays a vital role in allowing life on Earth. The ozone is concentrated in the stratosphere where many of the cancer-inducing ultraviolet rays, which would otherwise harm plants, animals, and humans, are absorbed by it.

Amounts of water vapour vary greatly from place to place. Water vapour is the source for cloud formation and precipitation in the troposphere. The percentage by volume can be as little as 0.20 in deserts; however, in tropical areas with active weather systems this can rise to as much as 4 per cent. Small amounts of tiny particles, such as dust, smoke, and salt crystals, have high local concentrations as well. Since the surface is the source, amounts of dust tend to be greatest in desert areas, smoke in industrial and urban areas, and salt in coastal locations with strong wave activity.

ACTIVITIES

1 Draw a pie graph to show the composition of dry air.

2 (a) What is the tropopause?

   (b) Make a table to show the differences between the troposphere and the stratosphere using these headings: amount, temperature, and composition.

3 Explain why atmospheric components present in small quantities

   (a) vary in amount and type from place to place;

   (b) have an importance greater than their percentages would suggest.

Atmospheric pollution: causes and impacts

In the natural Earth-atmosphere system everything is finely balanced, until humans upset this delicate system by increasing certain components (for example, carbon dioxide) and reducing others (for example, ozone: Table 7.2).

Humans use the atmosphere as a dumping ground just as much as the oceans and rivers. From the Industrial Revolution onwards, production of industrial goods and consumption of energy have increased dramatically. Due to all kinds of new technologies, the cocktail of gases emitted into the atmosphere keeps on growing both in quantity and variety. One of the greatest contributors is the internal combustion engine in cars. Another is fossil fuel-burning power stations. Together they are responsible for well over half of all emissions into the atmosphere.

People usually only notice the consequences of their actions after considerable damage has been done, by which time the unfortunate effects on natural ecosystems, climate, and health are difficult to reverse. Examples of some of these bad effects are included in Table 7.2.

Within countries, atmospheric pollution is most serious in urban areas, where emissions of smoke particles and exhaust fumes are most concentrated. Wind carries some types of pollution across borders into neighbouring countries, thus making it a regional problem. Acid rain is an example. Other types of pollution have now become worldwide problems, such as global warming and the hole in the ozone layer. International action is essential if their effects are to be reduced or eliminated.

TABLE 7.2   Summary of changes in the composition of the atmosphere caused by humans

People are increasing the amount of smoke and other solid particles suspended in the atmosphere	People are reducing the proportion of high level ozone
Causes ■ burning fossil fuels in power stations and exhaust fumes from cars, trucks, and buses ■ wastes burnt from chemical factories and other industries ■ bare soil in agricultural areas picked up and carried by the wind **Direct effects** ■ reduced visibility (haze, mist, fog, and smog) ■ poor air quality, especially in places where photochemical smog forms ■ formation of acid rain **Other effects** ■ health problems, particularly asthma, bronchitis, and other respiratory problems	**Causes** ■ use of chemicals, especially CFCs and halons **Direct effects** ■ depletes the ozone layer in the stratosphere, leading to 'ozone holes' ■ increases ultraviolet radiation that reaches the surface **Other effects** ■ Increased risk of cancers in people, especially skin cancer

TABLE 7.2 Summary of changes in the composition of the atmosphere caused by humans

People are increasing the proportion of carbon dioxide in the atmosphere	People are reducing the amount of water vapour returned to the atmosphere
Causes ■ deforestation and burning the wood ■ burning fossil fuels **Direct effects** ■ traps more of the heat radiated from the surface ■ increases the Earth's temperature (such as global warming) **Other effects** ■ rising sea levels ■ changes in world weather (such as more storms and droughts)	**Causes** ■ deforestation reducing transpiration ■ more bare surfaces on desert margins reducing evapo-transpiration **Direct effects** ■ less cloud formation and precipitation in areas already short of water ■ more likelihood of drought **Other effects** ■ lower crop yields and less agricultural output ■ reduced food supply, in extreme cases leading to famine

ACTIVITIES

1 From Table 7.2, identify and list

  (a) the five main human causes of air pollution;

  (b) the possible effects of air pollution on **(i)** people's health, **(ii)** ecosystems, **(iii)** water supply, and **(iv)** food production.

2 Study Figure 7.4.

  (a) Describe what is happening here.

  (b) State changes to the composition of the atmosphere that might result.

FIGURE 7.4 In the forested interior of Brazil

OXFORD
UNIVERSITY PRESS

Smog: causes and impacts

Smog is a combination of 'smoke' and 'fog' which lowers visibility and gives poor air quality. It is always likely to be more of a problem in urban than rural areas because many people, vehicles, and industries are concentrated in a relatively small space. Industrial processes release volatile organic compounds as well as dust and smoke particles. Traffic emissions are sources of gases and unburnt hydrocarbons, as well as smoke particles. These pollute the atmosphere and have adverse effects on people's health.

FIGURE 7.5 Traffic in Karachi: the labelling shows sources of pollution and effects on people.

When temperatures are high and there is strong sunlight, a photochemical reaction occurs which makes it even more unpleasant for city people. The 'chemical soup' from car exhausts, especially nitrogen oxides and hydrocarbons, can produce high levels of ground ozone. Haze and smog hang over urban areas, accompanied by an unpleasant smell. Ozone is the poisonous form of oxygen, beneficial to humans when in the upper atmosphere, but when present in the lower atmosphere it irritates the bronchial passages, lungs, and eyes.

Some of the world's large cities are 'famous' for their persistently high levels of air pollution and photochemical smog. These include Los Angeles and Mexico City, and Santiago (Chile); in Asia, Delhi and Beijing have the same problem. The first three of these five cities have certain physical characteristics that make pollutants hang around in the atmosphere instead of dispersing quickly (Figure 7.6). Pollutants are trapped by the surrounding high ground. The climate is hot, dry, and sunny for at least half of the year; because the pressure is high, the air sinks. Without rain and wind to clear them, smoke and dust particles are left to accumulate in the lower atmosphere, close to the ground.

An inversion of temperature often occurs, making it even less likely that pollutants can escape from the lower layers of the atmosphere. It is normal for temperatures to be highest at the surface and drop an average of 1°C for every 150 metres of height above the ground. In an inversion, the opposite happens; temperatures increase with height above the ground. An inversion occurs in Los Angeles on about half the days of the year. When the air above it is warmer, air from below is unable to rise. Therefore, none of the pollutants are dispersed to higher levels in the atmosphere. Instead, they are left to accumulate as a brownish-yellow haze below the inversion. Los Angeles is a 'city of freeways' (motorways), where the 'automobile is king'; car ownership is high and public transport is poor or non-existent. Hence, there is no shortage of pollutants.

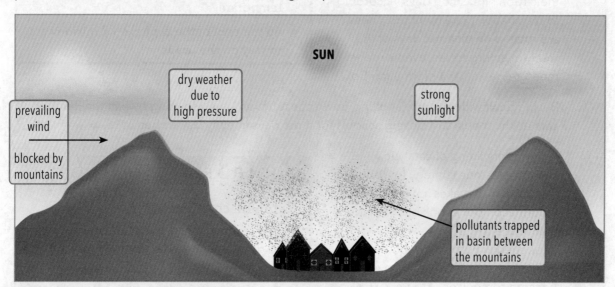

FIGURE 7.6 Physical factors which favour the build-up of pollutants in the atmosphere

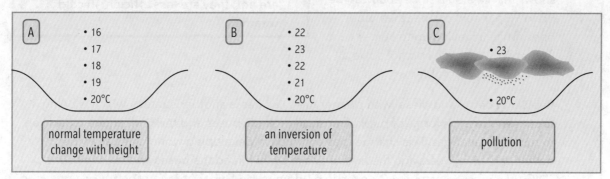

FIGURE 7.7 Inversion of temperature and air pollution

ACTIVITIES

1 **(a)** Name the pollutants from vehicle exhausts.

 (b) Describe how people's health can be affected by traffic emissions.

 (c) State how traffic emissions contribute to global as well as local pollution.

2 **(a)** What is meant by inversion of temperature?

 (b) Where and when is an inversion of temperature most likely to occur?

 (c) Why does it increase atmospheric pollution?

Smog: strategies to improve urban air quality

On bad smog days, people with chest problems, such as asthma, are warned to stay indoors in Los Angeles. In Santiago, Chile's capital city located in the Central Valley between towering Andean peaks and coastal mountain ranges, cars are banned from entering the city on high smog days, according to registration plate numbers. These are rotated on different days of the week. In emergencies, even stronger measures are taken (Information Box).

> **INFORMATION BOX**
>
> **Santiago—Environmental Emergency, June 2015 (mid-winter)**
> The Government ordered
> - over 900 industries to shut down temporarily;
> - 40 per cent of the capital's 1.7 million cars to stay off the roads.

Beijing dealt with smog by shutting down construction sites, reducing by half the number of cars on the roads, and closing schools for three days in early December 2016.

Compulsory fitting of catalytic converters is one strategy for reducing air pollution. It makes a big difference (Information Box). Look back to Figure 2.26 (page 57). It shows what happened in Europe around the year 2000 after use of catalytic converters became compulsory. Figure 2.26 also shows that cars built since 2000 can be up to 90 per cent cleaner than older ones, while travelling up to 50 per cent further. However, they do not solve all vehicle pollution problems.

> **INFORMATION BOX**
>
> **Catalytic converters**
> - They reduce emissions of pollutants such as oxides of nitrogen, carbon monoxide, and hydrocarbons.
> - They work most efficiently when engines are hot; they are less efficient in cold weather.

Replacing petrol and diesel with cleaner fuels like gas is another strategy which is being taken seriously. It is forms of public transport, notably buses and taxis, which are most likely to run on cleaner gas. This change is as common in developing world cities as in the developed. Many years ago the authorities in Delhi forced the buses and taxis to use CNG (compressed natural gas); even in oil-dominated Dubai, some buses are gas-powered. As long ago as 1996 the use of CBG (cleaner burning gasoline) was made compulsory in Los Angeles (and the rest of California); this fuel reduced ozone-forming emissions from road vehicles by 15 per cent.

Another approach is to improve public transport and make it a more attractive alternative to private car use. Cairo, Delhi, and Rio are just three of an increasing number of developing world cities to have recent or new bright, clean, and efficient metros (underground railways). A greater contrast cannot be imagined between travelling on a new metro and travelling on choked surface roads. However, a metro has a fixed route, whereas roads go everywhere. Persuading people to give up using their cars is not easy anywhere: buying a car is usually top of the wish list for people in developing countries as soon as they are wealthy enough.

ACTIVITIES

1 (a)   State three strategies for smog reduction in big cities.

   (b)   Outline the strengths and weaknesses of each strategy.

2 (a)   Number of high ozone days in Los Angeles:

       1994 – 270; 1997 – 190; 2000 – 160; 2006 – 145; 2009 – 140; 2012 – 125.

       Draw a graph to show these values.

   (b)   Describe the main trend shown.

   (c)   Suggest reasons for it.

   (d)   Why is the number of days unlikely to drop to zero?

3 Make a study of air pollution in a big city in your country or region. Look at causes and strategies to reduce pollution (if any). If there is none, give reasons why.

Acid rain: causes and impacts

Clean rain water has a pH value between 5 and 6, which makes it slightly acid. However, rainfall in many industrial regions has a pH value of between 4 and 5. Snow and rain in the industrial north-east of the USA have been known to have pH values as low as 2.1. The increased acidity comes from the presence of pollutants in the atmosphere, mainly sulphur dioxide and nitrogen oxides (Figure 7.8). Both are released when fossil fuels are burnt. Coal-fired power stations and vehicle exhausts are the main sources.

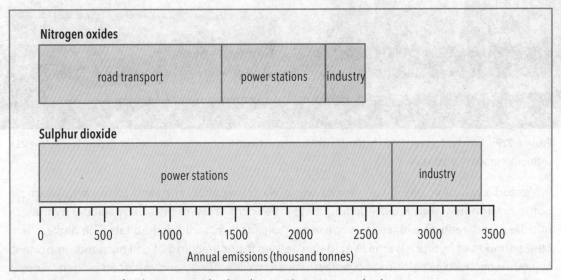

FIGURE 7.8   Sources of acid gases in one developed country (approximate values)

Once in the atmosphere, pollutants are carried by prevailing winds to other places, sometimes to other countries. Some are deposited directly onto the Earth's surface; this is known as dry deposition. The rest is converted into acids (sulphuric and nitric) which fall to the ground in rain, as wet deposition.

Impacts of acid rain

Acid rain is mainly a developed-world problem. It is most associated with the industrialized countries in Europe and North America, where the highest rates of fossil fuel use from power stations, industries, and cars are found. Increasingly, it is becoming an Asiatic problem as well, as countries like China and India industrialize and make use of their large coal deposits, some of which are very low grade with high sulphur content.

Because pollutants can be transported over long distances by the wind, other less industrialized countries are also affected. Acid rain is a major problem in Scandinavian countries (Norway and Sweden) because prevailing westerly winds carry the oxides of sulphur and nitrogen from the UK's coal-fired power stations (Figure 7.9).

FIGURE 7.9 Coal-fired power station in the UK—what comes out from the chimney, not from the cooling towers, is what contributes to acid rain formation.

Increased levels of acidity in soils are having devastating effects on land-based ecosystems. Some environmentalists are predicting that 90 per cent of Germany's trees will die by the middle of this century, with serious consequences for forest wildlife habitats. The high concentration of hydrogen ions in acid rain causes faster leaching of soil nutrients. Important soil nutrients, such as calcium and potassium, are washed away and replaced by manganese and aluminium, which are harmful to root growth. After a time, trees shed their leaves and needles and become less resistant to drought, frost, and disease, and eventually die.

In Scandinavia high acidity is damaging aquatic (water-based) ecosystems as well, resulting in the deaths of fish and plant life in rivers and lakes. Many fish cannot tolerate low pH values. Fresh water supplies are polluted.

Acid rain also has effects on people which are more direct. Farmers must buy more fertilizers to offset increased soil acidity and maintain crop yields. Acid rain has been linked to a decline in human health as one of the factors contributing to the increased number of cases of bronchitis and lung cancer. Some of the world's best known buildings, such as the Taj Mahal in India and the Acropolis in Athens, are 'rotting away' in the acid atmospheres that humans have created around and above them.

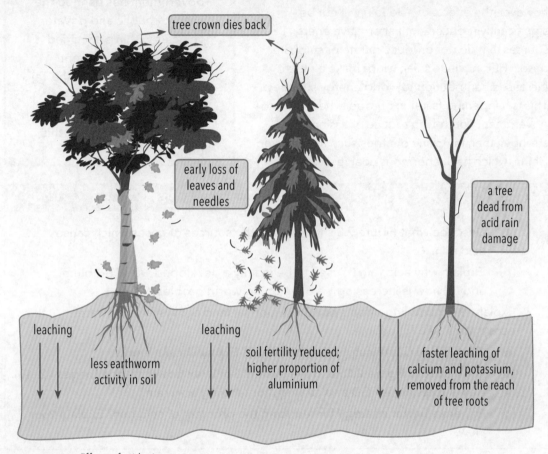

FIGURE 7.10   Effects of acid rain on trees

Acid rain: strategies to reduce its impacts

Some methods are used to try to reduce its damaging effects, such as adding limestone in powdered form to increase pH values in lakes. However, the only effective long-term strategy is to cut emissions of the gases doing the damage.

In coal-fired power stations sulphur can be 'scrubbed' out of the **flue gases** (gases going out of the chimney) by using a mixture of limestone and water which converts the sulphur dioxide into calcium sulphate. The proper name for this process is flue gas desulphurization (FGD). Nitrogen oxides in flue gases can be reduced by 'selective catalytic reduction'—adding ammonia and passing it over a catalyst to produce nitrogen and water. Both cost money and increase the cost of electricity, which explains why most power stations are not as clean as they could be.

There has been a switch from coal-fired to natural gas-fired power stations in some developed countries such as the UK, because the sulphur content of natural gas is so much lower than that of coal. Fitting catalytic converters reduces nitrogen oxide emissions from cars. In reality, however, the effects of acid rain will not be significantly reduced until alternative energy sources that do not produce nitrate or sulphate gases (HEP, nuclear, solar, wind) make a much increased contribution to world energy supplies. This is happening faster in Europe, where EU and government controls to reduce emissions are stronger, than in Asian countries such as India and China, which have enormous coal reserves.

INFORMATION BOX

- In an effort to save the pristine white marble of the Taj Mahal from discolouration due to pollution, the Indian government has banned the entry of public and private vehicles within a specified radius of the monument. Visitors can approach the Taj Mahal only in the battery-powered, smoke-free cabs especially provided for this purpose.

ACTIVITIES

1 (a) Describe what Figure 7.8 shows about the sources of gases which cause acid rain.

   (b) Explain why acid rain (i) used to be mainly a developed world problem, and (ii) now is increasingly a developing world problem.

2 Explain the damaging effects of acid rain on (a) land ecosystems (b) water ecosystems, and (c) people.

3 (a) What is flue gas desulphurization (FGD)? Explain how it works.

   (b) Look back to Figure 2.15 and the example of Drax power station (pages 42–43). How successful is FGD as a strategy for tackling acid rain?

   (c) Is there a better strategy for reducing the problem of acid rain? Explain your view.

Ozone layer depletion: causes and impacts

As already shown in Figure 7.3, the major concentration of ozone is in the stratosphere 25–30km above sea level. By absorbing incoming UV (ultraviolet) radiation from the Sun, ozone acts as a shield, protecting life on Earth from the damaging effects of high levels of UV radiation. It prevents 97 per cent of the Sun's UV light from reaching the Earth's surface.

There is serious concern that the ozone shield is breaking down. Signs of ozone depletion were first noticed over Antarctica in the 1980s; this has become known ever since as 'the hole in the ozone layer'. Thinning of the ozone layer happens during the winter in polar lands and is noticed most in spring and early summer, once daylight returns. By 1993, ozone had been reduced to between one half and two-thirds of the amount present in 1970, with most of this depletion occurring after 1990. Since 1989, depletions have also been recorded over the Arctic as well. Increased levels of UV radiation reaching the surface have been linked to increases in skin cancer and cataracts, and to a reduction in immunity to disease.

Causes

It is generally agreed that the release of a family of chemicals which contain chlorine, the so-called CFCs (chlorofluorocarbons), and halons into the atmosphere are the main causes. CFCs are used as the propellants in aerosol spray cans, which are widely used for hair-spray, deodorants, and insect killers. Coolants used in refrigerators and air-conditioning systems also contain CFCs. Halons are very useful in fire extinguishers, especially in ships, aircraft, and computer rooms. World production of CFC gases increased quickly from about 180 million kg per year in 1960 to over 1000 million kg by 1990.

They have valuable properties—they are stable, non-flammable, and non-toxic. They are also cheap. However, the fact that they are stable means that they persist in the atmosphere for a long time; this enables them to reach the ozone layer without being destroyed. Ultraviolet radiation sets off a chain of chemical reactions in which the chlorine converts the ozone into oxygen.

Although the hole in the ozone layer was first detected over Antarctica, the problem did not originate there. This is because no one lives permanently in Antarctica. Pollutants in the atmosphere travel around the world with the winds. It is an international problem.

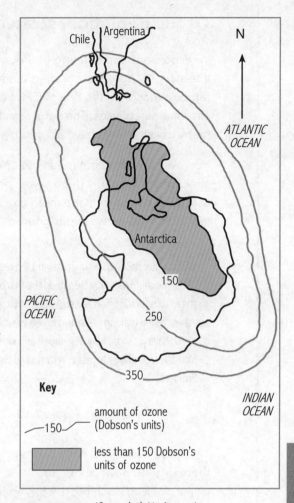

FIGURE 7.11 'Ozone hole' in Antarctica

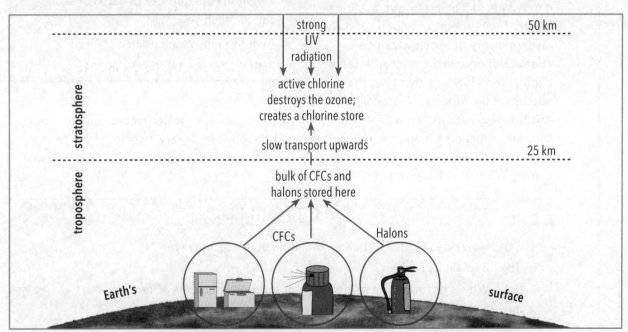

FIGURE 7.12 Causes of ozone depletion in the stratosphere

Ozone depletion: strategies for ozone recovery

In response to the thinning of the ozone layer, many governments signed up to an international agreement called the Montreal Protocol in 1987. They made pledges for a rapid reduction in the use of CFCs and halons and to stop using them by 2000, except for essential safety uses. The substantial reduction in output of CFCs since 1990 suggests that many governments have abided by the agreement.

However, this does not mean the end of the problem. These gases will remain in the atmosphere for many more years, possibly for hundreds of years. Even with total bans on their use, it will not be until the middle of this century that the chlorine content of the stratosphere falls below the levels that triggered off the formation of the Antarctic ozone hole.

'Our country has just begun installing the technology to make CFCs, the chemicals which enabled the rich countries to have cheap refrigeration and air conditioning. Now we have been asked to stop making them and to use expensive substitutes, which have yet to be fully developed and which we do not have the technology to make. Why should we agree to this Protocol?'

'The agreement is still not strong enough. Chlorine in the atmosphere will grow during the next ten years. I calculate that it will be 2030 before the chlorine level goes down to the level in 1986 when the ozone hole was first announced.'

FIGURE 7.13   Comments made in 1990 about the Montreal Protocol.

The good news—and it is not often there is good news about air pollution—is that scientists working in Antarctica announced in 2016 that the ozone hole had at last begun to shrink in size. They expect continued ozone layer recovery, albeit slowly since chemicals linger in the atmosphere for a long time. However, thanks to the success of the Montreal Protocol at

INFORMATION BOX

Phasing out of CFCs

- 2 million—the number of cases of skin cancer each year
- Avoidable by reduced use of CFCs
- Estimate made by the UN in 2016

encouraging nations to eradicate the use of CFCs in products, scientists are confident that they are detecting a long term downward trend, despite temporary increases from time to time due to natural causes such as chlorine gases released during periods of high volcanic activity in Chile, as happened in 2015.

ACTIVITIES

1 (a)   How does Figure 7.11 show the 'hole in the ozone layer'?

   (b)   Explain its causes.

   (c)   Why is its formation an example of an international problem?

2 (a)   What was the Montreal Protocol?

   (b)   How successful has it been? State and explain your view.

Enhanced greenhouse effect: causes and impacts

Global warming and the greenhouse effect

There is no argument that global warming is happening, although there are arguments about its causes.

Look at Figure 7.14. The average temperature of the Earth was about 14°C about 150 years ago. Between then and 2015, it has slowly increased by 0.76°C. This may not sound like much, but it really is a very significant increase. Scientists tell us that a global cooling of 3°– 4°C brought on the last Ice Age. If warming carries on at the same rate as during the last 150 years, how much warmer will the world be in 2100?

Repeat Warning

EXAM TIP

- Many students in writing examination answers confuse the hole in the ozone layer with the greenhouse effect and global warming.

- The hole in the ozone layer allows more of the Sun's UV rays through, not more light rays. Therefore insolation (heating from sunlight) is not increased. The Earth is not heating because of the hole in the ozone layer.

- The one and only thing in common between the ozone hole and greenhouse effect is that CFCs are partly responsible for the formation of both of them.

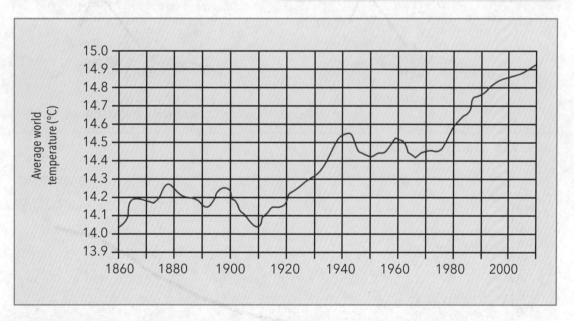

FIGURE 7.14   Change in average world temperature 1860 – 2010

However, Figure 7.14 also shows that since 1980 the rate of global warming has been speeding up. The ten hottest years on record have all happened since 2000; 2014, 2015, and 2016 were the hottest so far. General world temperatures have been rising since the end of the Ice Age 10,000 years ago, but in the last 35 years the rise has been faster than ever before.

OXFORD
UNIVERSITY PRESS

The greenhouse effect is a natural process, as was made clear earlier in this chapter. Figure 7.15A shows how it works. Although a few scientists remain unconvinced, the overwhelming majority believe that the speed at which the world is warming up at present is not entirely natural and that rising levels of greenhouse gases in the atmosphere are to blame, at least in part.

Human activities have sent levels of greenhouse gases in the atmosphere soaring. It is expected that by 2080 concentrations of carbon dioxide will be double what they were before the Industrial Revolution (Figure 7.16). What is likely is that this is creating what is known as the 'enhanced' or 'accelerated' greenhouse effect, which is shown in Figure 7.15B. In other words, humans are not responsible for creating a new atmospheric process, but are responsible for increasing the proportion of greenhouse gases, which is upsetting the natural balance of gases in the atmospheric system.

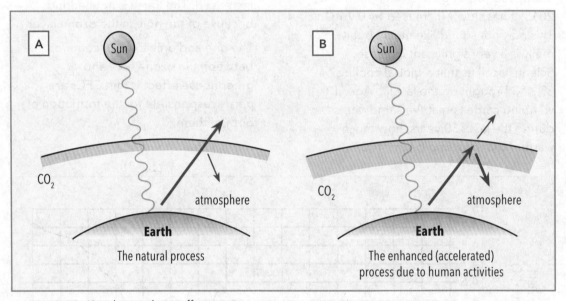

FIGURE 7.15 How the greenhouse effect operates

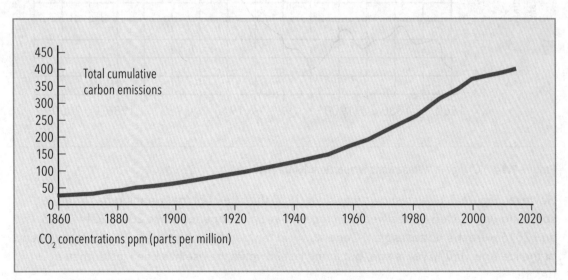

FIGURE 7.16 Growth in concentrations of carbon dioxide in the atmosphere

Information about greenhouse gases is given in Table 7.3. In percentage terms, by far and away the largest contributor is carbon dioxide. The main reason for this is that global energy use is absolutely dominated by fossil fuels. Since the start of the Industrial Revolution, humans have been taking stored carbon out of the Earth in the form of fossil fuels and releasing it back into the atmosphere when these fuels are burnt.

What is also significant is the number of years the gases remain in the atmosphere before being absorbed or dispersed. Which one of the greenhouse gases is much more dangerous than its percentage contribution suggests?

TABLE **7.3** Greenhouse gases

Greenhouse gas	Sources	% contribution to the greenhouse effect	Number of years it stays in the atmosphere
Carbon dioxide	Burning fossil fuels, deforestation and burning wood	64	up to 200
Methane	Deforestation, decomposition of waste, rice and cattle farming generating methane from rotting vegetation	18	12
CFCs	Used in aerosols, refrigeration	14	45 - 1700
Nitrogen oxides	Use of chemical fertilizers on farms, motor transport burning fuels, deforestation, and burning vegetation	4	114

ACTIVITIES

1 Draw labelled sketches to show **(a)** how the natural greenhouse effect operates and **(b)** how it can be speeded up by humans.

2 State the evidence that the Earth is warming up faster than ever before.

3 Explain the human causes of increased greenhouse gas emissions using these headings:

   (a) burning fossil fuels, **(b)** cutting down forests, and **(c)** making changes in agriculture.

4 Why is it good news for the world that use of CFCs has been greatly reduced?

OXFORD
UNIVERSITY PRESS

Effects of global warming

Since the year 2000 carbon dioxide has been released in record amounts, so that the effects of global warming can only get worse before they get better. Figure 7.17 shows carbon emissions (metric tonnes) per head for various countries and regions of the world. The USA by itself, with less than 5 per cent of world population, is responsible for over 20 per cent of world emissions. The fastest increase in emissions has been from China due to the size and speed of its industrial and economic growth. Given its huge population, however, its emissions per head are only 6.1.

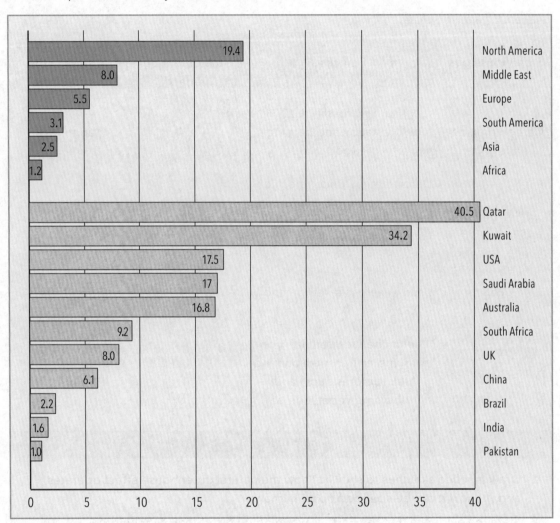

FIGURE 7.17   Carbon emissions per head for various countries and regions (2014)

Global warming is already having impacts that can be observed and measured. The Arctic ice cap is thinning by 10cm a year. Icebergs of record sizes are breaking off the Antarctic ice sheet during summer. Glaciers in high mountain areas are retreating to ever higher levels and some are disappearing. Permafrost in the Arctic will thin and melt. Sea levels are already 18cm higher than they were 100 years ago. Therefore, the sequence of events shown in Figure 7.18 is already happening and is expected to continue and become more widespread in its effects during the rest of the century.

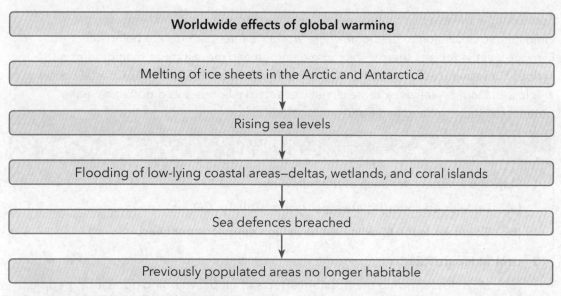

Worldwide effects of global warming

Melting of ice sheets in the Arctic and Antarctica

Rising sea levels

Flooding of low-lying coastal areas—deltas, wetlands, and coral islands

Sea defences breached

Previously populated areas no longer habitable

FIGURE 7.18   Worldwide effects of global warming

FIGURE 7.19   Iceberg from the Antarctic ice sheet–the increase in their size and numbers is evidence of global warming.

Rises in temperature are not expected to be the same across the globe; they are expected to be greatest in high latitudes and near the poles. It is possible, for example, that local warming over Greenland will be one to three times greater than the global average. If so, a complete melting of the Greenland ice cap would result in a sea-level rise of about 7 metres. This would be more than enough to drown many of the world's major cities! It is no surprise that island countries, like the Maldives and Seychelles in the middle of the Indian Ocean, are very alarmed at the prospects of global warming, as also are delta countries such as Bangladesh and the Netherlands.

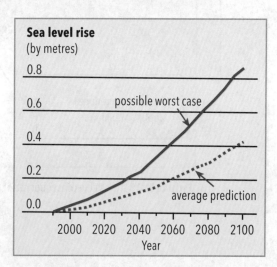

FIGURE 7.20   Predicted and possible rises in sea level, 2000-2100

Some people believe that global warming is already causing major changes in the atmospheric circulation to the point where world weather patterns are being affected. Extreme weather events seem to be more common and more intense than before, with serious consequences for people living in the areas affected (Chapter 6). Coastal flooding and loss of land, as well as extreme climatic events like floods and drought, have the potential to cause widespread human migrations.

ACTIVITIES

1   State the evidence for each of the following:
    (a)   Developed countries are most responsible for CO_2 emissions.
    (b)   Countries in the Middle East have high emissions per head.

2   Look at Figure 7.21.
    (a)   Make lists showing the possible effects of global warming upon jobs, people, and countries.
    (b)   Which of these are most likely to affect your country or region? Explain.
    (c)   Explain why governments and people in some countries have more to fear from global warming than in others.

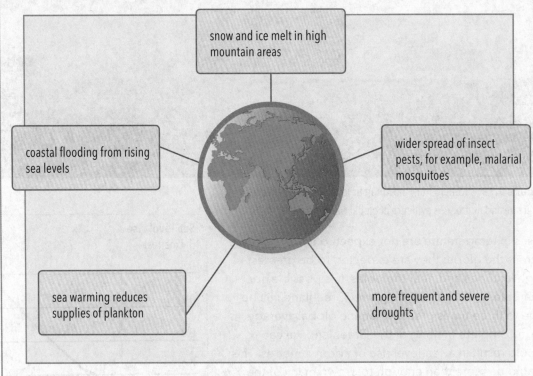

snow and ice melt in high mountain areas

coastal flooding from rising sea levels

wider spread of insect pests, for example, malarial mosquitoes

sea warming reduces supplies of plankton

more frequent and severe droughts

FIGURE 7.21   Possible consequences of global warming

Enhanced greenhouse effect: strategies to deal with its causes and impacts

Most scientists are convinced of the human role in global warming because of the size of the changes. Some politicians are less easily convinced because they are usually more interested in re-election and look mostly at the economic costs of cutting emissions. Against this kind of background international strategies to control greenhouse gas emissions have limited chance of success.

The issue of climate change was first discussed at the Earth Summit in Rio in 1992; although some 150 countries signed treaties aimed at reducing the greenhouse effect, they were not compulsory.

The Kyoto conference in 1997 was more tightly focused on climate change and proposed compulsory reductions of carbon dioxide emissions of 5 per cent by 2010, compared with 1990 levels for all developed countries. The US Senate refused to ratify the agreement and since then the USA's emissions have increased by 3 per cent per year. Developing countries were deliberately excluded so as not to hinder their economic development, although some of them, such as India and China, are industrializing rapidly and have considerable coal deposits of their own.

Everyone knew that the level of reduction agreed at Kyoto was not enough. Since then international conferences on global warming have come and gone, with little agreement and real change. The one held in Paris in 2015 led to more agreement as this time the big emitters, USA and China, signed up to the proposed reductions. However, the general feeling among scientists and environmentalists can be summed up as 'too little' and 'too late'. In the intervening years, the EU has been more active than most national governments in setting strict targets for CO_2 reductions. Countries such as Germany and Denmark have led the way in increased use of clean renewables, notably wind and solar power (Chapter 2, pages 44–46). More details of the strategies listed in Table 7.4 have been given in Chapter 2 as well as earlier in this chapter.

TABLE 7.4   Strategies to reduce greenhouse gas emissions

Strategy	How it reduces greenhouse gases	Other benefits
Tree planting	Increases size of the CO_2 store in the biosphere	Reduced soil erosion; lower risk of flooding; improved habitats for species
Alternative sources of energy	Replace fossil fuels with clean energy sources	Conservation of non-renewable resources for future generations
Energy conservation measures	Reduce amount of fossil fuels burnt	Cleaner air and less acid rain
Ban on use of CFCs in aerosols and fridges	Cuts emissions of CFCs	Reduces health risks, for example, skin cancer

The big hope for the future is greater use of renewables, especially as costs are coming down and making them more competitive with fossil fuels than ever before (Figure 2.21, page 49), and the governments of some developing world countries are showing more interest in harnessing their natural resource potential for renewables, such as Morocco and Kenya (Chapter 2). Much research is being channelled into developing bigger and better batteries so that power generated during favourable weather conditions can be stored for later use. This will help to overcome one of the main problems of renewable sources, namely intermittent supply.

Some people are keen on other options. One of these is carbon capture and storage. The CO_2 is captured as it leaves the coal burning power station and buried underground in aquifers or tunnels no longer used for mining. Not everyone is convinced about its viability and desirability. Critics mention the practical difficulties, the cost, and the fact that a very dangerous toxic gas is being stored.

Another option is nuclear. A newspaper headline in May 2004 read '**Only nuclear power can now halt global warming**'. Some of the supporting arguments are listed in Figure 7.22, followed by a reply from a member of the Green movement. The nuclear disaster at Fukushima in 2011 badly hit support for the nuclear lobby (Chapter 2, page 38) and many governments have cut back. Even so, some are to go ahead with new nuclear power stations, such as the UK in 2016. It used the argument that a mix of sources of electricity supply is needed to secure future supplies and it will help its commitment to meet lower and lower carbon emissions targets.

Nuclear power is needed

- Temperatures are already rising more rapidly than the UN's scientists realized at their meeting in 2001.

- There is not going to be enough time for renewable energy sources, the favoured solution of the Green movement, to replace fossil fuels and halt these changes.

- Nuclear power produces no CO_2; only by a massive expansion can runaway global warming and all the damage it will cause, be checked.

- Fears about the safety of nuclear energy are exaggerated and the Green movement should drop its opposition to nuclear power.

... a scientist speaks out

Nuclear power is not needed

- A dramatic response to climate change is needed.

- Although right to question previous assumptions, the scientist is wrong to think that nuclear power is any part of the answer.

- Nuclear power creates enormous problems—waste we do not know what to do with, radioactive emissions, unavoidable risk of accidents and terrorist attacks.

... a reply from the Greens

FIGURE 7.22 Is nuclear power needed?

ACTIVITIES

1 Study Figures 7.23 and 7.24.

Explain why countries have different views about the importance of global warming.

A Delegate from AOSIS (Alliance of small island states):

'We want at least a 20 per cent reduction in CO_2 emissions within the next 10 years.'

B Delegate from an oil producing and exporting country:

'I will support a delay in introducing new measures for reducing CO_2 emissions until all countries have agreed.'

C Delegate from the EU (European Union):

'The EU sets targets for CO_2 reductions in its member countries. We want other countries to do the same.'

D Delegate from the USA:

'We do not acknowledge that humans burning fossil fuels are the cause of global warming.'

E Delegate from a developing country in Asia:

'It is not our problem. It is not our fault. We want industrialized countries to take CO_2 cuts seriously.'

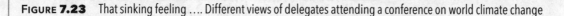

FIGURE 7.23 That sinking feeling …. Different views of delegates attending a conference on world climate change

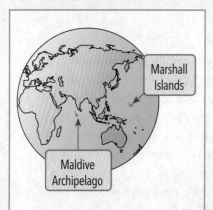

Marshall Islands

Maldive Archipelago

FIGURE 7.24 Island states most at risk from global warming

2 Choose two different strategies for reducing CO_2 emissions. For each one, state **(a)** how it helps and **(b)** why it is not being used more.

3 Answer the following questions, explaining as fully as you can.

(a) Are you for or against the building of more nuclear power stations?

(b) Do you believe that there will be a big reduction in CO_2 emissions in the world by 2030?

(c) Is global warming a big issue in your home country?

OXFORD
UNIVERSITY PRESS

Managing atmospheric pollution

The strategies listed in the syllabus to reduce the effects of atmospheric pollution are named in Figure 7.25. One or two are more the responsibility of individuals, such as not wasting energy at home, and by walking, cycling, or using public transport to travel to work (instead of going by car). All strategies contribute to energy efficiency and lower energy use.

FIGURE 7.25   Strategies to reduce the effects of atmospheric pollution

Many of the others are more the responsibility of governments. Only governments can implement transport policies, force manufacturers to stop using CFCs in their products, make catalytic converters compulsory on all vehicles, and instruct the owners of coal-fired power stations to instal Flue Gas Desulphurization (FGD) systems. Governments have the power to pass laws and enforce regulations. Unfortunately, many governments are better at passing laws than enforcing regulations. Governments also control taxation. Governments in the EU have led the way in using tax concessions to encourage a greater take-up of renewable energy sources. They needed to do this to reduce their carbon footprints and help them meet EU and other international targets for CO_2 reduction. Only by giving subsidies for wind and solar power could the initial higher costs of producing electricity from these, compared with fossil fuels, be reduced to make it worthwhile for companies to invest. Tax subsidies have been progressively reduced as new technology lowers the costs of renewables.

International climate change meetings have increased worldwide awareness of climate change and related issues, even though they have not led to agreements strong enough to stop global warming. They have raised the profile of atmospheric pollution as a major world issue. It is never going to be easy to get agreement for anything from the world's 170+ countries. The world has come closest with the Montreal Protocol and eradication of harmful CFCs hence the good news about the ozone hole recovery. Clearly, the economic consequences of getting rid of all dirty fossil fuel use are enormous and on a different scale in terms of need and worldwide use, from CFCs used only in a limited range of products.

ACTIVITIES

1 Exam watch: Check that you understand what is meant by the 11 strategies listed in Figure 7.25 by writing a definition or brief statement about each one. For some, it will be helpful to look back at Chapter 2 as well.

2 Look back at Table 7.2, and the answers you gave to Activity 1(a), page 201. Make a table listing the strategies reducing the effects of air pollution from Figure 7.25. Use a layout like the one below and list all the strategies which apply.

Causes of air pollution—strategies to reduce their effects				
Chemicals such as CFCs				
CFC replacement				

3 (a) For your home country, can you see evidence of any of these strategies being used?

(b) Explain why, or why not.

Case study: New Delhi's smog

In 2015 the WHO (World Health Organization) found that 13 of the 20 cities with the most polluted air were in India. Top of the international league table for high and dangerous rates of atmospheric pollution was New Delhi, even worse than Beijing with its terrible reputation for smog. The WHO was particularly worried about tiny cancer-causing particulates known as PM2.5–tiny dust and smoke particles more likely to kill because they go deeper into the lungs. Levels of PM2.5 in Delhi's air are frequently 15 times higher than the WHO considers safe.

Residents thought that they had defeated the problem of air pollution years ago. Delhi's air improved sharply after 2001 when regulations were enforced to make all public transport vehicles convert to running on CNG (Compressed Natural Gas), with tiny emissions compared with petrol and diesel engines. So what has changed? Delhi has grown, with 18 million city inhabitants, and more in the surrounding metropolitan area. The number of cars and trucks have increased–Delhi has more than 8 million registered vehicles. Increasing numbers of these have diesel engines, the worst type for emitting particulates. Convoys of trucks converge on Delhi every morning; it is the trucks that are most to blame for Delhi being at the top of the world's cities' pollution league table. India's low emissions and fuel quality standards do not help.

One estimate is that air pollution kills 10,500 people a year in Delhi. Breathing problems and respiratory illnesses trigger heart and asthma attacks. Particulate matter causes cancer. Reported cases of asthma and bronchitis among children increase every year. As always, it is Delhi's poor who are the most vulnerable, especially those who live and work on the toxic traffic-choked streets.

FIGURE 7.26 New Delhi smog

FIGURE 7.27 Delhi, November 20, 2015: Crowded traffic with colourful Tuk-Tuks, vehicles, and visible smog of air pollution behind them

The Delhi government has plenty of ideas about what to do. It wants to speed up closures of old coal-fired power stations. It intends to plant trees along the main roads to reduce dust. It has a target to introduce European vehicle emissions standards by 2017. It did build the new metro. But such is the scale of the problem that it still has to resort to temporary measures on winter mornings when the smog is particularly bad, such as banning vehicles on certain days according to their registration numbers.

As in many big cities in the developing world, the intention to tackle air pollution is often greater than implementation.

ACTIVITIES

Make brief case study notes for atmospheric pollution in Delhi using these four headings which are most likely to be used in examination questions.

A: Causes of air pollution

B: Effects of air pollution

C: Management strategies for reducing air pollution

D: Evaluation of the success of these policies (i.e how successful have they been; if not, why not?)

CHAPTER **8**

Human population

OBJECTIVES

In this chapter you will learn about

- distribution and density of population
- growth of the human population
- population structure
- managing human population size

FIGURE 8.1 Pedestrians at the Shibuya crossing, Tokyo—this famous crosswalk is used by over 2.5 million people daily.

INTRODUCTION

The growth in the world population over the last 200 years has been spectacular (Figure 8.2) and has not stopped yet. The total of 7.6 billion people in the world was reached in 2018. Although estimates for the future rates of population growth vary, there is no doubt that it will be in the same direction, upwards, for at least the next 30 years.

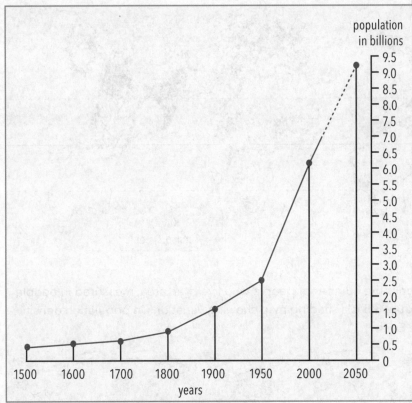

FIGURE 8.2 World population growth since 1500

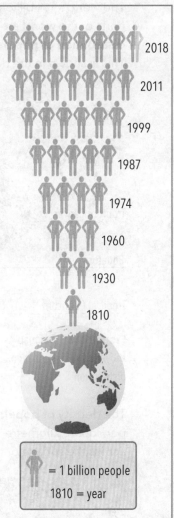

FIGURE 8.3 Total world population (billions)

Population growth has, and is, putting great pressure on the Earth's resources. More and more food is needed to feed ever increasing numbers of people. On land, the need to grow more food has led to overcultivation and overgrazing. This in turn has increased rates of deforestation, soil erosion, and desertification. At sea, the oceans have been overfished.

The increase in population increases the demand for fuel and mineral resources for industrial growth and for domestic cooking and heating. Increasing numbers and a higher proportion of the world's population now live in cities (urbanization). This has led to habitat loss and created major problems such as land and water pollution from waste disposal.

OXFORD
UNIVERSITY PRESS

Human population distribution and density

The world's 7.6 billion plus people are very unevenly spread across the Earth's surface. Some parts of the world are very densely populated, while others are almost totally empty. The **distribution of population** is the way people are spread out across the surface of the Earth. This is shown in the dot map in Figure 8.4.

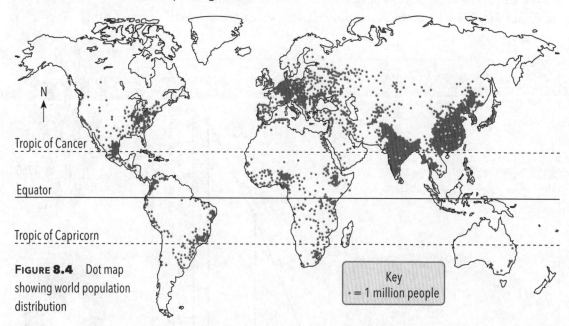

FIGURE 8.4 Dot map showing world population distribution

Key
• = 1 million people

The **density of population** is the number of people who live in an area, measured in people per square kilometre. Figure 8.5 is a shading map showing variations in population density across the surface of the Earth.

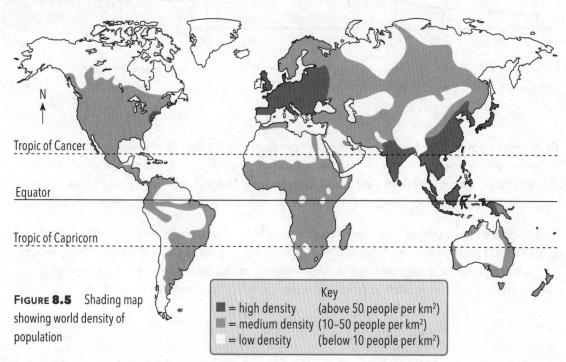

FIGURE 8.5 Shading map showing world density of population

Key
■ = high density (above 50 people per km²)
■ = medium density (10–50 people per km²)
□ = low density (below 10 people per km²)

To explain the patterns of world population distribution and density it is necessary to look at both physical and human factors. Densely populated areas are most likely where there are

- areas of low, flat land with fertile soils,
- a hot or temperate climate with at least one season of rain,
- places in which farming is intensive and crop output is high,
- urban areas of great economic activity (both industrial and commercial).

Together, the continents of Asia and Europe house over 80 per cent of the world population. They have been inhabited for a long time. Some of the highest densities are in the great river valleys of Asia (Chapter 4, page 111), explained by a combination of flat land, fertile silt soils, water supplies, growth of high yielding crops such as rice, rivers for transport, and recent big city industrial growth.

Physical factors alone go a long way to explaining low population densities. In Figure 8.6 the main factors which limit how many people can live in the area are highlighted. In northern Canada and Russia, it is extreme winter cold and very short cool summers (tundra climate) that prevent crop growth. In the deserts of North Africa and Western and Central Asia, it is lack of rainfall which makes farming impossible over wide areas. Even so, where water is available for irrigation, high population densities exist, as in the Nile Valley in Egypt (Chapter 4, page 119).

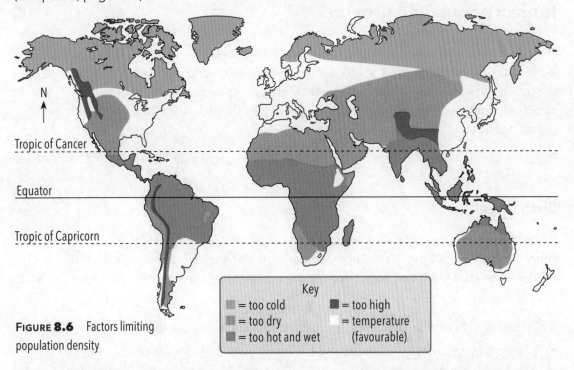

FIGURE 8.6 Factors limiting population density

Key
- = too cold
- = too dry
- = too hot and wet
- = too high
- = temperature (favourable)

Densely populated areas must not be confused with areas described as overpopulated. **Overpopulation** only exists in places where too many people live to be well provided for by the available resources. Thus an area with 10 people per hectare may be overpopulated because its resources are too few to support a good living for its inhabitants, whereas people living in another area with more than 500 people per square kilometre may be prosperous because of good resources.

ACTIVITIES

1 Study Figures 8.4 and 8.5.

  (a) Describe what they show about the distribution and density of population in **(i)** Asia and **(ii)** Europe.

  (b) Describe the similarities and differences in population between South America and Africa.

2 **(a)** Investigation: From Figure 8.5, choose one area of high density and one area of low density. Find out the reasons for the difference in density between them.

  (b) How useful is Figure 8.6 to explain the difference in density between your two chosen areas? Elaborate your answer.

3 'Most of the world's people live within 300 kilometres of the coast.'

  (a) From Figures 8.4 and 8.5, write down evidence for and against this statement.

  (b) In your view, how true is it as an overall summary of world population distribution?

Human population growth

The growth of world population during the last 100 years is clearly shown in Figure 8.2. The really rapid growth since 1950, shown by the change in direction of the line in Figure 8.2, is described as an exponential rate of growth. More young people in the world meant more people starting their own families once they grew up. This is why the rate of population growth speeded up so much.

Population growth can be explained by looking at birth and death rates.

Birth rates

The average birth rate in developed countries is about 12 or 13 per 1000; in developing countries it is 23 or 24 per 1000. There is a general relationship between the level of economic development and birth rate: the more developed the country is, the lower is its birth rate.

Birth rates in all European countries, not just those in Table 8.1, are low because

- family planning is widely available and practised by nearly all married couples;
- women are well educated and wish to pursue their own careers;
- socially, having one or two children is accepted as the normal family size;
- economically, children cost their parents money and do not contribute to the family income, if at all, until they have grown up into adults.

TABLE **8.1**	Countries with the world's highest and lowest birth rates (per 1000) 2010 – 2017				
	Country	Highest	Country	Lowest	
1	Niger	44.2	1	Japan	7.7
2	Mali	43.9	2	Germany	8.6
3	Chad	35.6	3	Portugal	9.0
4	Burundi	41.3	4	Taiwan	8.3
5	Angola	44.2	5	Italy	8.6
6	Somalia	39.6	6	Malta	10.1

In contrast, many countries in Africa have birth rates well over 40 per 1000. This is because

- family planning is not always available, especially in rural areas;
- many women receive little education and marry young;
- socially, families of five or more children are considered to be quite normal;
- economically, many children work to supplement the family income;
- some governments and religions do not support or approve of birth control.

Birth and fertility rates are linked. Niger has the highest fertility rate in the world with an average of 7.6 children per woman; Japan has one of the lowest with only 1.4 children per woman. A fertility rate of 2.1 per 1000 is the natural replacement rate to keep the population total in a country stable. Lower than this and the population total can be expected to start to decline.

Death rates

Unlike birth rates, death rates are similar between developed and developing countries; the world average for both is between 9 and 10 per 1000. In the second half of the last century, death rates fell everywhere due to the spread of medical knowledge and improvements in both primary and secondary healthcare. Primary healthcare is preventing disease, for example, by vaccination; secondary healthcare is the treatment of illnesses by doctors and nurses in clinics and hospitals.

The only exceptions are in poor countries with high levels of disease, mainly in Africa. Chad has one of the world's highest death rate (13.8 per 1000) and the highest infant mortality rate (85.4 per thousand). In 2014 and 2015 Sierra Leone was ravaged by the outbreak of Ebola, a viral disease. Some countries, such as the Central African Republic, are being torn apart by conflicts and war. Another factor of great importance is high rates of HIV / AIDS, particularly in countries of Southern Africa. For some time, death rates have been rising in countries such as Zimbabwe and Botswana.

INFORMATION BOX

Understanding population terms

Crude birth rate:
- number of live births per 1000 people per year

Crude death rate:
- number of deaths per 1000 people per year

Fertility rate:
- average number of children born to a woman in her lifetime

Natural increase:
- population growth because the birth rate is higher than the death rate

Infant mortality rate:
- number of deaths of children under one year old per 1000 people

TABLE **8.2**	Countries with the world's highest death rates (per 1000) 2010 – 2017			
1	Lesotho	15.0	6	Belarus	13.2
2	Bulgaria	14.5	7	Central African Republic	13.2
3	Latvia	14.5	8	Sierra Leone	10.4
4	Ukraine	14.4	9	Botswana	9.6
5	Russia	13.5	10	Democratic Republic of Congo	9.5

Natural increase

When birth rates are higher than death rates there is a natural increase in population. In Niger the birth rate is 44.2 (Table 8.1); the death rate is 11.8. This gives the country a natural increase of 32.4 per 1000, which is very high. The natural increase is often expressed as a percentage; for Niger it is 3.2 per cent. Birth rates in Japan and some European countries are now so low, below the death rates, that there is natural population decrease. The death rate in Japan is 9.8 per 1000, whereas its birth rate is only 7.7 per 1000 (Table 8.1). This gives a natural decrease of 2.1 per 1000.

ACTIVITIES

1 (a) Describe what Figure 8.7 shows about population growth between 1950 and 2000.

   (b) For 2000, give the difference in population numbers between developed and developing countries.

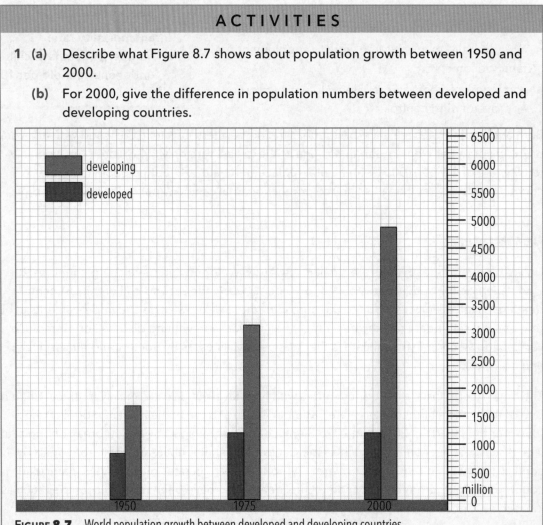

FIGURE 8.7 World population growth between developed and developing countries

2 Estimated world population data

A		B	
Total population (billions)		Population in 2025 (billions)	
2018	7.6	World total	8.2
2023	8.0	Developed countries	1.2
2050	9.0	Developing countries	7.0

(a) Show this estimated data for future world population by drawing two separate graphs for columns A and B.

(b) State the evidence from the data that the rate of population growth is expected to slow down by 2050.

3 Birth and death rates (per 1000) for three countries:

	BR	DR
Pakistan	22	6
China	12	7
UK	12	9

(a) Calculate the natural increase in each country.

(b) Are there any surprises in the data? Explain.

Migration

Migration is another factor which affects population size, i.e. how many people are living in an area. Migration is the movement of people to live in a different place. What makes a person move?

In most decisions several factors are involved, which are likely to be a mixture of push and pull.

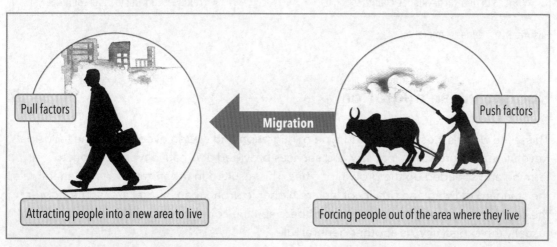

Pull factors

Migration

Push factors

Attracting people into a new area to live

Forcing people out of the area where they live

FIGURE 8.8 The push-pull model of migration

OXFORD
UNIVERSITY PRESS

Push factors are the dislikes about where they live: the disadvantages. There may be no work, or what work there is may be badly paid or available only for part of the year. Public services and utilities such as schools, hospitals, electricity, and clean water may not be widely available. A natural disaster such as an earthquake or flood might force people to move out immediately as the push factor is so strong that people do not even think about staying.

Pull factors are attractions of the place they are moving to: the advantages. The new location may offer physical advantages such as a wetter climate and more fertile soils, or it could offer economic advantages, such as work opportunities leading to an improved standard of living. Attractions can also be social, like moving closer to family and friends.

However, there are obstacles to the free movement of people. Between countries these are border controls and the need for visas and entry permits. Within a country, availability and cost of transport may be more significant; the level of migration is lower in places where roads are non-existent or poorly maintained. Social obstacles, such as leaving family behind and fear of the unknown, affect all would-be migrants but their strength and the importance of migration varies from person to person.

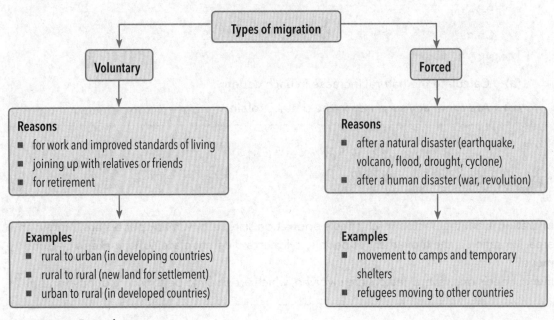

FIGURE 8.9   Types of migration

Rural to urban migration

This is the world's most widespread type of migration and was so even before the Industrial Revolution. The growth of industry and services provided alternative types of work to farming and speeded up the growth of cities. This resulted in urbanization. As a general rule, the standard of living and quality of life are higher in urban than in rural areas. The poorer the country, the greater the gap in wealth between the countryside and the largest city (usually the capital city), is another general rule.

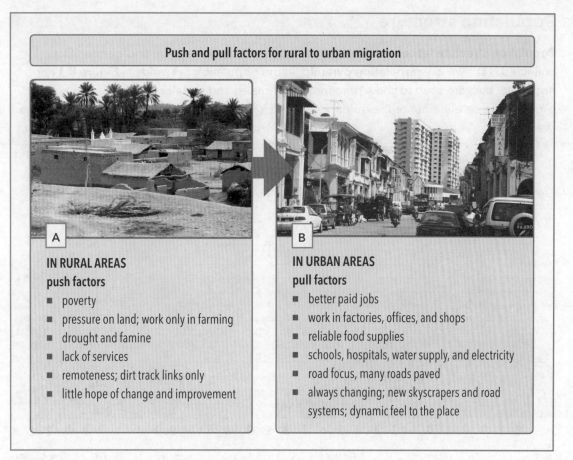

FIGURE 8.10   Push and pull factors for rural to urban migration

Thus, people are 'pushed' out of rural areas by poverty and limited opportunities and 'pulled' towards urban areas by the dream of wealth and perceived unlimited opportunities for personal improvement. While the urban dream does not always become reality, it has already been shown that the standards of living and provision of essential services are higher in urban areas in developing countries.

ACTIVITIES

1   Three factors for migration are work, food, and schools.

   Explain each one out first as a push factor, and then as a pull factor.

2   Draw a labelled push-pull model (as in Figure 8.8) for rural to urban migration between the places shown in photographs A and B in Figure 8.10.

3   For your home country,

   (a)   name the types of migration;

   (b)   state the main factors for these migrations;

   (c)   describe how they are changing the population distribution.

Population structure

Population structure is the make-up of a country's population by age and gender. Data collected is shown in a **population pyramid**. In the population pyramids in **Figure 8.11**, horizontal bars are used to show percentages of males and females in each 5-year age group. (Take careful note of the guidance in the Exam Tip about how best to interpret these graphs.)

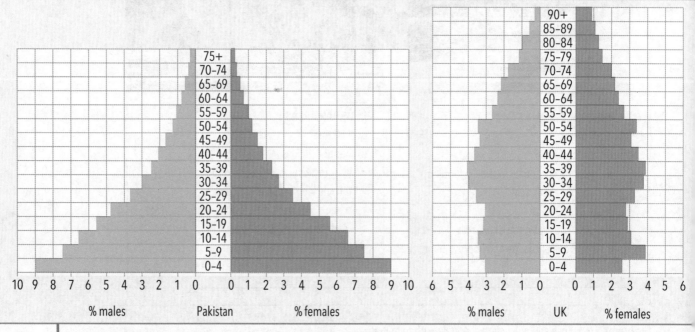

FIGURE 8.11 Population pyramids of Pakistan and the UK

EXAM TIP

How to describe and interpret population pyramids

1 Look first at the base.
  ■ If it is wide, there are many children, suggesting a high birth rate.
  ■ If it is narrow, a low birth rate is suggested.

2 Look at the top.
  ■ If it is high and wide, there are many old people, suggesting long life expectancy.
  ■ If it is narrow and goes to a point, low life expectancy is suggested.

3 Look at the overall shape.
  ■ If it is like a triangle, it is likely to be for a developing country.
  ■ If it is more straight up and down, it is likely to be for a more developed country.

4 Separate out age group ranges by drawing lines across between the three groups below
  ■ 0–14 young and part of the non-working population
  ■ 15–64 with the middle-aged making up the working population
  ■ 65+–old aged, no longer part of the working population

5 Quote supporting percentages to make your descriptions more precise e.g. state the percentage for the largest age group, or the total percentage for all below 15, or all above 65.

The pyramid for Pakistan shows many of the characteristic features of a developing country, particularly its wide base showing a population structure dominated by young people due to high birth rates. In the pyramids for developed countries, like the UK, percentages are more evenly distributed between different age groups. The middle-age groups, not children, dominate. Look at the tops of the pyramids in Figure 8.11. What is the other big difference that is shown between developing and developed countries?

It is customary to subdivide the structure of a country's population into three groups on the basis of age–young (0–14), middle-aged (15–64) and old (above 65). The middle-aged are distinguished as the **working** or **independent population**; they are working, earning money, and paying taxes. The young and old have in common that they are **dependants**; although some of them work, the majority *depend* upon services such as education and healthcare, paid for by taxes taken from the working population.

Young and ageing populations

Pakistan has a young population. The UK has an ageing population. The key difference between them is the size of the fertility rate. In Pakistan it is 3.2 children per woman, lower than it used to be, but still high. In the UK it is 1.9. In order to maintain a country's population size naturally (without any effects from migration) an average fertility rate of 2.1 is needed. Above this, the population increases and young people dominate. Below this, a country's population size decreases and middle-aged people dominate.

INFORMATION BOX

Natural decrease

	BR	DR	ND
	(per 1000)		
Germany	8.6	11.7	3.1
Hungary	9	12.8	3.8
Italy	8.6	10.4	1.8

Most of the world's lowest fertility rates are in Europe. Some countries are experiencing a natural decrease in population (Information Box). Life expectancy is high (over 75 years in most European countries) and rising, as medical science continues to improve. In developing countries, infant mortality rates are falling, which is contributing to the increased size of young populations. Couples are continuing to have the same number of babies despite lower rate of infant losses.

Although the contrast between Europe's ageing populations and the young populations in Africa and the Middle East is striking, one population measure is similar–the death rate (See Table 8.2). Why should death rates be similar in developed and developing countries? Medical facilities, access to clean water and the amount of food available are all known to be better in developed countries. The answer is that developed countries have higher proportions of old people. Although these people are living longer, out of every 1000 people there is a larger number who will reach the age of dying. In developing countries, the higher percentage of young people keeps the death rate down.

ACTIVITIES

1 Describe what the population pyramids show for **(a)** Pakistan and **(b)** the UK, using the exam watch advice as a guide.

2 **(a)**   What is the difference between a young population and an ageing population?

   (b)   Explain why many countries in Europe have ageing populations.

Managing human population growth

Many governments in developing countries now recognize high birth rates as a problem, and have family planning and population policies in place. Some of these strategies for managing population growth are shown in Figure 8.12. There are many different ways. Looking at them, can you understand why people who are better off in terms of income and education are more likely to use one or more of these ways? Can you also understand why the practice of family planning is more evident in urban areas than in the countryside in developing countries?

FIGURE **8.12** Ways of reducing birth and fertility rates

As for national population policies, these vary from the very weak, emphasizing education and persuasion, to the very strict, backed up by punishments (Figure 8.13) and penalties, as in China. A few countries have shown little interest in controlling their population, such as Saudi Arabia and Niger, and have no policy. Religious teaching opposes the use of artificial means of contraception in most Muslim and Catholic countries; poverty is also a factor in Niger and some other African countries.

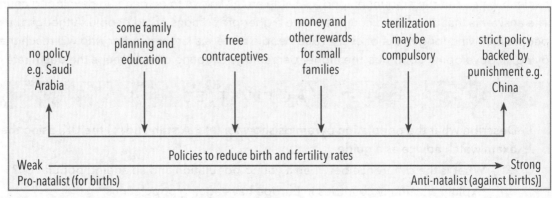

FIGURE **8.13** Strength line for national population policies

Case study: China and its 'one child' policy

The 'one child' policy

Until the 1970s the communist government of China promoted the idea that a nation with many people is a strong nation. In 1965 the fertility rate was 6.5 births per woman (Figure 8.14) Then in the 1970s, with a population of almost one billion, the government calculated just how large China's population could become. What began as a 'two child' policy in the 1970s became the 'one child' policy in 1979.

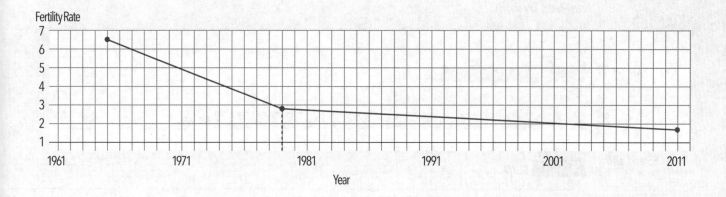

FIGURE 8.14   Fertility rates in China 1961 – 2011

The policy of 'one couple, one child' was very strict. With one child, education was free; parents benefited from family allowances, priority housing, and enhanced pensions. But in case of two or more children, there was a range of sanctions, from fines on the rich to cruel punishments such as being sent to re-education centres and labour camps. The government supported the policy with family planning services free to all.

Among ordinary Chinese, the policy was desperately unpopular. Most Chinese live in the countryside. As with peasant farmers everywhere, they want large families to help with work in the fields and to look after them in old age. The rules were relaxed to allow up to two children per family in rural areas. This was almost forced on the government because of one of the bad consequences—parents in the countryside killing baby girls because they wanted a boy so much. City couples found it easier to abide by the law. Everything in China is centrally planned, which is why the government could force through an unpopular policy.

The original aim of the policy was to stabilize the population at about 1.2 billion in 2005. As a result of relaxing parts of the policy, the population has now reached just over 1.3 billion. China's rate of population increase remains one of the lowest among developing countries.

Problems

The government officials who made the policy in the 1970s never thought about the problems it was going to create by 2030. According to some, China is sitting on a demographic time bomb, likely to explode during the next 20 years—too few young people, too few women, too few workers, and too many old people. China's great economic growth from 1970 was based around masses of cheap labour. Looking at Figure 8.15 and the Information Box, what do you think is expected to happen to the plentiful supply of workers by 2030?

INFORMATION BOX

Population data

	Boy : Girl ratio
2015	118 : 100
	Workers : Retired ratio
2000	6 : 1
2030	2 : 1

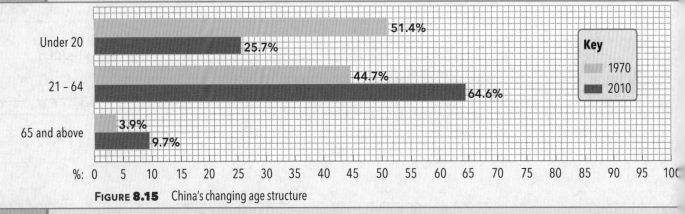

FIGURE 8.15 China's changing age structure

By 2015, over-60s made up almost 15% of the total Chinese population. An ageing population costs money. It increases the demand for pensions, medical services, and care provision. Per capita, China is not as wealthy as a developed country like Japan. Will the government be able to afford all the services the elderly population is going to need? How well is the single child, (more likely male than female), going to be able to look after parents' needs as they grow old?

It came as no surprise in 2013 when the government announced that it was going to relax the one child rule and make it two for all couples. Many think that this may have come too late. It is unlikely that this change will lead to a baby boom. Especially in the cities, people's attitudes have changed towards having many children.

ACTIVITY

- Make brief revision notes for China to be used in a case study question of a national population policy. Use these guidelines:
  - main features of the policy
  - changes over time
  - policy successes
  - policy failures
  - overall evaluation of how successful the policy has been

Population policies in other countries

Thailand has one of the world's most successful and effective family planning programmes, which uses a mixture of media, economic incentives, and community involvement to increase contraception use. The immediate benefits of lower fertility are stressed; the key message links family planning and low family size to high standards of living. To get everyone involved, even in remote rural areas, fun events are organized such as birth control carnivals. Farmers who have registered for family planning are given financial benefits, such as above-market prices for their crops and reduced transport costs to market. In Thailand, the message is carried everywhere, not just left in the cities.

Pakistan does not have a consistent population policy desipite some efforts on part of the government. Likewise in most African countries, population policies are either non-existent or given a low priority. This is due to a mixture of economic, political, and social factors:

- poverty—many countries are just too poor to provide the health services needed to support the policy, particularly in rural areas;

- political instability, wars and conflicts, as well as widespread corruption among government and local officials;

- Islam is the dominant faith in North Africa; some Muslim countries do not enforce family planning.

- Subsistence farmers everywhere view their children as assets.

INFORMATION BOX

Niger fact file, 2017

- Population: 19.2million
- Religion: 80% Muslim
- Birth rate: 44.2 per 1000
- Death rate: 11.8 per 1000
- Natural increase: 32.4 per 1000
- Infant mortality rate: 53.6 per 1000
- Population structure:
  - Under 15   50%
  - Over 65   3%
- Living in urban areas: 16.4%

Action plan for population – too little and too late

Niger is a country of young people. Its population is expected to double every 20 to 25 years.

At last someone in the government has a population plan – to bring the average fertility rate per woman down from 7.6, the highest in the world, to below 5.0 by the early 2020s.

All previous ideas for stopping the population explosion have failed. Male domination, lack of education for women, poverty, and repeated struggles against drought were to blame. The fact that 60 per cent of marriages involve girls under 15 does not help.

When some villagers were asked in a newspaper survey 'How many children would you like to have?', women said nine and men said twelve (on average). Some families even said 20 or more! This is a society that is pro-children. Subsistence farmers, making up 75 per cent of Niger's population, see the worth of children in a different way from city folk.

Only about 5 per cent of women in Niger use any form of contraception, mainly because their husbands forbid it. In the capital, Niamey, there are clinics where contraceptives are given out free. One mother of 10 children said that she had been taking the pill without telling her husband; but he found out, and forced her to stop. What hope is there for reaching the action plan target of 15 per cent by the early 2020s?

FIGURE 8.16   Niger – the country with the world's highest birth rate and natural increase

OXFORD
UNIVERSITY PRESS

ACTIVITIES

1 (a) Name and briefly describe the different methods for controlling population numbers.

   (b) Choose the two which you consider to be the most important. Give reasons for your two choices.

2 With the help of examples, explain why national population policies are more successful in some countries than in others.

3 (a) What is the national population policy in your country? Give details.

   (b) Where would you place it on the strength line (Figure 8.13)?

   (c) How successful is it?

Natural ecosystems and human activities

OBJECTIVES

In this chapter you will learn about

- natural ecosystems and how they operate
- natural ecosystems under threat
- causes and impacts of deforestation
- sustainable management of forests
- measuring and managing biodiversity

FIGURE 9.1   Ecuador in South America: inside the tropical rainforest, the world's most productive and biodiverse ecosystem. Can you detect the different layers of vegetation within this forest?

INTRODUCTION

Large-scale ecosystems are known as biomes. They are identified and named according to their dominant vegetation cover, like tropical rainforest. The global distribution of some of the world's major biomes is shown in Figure 9.2. Notice how most of the zones are aligned east-west within continents. There is a good reason for this: the climate.

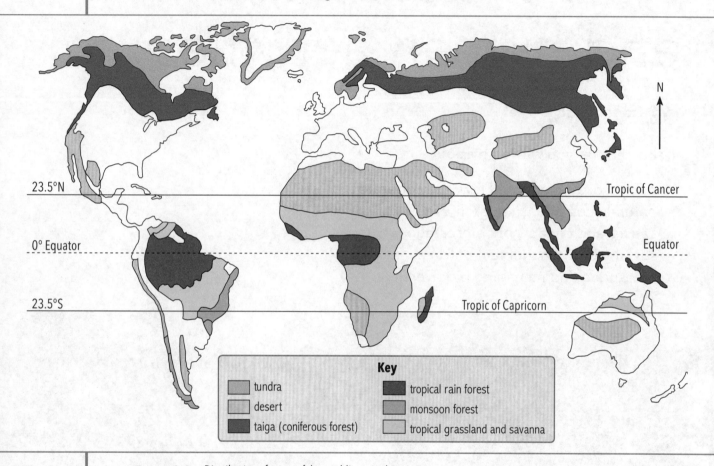

FIGURE 9.2 Distribution of some of the world's major biomes

On a global scale, climate exerts a strong control over vegetation characteristics. The height, variety, and density of the vegetation cover in Figure 9.1 are a direct response to the region's uniformly hot and wet Equatorial climate (Table 9.1). Non-stop plant growth is possible.

TABLE 9.1 Equatorial climate – Singapore												
	J	F	M	A	M	J	J	A	S	O	N	D
Temperature (°C)	27	27	28	28	28	28	28	28	28	27	27	27
Rainfall (mm)	252	173	193	188	173	173	170	196	178	208	254	257

For small-scale ecosystems, climate provides the overall framework, but other more local factors increase in importance. They determine why vegetation changes, say from trees to grasses or to marsh and reeds, within a short distance. Factors such as slope, soil pH, and drainage take over from climate.

Ecosystems

An ecosystem comprises all the living communities in an area together with its non-living natural environment. In other words, an ecosystem is composed of biotic elements (plants, animals, and other organisms) and abiotic elements (climate and soils). It is a system because all the elements are interlinked; they both affect and are affected by the other elements. These interrelationships are illustrated in Figure 9.3. More details about the living and non-living components of the ecosystem are given in Figure 9.4.

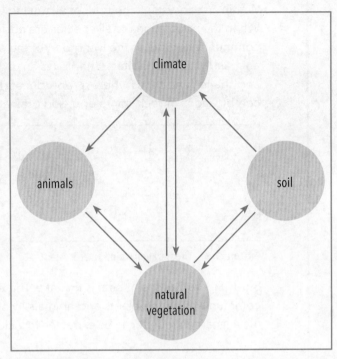

FIGURE 9.3   An ecosystem

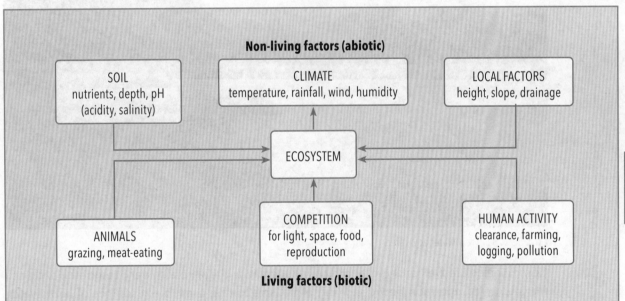

FIGURE 9.4   The living and non-living components of an ecosystem

Ecosystems are maintained by energy flows and the cycling of nutrients between the living and non-living matter. They are self-supporting and remain balanced with little change, unless and until a change occurs which affects one or more of the elements. Disruption to this balance (or equilibrium) may be for a variety of reasons, such as volcanic eruption, climate change, plant and animal diseases, and human activity.

Organization of ecosystems

Within an ecosystem, the total of all the individuals of the same species is its **population**. When the populations of all species are added together they form the **community**. The community comprises the living part of the ecosystem, being made up of all the plants and animals living in a **habitat**. A habitat is an organism's natural home; here it obtains its food and shelter, and this is where it reproduces. Each natural habitat is formed by unique combinations of rock, soil, slope, and drainage, under particular climatic conditions.

Individuals of the same species $\Big\}$ = POPULATION + populations of other species $\Big\}$ = COMMUNITY + non-living factors $\Big\}$ = ECOSYSTEM

FIGURE 9.5 Organization within an ecosystem

Study Figure 9.6: the habitat is the lake. The environment includes air, water, and sunlight. The community is all the plants and animals living in the water and on its edges. Within the lake, the animal community can be expected to include fish, insects, crustacea, molluscs, and protozoa.

FIGURE 9.6 Freshwater ecosystem

Communities are well ordered and highly integrated. They are also very competitive, due to the intense **competition** between living organisms for the available resources of light, water, soil nutrients, food, and space. All organisms produce more offspring than can ever survive so competition between them is unavoidable.

Every organism has a role in the functioning of the ecosystem, which is known as its **niche**. It is an important rule of nature that any stable community must be made up of species that have different needs for resources, so that each can occupy a different position or niche. This allows them to interact with others as part of a working system, as well as ensuring that as many of the natural resources available are consumed for the benefit of all.

ACTIVITIES

1 Describe fully the difference between biotic and abiotic factors in an ecosystem.

2 Know the key terms. Give definitions for the five key terms shown in bold in the text about the organization of ecosystems.

3 **(a)** Draw a large frame and sketch the main features shown in Figure 9.6.

(b) Add labels using different colours for the living and non-living elements shown.

(c) Describe **(i)** the habitat and **(ii)** the community shown in this area.

Adaptations to physical factors and relationships of living organisms

All life on Earth depends upon a single source of energy—the Sun. The Sun has direct control over variations in light and temperature across the Earth's surface. Not only this, but it also has a powerful influence over water, humidity, nutrients, and soil, which are the other principal ingredients of life on Earth. The availability of these physical factors varies greatly from place to place. Members of the plant and animal community must adapt both to climatic conditions and to living within a competitive community for successful survival.

FIGURE 9.7 Elephants on a Kenyan reserve

In the course of evolution, changes in organisms have occurred which have increased their chances of success even in some of the world's most challenging environments. Plants have developed special characteristics which have adapted them to life in places where physical factors are unfavourable, such as in areas of mineral-poor or salty soils, or where there is limited time for growth each year due to factors such as drought or cold. Animals have changed their ways of finding and digesting food, and have developed characteristics to withstand the worst physical conditions.

At the local level, competition means that the physical factors of light, temperature, humidity, water supply, wind speed, and soil are not the same for all members of the community. Nowhere is this more clearly demonstrated than in tropical rainforests (see Figures 9.8 and 9.9).

FIGURE 9.8 At the top of one of the rainforest's tallest trees with a view of the canopy

FIGURE 9.9 At the foot of one of the rainforest's tallest trees with a view of the forest floor

Tall trees need access to great amounts of sunlight in order to produce large amounts of food sufficient to satisfy energy needs for the formation of woody tissues. These must be capable of supporting crowns of leaves 30 metres or more above the ground. Broad leaves enable them to intercept great amounts of light. Without adaptations to the physical conditions experienced in the forest top, they cannot compete and survive. These include leaves that are leathery to survive the daytime heat and rapid water loss; leaves also have drip tips at the end to shed water quickly during the torrential tropical downpours.

Physical conditions on the forest floor could hardly be more different. Here it is dark, humid, and without wind. For vegetation growth on the forest floor access to sunlight is strictly limited. Plants cannot afford to use up their precious food reserves on woody organs of support like the trees above them. Animals in turn exploit the variety of niches found in these forests. Monkeys, butterflies, macaws, and hosts of insect species live in the canopy layers and they may never visit the lower layers. Living on the ground are jaguars, tapirs, anteaters, deer, ants, and termites.

Living organisms depend on each other in order to survive, grow, and reproduce: they are **interdependent**. A simple illustration is the dependence between bees and flowers. Bees depend on pollen and nectar from flowers for their food, but flowers in turn depend upon bees for pollination.

Living organisms depend on each other in several different ways.

- Pollination: birds and insects transfer pollen between plants.
- Dispersal of fruits and seeds: birds and animals carry these away from the parent plant so that competition for light and water between members of the same species is reduced.
- Food supply: numerous food chains exist. Small birds live off flowers, seeds, fruit, and nuts from plants, but they can be caught and eaten by larger birds of prey. Zebras eat grass, but can be on the menu of a family group of lions.

Flowering plants need fertilization before they can produce seeds. This involves the transfer of pollen from the anthers to the stigma in flowering plants. The anthers split open, exposing the microscopic pollen grains. The pollen grains can simply be blown away, but insects (such as bees) and birds (such as humming birds in the Tropics) play a major role in transferring pollen from the anthers of one flower to the stigma of another to complete pollination.

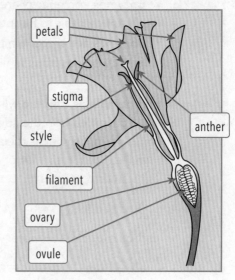

FIGURE 9.10   Pollination

Flowers that rely upon insects for pollination have adapted in ways that improve their chances of successful pollination by insects, for example by having a strong scent or brightly coloured petals, or by producing nectar. Many have modifications which adapt them to pollination by only one type or species of insect, emphasizing the importance of the relationship. Flowers with narrow, deep petal tubes, such as honeysuckle, are adapted to pollination by moths or butterflies, whose long 'tongues' can reach down the tube to the nectar.

When the seeds are mature, the whole fruit or the individual seeds fall from the parent plant to the ground, where the seeds may then germinate. However, in many plants the fruits and seeds are adapted in such a way that they are carried a long distance away from the parent plant to avoid competition. Wind and animals are the main agents of dispersal. Some fruits grow hooks; the hooks catch in the fur of passing mammals and the seeds fall out as the animal moves about. Many fruits are eaten by birds and mammals; their hard pips containing the seeds are not digested. They pass out with the droppings and dung, often well away from the parent plant.

ACTIVITIES

1 **(a)** Describe how physical conditions differ between forest top and forest floor in tropical rainforests.

   (b) Why do herbs replace woody plants on the forest floor?

2 Describe an example of each of these biotic interactions.

   (a) competition   **(b)** predation   **(c)** pollination

3 Explain

   (a) why animals need plants;

   (b) how plants make use of the animals that feed on them.

OXFORD
UNIVERSITY PRESS

INFORMATION BOX

Photosynthesis

- 'Photo' means life.
- 'Synthesis' means building-up of complex food molecules from simpler substances.
- Enzymes and energy are needed for photosynthesis to happen.
- Enzymes are present in the plant cells.
- Energy comes from sunlight.

Photosynthesis, energy flows, and the carbon cycle

All living organisms need food to build new cells and tissues for growth and as a source of energy. All ecosystems are sustained by a flow of energy through them. Energy to 'drive' the systems comes from sunlight (short wave solar radiation). Green plants use carbon dioxide, water, and sunlight to make glucose. The process by which they achieve this is **photosynthesis**.

In photosynthesis, chlorophyll-bearing organisms in plant cells absorb light energy from the Sun to convert carbon dioxide and water into carbohydrates which now store the energy in chemical form. Oxygen is released as waste from this process, but it is essential to animal and human life. The formula for photosynthesis is:

$$6CO_2 + 6H_2O \xrightarrow{\text{light energy}} C_6H_{12}O_6 + 6O_2$$

| carbon dioxide | water | | sugar / glucose (carbohydrates) | oxygen |

In plants, the process mainly takes place in the cells of the leaves and is summarized in Figure 9.11. Carbon dioxide is absorbed from the air through stomata, the pores in the leaf. On land, water is absorbed by the plants from the soil through the roots and carried in the water vessels of the veins, up the stem and to the leaf. Carbon dioxide and water are combined in the cells to make sugar. Energy for this reaction comes from sunlight which is absorbed by the green pigment chlorophyll, which uses light to split water molecules into hydrogen and oxygen. The hydrogen is added to the carbon dioxide molecules to form sugar and other carbohydrates, while oxygen escapes from the leaf.

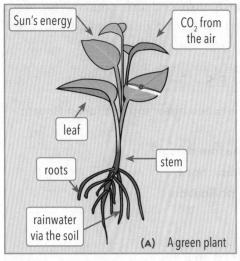

(A) A green plant

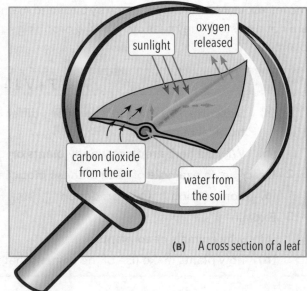

(B) A cross section of a leaf

FIGURE 9.11 The photosynthesis process

In daylight, when photosynthesis is taking place, green plants are taking in carbon dioxide and giving out oxygen. This exchange of gases is the opposite of the one that results from **respiration**, which is the chemical process by which energy is produced from food. Glucose is the food mainly used for energy in cells. All food molecules contain carbon, hydrogen, and oxygen atoms. By the process of oxidation carbon is converted to carbon dioxide, and hydrogen to water. At the same time, energy is released which can be used to drive other reactions. The formula for respiration is:

$$C_6H_{12}O_6 \quad\quad + 6O_2 \longrightarrow 6CO_2 \quad\quad +6H_2O \quad\quad + \text{release of energy}$$

| glucose | oxygen | carbon | water | respiratory heat |
| (new production) | dioxide | dioxide | (lost to ecosystem) | |

Plants reuse some of the energy produced from respiration to carry out normal functions such as absorbing nutrients and repairing cell damage. Even so, some of it always appears as heat and is lost to the surrounding air as soon as it is produced. However, in warm-blooded animals, like birds and mammals, some of the heat from respiration is retained to keep up body temperature.

Energy flows in food chains

Solar energy is held only briefly in the biosphere before it is re-radiated as heat and lost into space. Plants and their photosynthetic production of organic matter are the only way that this energy can be stored in the biosphere. This energy is released when green plants are consumed by organisms higher up the food chain. Each stage in the chain where energy is exchanged is called a **trophic level**. Green plants such as grasses, bushes, and trees are in trophic level 1, herbivores in level 2, and carnivores in level 3 or higher.

Most food chains have no more than four levels. At every stage in the food chain there is a great loss of total energy passing along the chain. During photosynthesis plants themselves take in only 1 per cent of total light reaching the ground. Between each trophic level the loss is about 90 per cent, leaving only 10 per cent to be passed on to the next stage for growth (Figure 9.12). This is the so-called '10 per cent rule'. Energy is used in life processes, such as breathing, generating heat, growing, and moving around, which is why a smaller number of organisms can be supported in the chain shown.

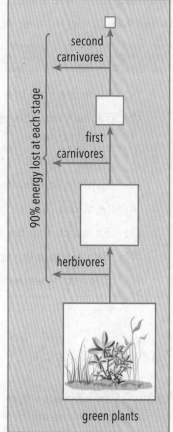

FIGURE 9.12 Relative amounts of energy passing along the food chain in a natural ecosystem

OXFORD
UNIVERSITY PRESS

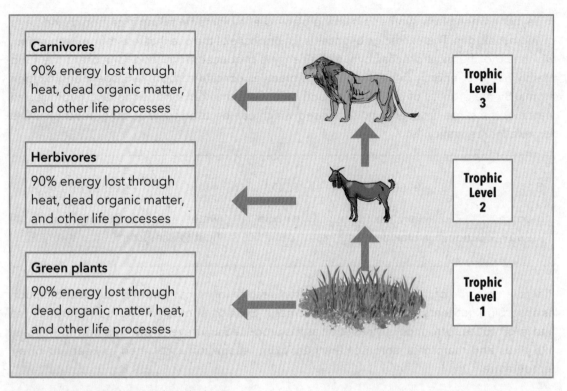

FIGURE 9.13 Energy loss at each trophic level

ACTIVITIES

1 **(a)** With the help of a labelled diagram, explain the process of photosynthesis.

  (b) Explain why this process is vital to **(i)** animal life in general and **(ii)** human life in particular.

2 **(a)** What is meant by the 10 per cent rule?

  (b) Explain how it affects the numbers of species at each trophic level.

3 Investigation:

  (a) Research and draw a food chain and a food web found in your home area.

  (b) Explain how the species shown are interdependent.

  (c) Draw another version of Figure 9.13 using home country species.

The carbon cycle

Carbon is an element which is present in all living organisms. It is obtained by plants from carbon dioxide in the atmosphere as a result of their photosynthesis. When the plants are eaten by animals, the organic plant material is digested, absorbed, and built into compounds making up the animal's tissues; carbon atoms from the plant become part of the animal. The carbon cycle, therefore, is about the intake and re-release of carbon dioxide (Figure 9.14).

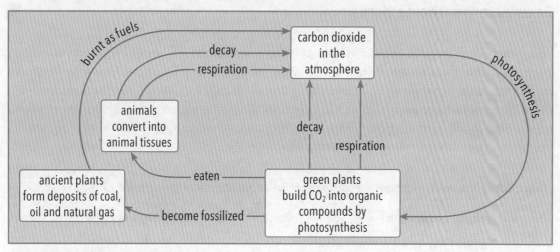

FIGURE 9.14 The carbon cycle

Carbon is added to the atmosphere in three main ways.

1. **Respiration**: Plants and animals obtain energy by oxidizing carbohydrates in their cells to carbon dioxide and water, which are excreted. The carbon dioxide returns again to the atmosphere.

2. **Decay**: Organic matter from dead plants and animals is used by decomposers as a source of energy. The micro-organisms turn the carbon compounds back into carbon dioxide, which goes back into the atmosphere.

3. **Combustion** (burning): Wood, coal, oil, and natural gas are all fuels which contain carbon. Oxygen is needed for burning; when burned, carbon is oxidized to carbon dioxide. Coal, oil, and gas were formed from ancient plants and creatures which have only partly decomposed over the millions of years since they were buried.

ACTIVITIES

1 Explain how respiration is different from photosynthesis.

2 **(a)** Why do living organisms need a supply of carbon?

 (b) Where do **(i)** plants and **(ii)** animals get their carbon from?

3 Forests are often described as carbon stores (carbon sinks). Explain why.

4 Study Figure 9.15.

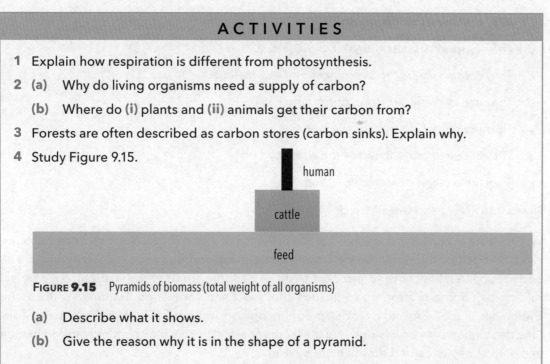

FIGURE 9.15 Pyramids of biomass (total weight of all organisms)

(a) Describe what it shows.

(b) Give the reason why it is in the shape of a pyramid.

Ecosystems under threat

Ecosystems both large (e.g. biomes) and small (e.g. wetlands) are under increasing threats of destruction due to population growth and intensive agricultural practices. However, losses to the world's large ecosystems have been very uneven (Table 9.2). World distributions for these biomes were shown in Figure 9.2. Compare the percentages in the table with locations on the map. Work from the Equator towards the Poles. What do you notice? Why must the explanation be about farming and making a living?

TABLE 9.2 Estimates of percentage losses of the area of five natural ecosystems (biomes) up to 2010

Natural ecosystem	Percentage loss
Tropical rainforest	42
Savanna	56
Hot deserts	25
Coniferous forests (taiga)	5
Tundra	2

Deforestation (clearing forests and woodlands) is the most visible way in which people have changed the face of the Earth. Forests are plundered for their valuable natural products. Wood is useful for construction, shelter, furniture, tools, and paper, as well as being a fuel. Once cleared, many forest soils can be used for cultivation and food supply. Other human activities, such as livestock grazing and burning vegetation in the dry season, prevent the return of forests over wide areas.

Why are forests worth saving?
■ They support habitats with high biodiversity.
■ They contain useful food resources and raw materials.
■ They improve soil structure, depth, and fertility.
■ They prevent or slow down soil erosion.
■ They are an important part of the water cycle.
■ They are a major carbon store / sink.

FIGURE 9.16 Why are forests worth saving?

Wetlands are ecosystems dominated by the presence of water. They include swamps, marshes, lakes, and deltas. The water can be flowing or stagnant, and fresh or salty. When they are all added together, they cover 6 per cent of the land surface (not much less than the tropical rainforests). Some big examples include the Sudd and Okavango swamps in Africa, the Everglades in the USA, and river deltas and mangrove swamps in south and south-east Asia. One description of them is 'kidneys of the landscape' for the role they play in cleansing human and natural wastes carried downstream by rivers.

Why are wetlands worth saving?

- They sift waste and suspended silt from floodwaters, maintaining water quality and encouraging plant growth.
- They are highly productive ecosystems rich in plants, fish, and water fowl for which they are rich breeding grounds.
- They absorb and store water, reducing flood peaks, and act as barriers against storm surges, protecting shorelines.
- They absorb and store carbon.
- They have economic uses—rich fisheries, reeds and other building materials; they are also used for recreation.

FIGURE 9.17   Why are wetlands worth saving?

Threats to wetlands have increased due to intensification of agriculture and the need for more land. Water is drained, sea walls and dams are built to keep out the water, and the land to be reclaimed is surrounded by dykes. For free drainage the dykes are regularly dredged of all vegetation. Other threats to wetlands are from human discharges of pesticides, sewage, and toxic substances, as well as from the extraction of resources such as groundwater, oil and gas, gravel, and peat.

FIGURE 9.18   Wetland of coastal salt marsh—not much to look at, but ecologically productive and environmentally useful

Loss of natural ecosystems is accompanied by loss of biodiversity, genetic depletion, and species extinction. **Biodiversity** refers to the numbers and variety of living species, plants, and animals, and includes the whole range of species in the world. Also included are the different kinds of ecosystems which are valuable not only for the species they contain, but also as unique living communities of plants and animals in harmony with their surrounding environments.

OXFORD
UNIVERSITY PRESS

One of the most characteristic features of tropical rainforests is the enormous diversity of species they contain. A wide range of tree species provides a habitat which supports a great diversity of animal species. It is estimated that 50 per cent of the world's 10 million species live in tropical rainforests, despite the latter covering only about 7 per cent of the land surface.

Species becoming extinct is a natural process; it is part of evolution. At one time dinosaurs ruled the world, but they suffered a mass extinction about 65 million years ago. The worry today is the alarming increase in the rate of extinction as a result of human actions. Current species loss is estimated at one a day.

INFORMATION BOX

Ecuador: tropical rainforest biodiversity

A typical 5-hectare patch of rainforest, as in the area shown in Figure 9.1, is species-rich containing

- 750 species of tree
- 1500 species of flowering plant
- 400 species of bird
- 150 species of butterfly
- 100 species of reptile
- 60 species of amphibian
- 40,000+ species of insect

The dodo, a big flightless bird that lived on the island of Mauritius, was wiped out by sailors and settlers by the end of the seventeenth century. Once gone, it is gone for ever. Other species have shrunk to such dangerously low numbers of individuals that they are now classified as endangered. Although there is more than one reason for loss of species, the most important is undoubtedly loss of habitats including their sources of food.

When all living things are part of functioning ecosystems, it follows that one alteration in the balance of nature is enough to trigger off a chain reaction that runs through the whole system. The great increase in human population over the years has been at the expense of other species. In order to obtain land for agriculture, industry, and cities, natural vegetation has been cleared and neighbouring habitats changed or destroyed. Humans have a long history of ignoring the complex structures of natural habitats.

FIGURE 9.19   In the last one hundred years, the world tiger population has fallen from 120,000 to just 6000.

ACTIVITIES

1 **(a)** Draw a graph to show the data in Table 9.2 about ecosystem losses.

  (b) What is the main reason for the big differences between the percentages? Explain briefly.

2 **(a)** What is meant by biodiversity?

  (b) The land ecosystem with the greatest biodiversity is the tropical rainforest. Give information which supports this statement.

  (c) Describe how Figure 9.1 and Table 9.1 help to explain why rainforest biodiversity is so great.

3 From the list in Figure 9.16, choose what you consider to be the top three reasons for saving forests. Explain your choices.

4 Design a poster to support the campaign to save the world's wetlands.

Deforestation: causes and impacts

It is estimated that at least one third of the world's natural forests have already been destroyed by a mixture of felling, burning, or grazing. Before 1950, the greatest impact from forest destruction was felt in temperate latitudes, mainly in Europe and North America, and also in monsoon Asia. The Industrial Revolution led to the growth of industry and population with their increasing demands for natural resources and food. Forests were cleared to make way for farms, factories, and cities.

By 1950, great expanses of natural forests were left in only two world zones—the coniferous forests across North America and Eurasia at about 60°N, and tropical rainforests around the Equator in Central and South America, Africa, and South-east Asia. Soils that form under coniferous forests are infertile. Needles from conifers decompose slowly and release few minerals into the soil; any minerals present in the soil are soon washed out by leaching. With poor soils and a cold climate, in most places it is not worth clearing coniferous forests for farmland.

This leaves tropical rainforests as the ones most vulnerable to present and future deforestation. Today they cover under half the area they did before. Over 100,000km² of rainforest disappears every year. Rainforests are concentrated in developing countries (Figure 9.20). Governments seeking economic growth and development are attracted by their great untapped resources of timber and minerals, as well as their agricultural potential.

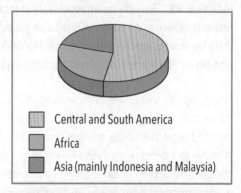

Central and South America

Africa

Asia (mainly Indonesia and Malaysia)

FIGURE 9.20 Distribution of remaining areas of tropical rainforest between continents (2011)

The biggest cause of recent rainforest destruction is **commercial farming**, both cultivation and ranching.

Cultivation is responsible for as much as 80 per cent of forest losses. Traditional subsistence farming clears relatively small plots of land by slash and burn. Population pressure has meant larger plots and plots used more frequently so that farming in many areas has become more permanent than shifting. In some places much larger areas of forest have been cleared by big companies for setting up plantations, such as bananas in Central America (Figure 3.11, page 77) and rubber in Brazil (Figure 9.21).

Ranching has been a major factor for forest clearance in the Americas. Almost 1,000,000km² of rainforest was burnt in Brazil between 1965 and 1980 solely for large cattle ranches with six million beef cattle. These were owned by major companies, often having nothing to do with farming, such as banks and car companies in Brazil; they existed mainly for the tax concessions offered by the government of Brazil as part of its policy of opening up the interior to development. Incredibly, most timber is just burnt, not even collected and sold (Figure 7.4, page 201). Tropical pastures are easily damaged and new forest is cleared so that cattle numbers can be maintained at the same levels.

FIGURE 9.21 Recently transplanted saplings for a new rubber plantation in the interior of Brazil. Can you believe that a few months ago this area was covered by rainforest? How big are the commercial and environmental risks?

FIGURE 9.22 Cattle rearing in Central America – is any risk to the environment suggested?

Logging for valuable hardwoods is a growing threat to rainforests. Multinational companies have the technology to clear extensive areas. The heavy machinery used frequently causes widespread damage as the small numbers of commercially valuable trees are sought out. Although companies begin with legal rights, they often ignore regulations and controls: they devastate large areas, taking no notice of protests from local people who have lived off the forest resources for thousands of years.

Minerals are high value resources. No matter how remote the location, or how far inside the rainforest regions the mineral lies, the big mining companies will be interested. They have the resources and technology to discover it, mine it, and build the transport infrastructure (pipelines, railways, and roads) to take it to the market. Some rainforest regions are rich in minerals. There is oil in tropical Africa (e.g. Nigeria, Chapter 2, page 66) and in the Amazon

Basin in interior Ecuador and Peru. In Brazil, the greatest concentration of mineral resources is at Carajas (Figure 9.23), where there are major deposits of iron ore, bauxite, nickel, copper, and manganese, to which there are both road and rail links. These roads open up previously untouched inaccessible areas of forest to new settlers, farmers, and loggers.

Roads like the one shown in Figure 1.12 (page 12) allow both easy access for forest clearances, and an export route for timber, farm produce and minerals from the cleared land. The persistent rainforest losses in the Amazon Basin of Brazil (Table 9.3) follow from the road building programme begun in the 1960s as part of the government plan to open up its vast, empty interior to economic development. The roads shown in Figure 9.23 provide the framework for access into the Amazon rainforest. The road links have been progressively extended northwards and westwards from Brasilia, the capital city.

Brazil is a great exporter of minerals; they are a major source of foreign exchange income. However, it is also a great exporter of agricultural products, notably beef and soybeans. Much of the advance of agriculture northwards and westwards from Brasilia since 2005 has been led by farmers growing soybeans. This crop offers farmers large profits. Most are exported to places such as Europe, where they are in high demand for animal feed.

TABLE 9.3 Estimated annual rainforest losses in the Amazon Basin of Brazil (km²)

1996	30,000	2002	24,600
1997	12,600	2003	23,400
1998	16,200	2004	23,200
1999	16,700	2005	17,800
2000	19,200	2006	11,200
2001	17,600	2007	16,800

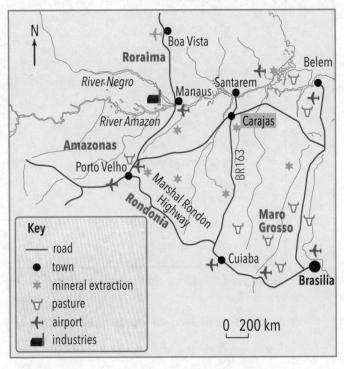

FIGURE 9.23 Road network in the Amazon Basin of Brazil

ACTIVITIES

1 State two different reasons why the threat to rainforests is greater than to other types of forest (such as coniferous forests).

2 Answer the question in the caption to Figure 9.22.

3 (a) Use the data in Table 9.3 to draw a bar graph showing rainforest losses in Brazil.

  (b) On your graph, draw a summary line linking the tops of the bars.

  (c) Describe what your graph shows.

4 (a) Study Figure 9.23. Describe the road pattern shown in the Amazon Basin of Brazil.

  (b) Explain how building a road leads to more and more forest destruction.

  (c) Identify and explain two economic reasons for forest clearances in Brazil.

OXFORD
UNIVERSITY PRESS

The **impacts** of deforestation are many and varied. They are listed in Figure 9.24. It shows just how great they are. All the natural elements of the ecosystem that were shown in Figure 9.3 are affected—the climate, soil, natural vegetation, animals, and people.

Physical impacts

A   Impact on atmosphere

- decreased rainfall
- tree-burning releases CO_2, contributing to global warming
- reduced production of oxygen

B   Impact on water cycle

- less precipitation intercepted and transpired
- increased surface run-off
- increased flood risk from rivers

C   Impact on soils

- increased soil erosion through surface run-off and gulleying
- increased leaching causing loss of soil nutrients
- disruption of nutrient cycle
- reduced soil fertility

D   Impact on plants and animals

- reduced biodiversity
- threatened extinction of species
- forest replaced by anything from bare ground to species-poor forest

Human impacts

E   Local people

- indigenous people displaced from their lands
- loss of traditional way of life
- lack of fuelwood

F   All people in the world

- genetic pool of plants reduced
- loss of climatic stability

FIGURE 9.24   Summary of the consequences of the clearance of natural vegetation

You can find more details about some of them in other places in this book.

- Impact on the atmosphere, including climate change—see Chapter 7.
- Impact on the water cycle—see Chapter 4.
- Impact on soils, including soil erosion and desertification—see Chapter 3.
- Impact on plants and animals, including reduced biodiversity and genetic depletion—earlier and later in this chapter.

ACTIVITIES

1   Exam watch: Impacts of deforestation which are listed in the syllabus:

habitat loss; soil erosion; desertification; climate change; loss of biodiversity; genetic depletion.

(a)   State briefly what each one means.

(b)   Explain briefly how deforestation causes it.

Case study: The causes and impacts of deforestation in Indonesia

FIGURE 9.25 Indonesia

Indonesia is a country of islands—over 3000 of them including Java, Borneo, and Sumatra (Figure 9.25). All lie on or close to the Equator, which means that everywhere one experiences a hot and wet equatorial climate. Tropical rainforest is the natural vegetation cover in lowland areas throughout, which is why it is sometimes called the 'Amazon of South-east Asia'. Rates of deforestation are increasing and tropical rainforest destruction is a major issue in Indonesia.

There is some debate about who is most responsible. Some blame the government and its large-scale development projects. Others point the finger of blame at the greed of big logging companies. Some claim that population growth is the main cause; increasingly high population densities have led to an expansion of slash and burn farming to increase food supply. That is everyone's responsibility.

TABLE 9.4 Estimated amounts of deforestation in Indonesia

2000 – 2004	310,000 hectares of forest lost per year
2005 – 2009	690,000 hectares of forest lost per year
2010 – 2014	840,000 hectares of forest lost per year

TABLE 9.5 Indonesia–population data (2017)

Total population	260.5 m (4th largest in the world)
Birth rate	16.2 per 1000
Death rate	6.5 per 1000
Natural increase	9.7 per 1000 (or 0.97%)

Causes of deforestation

1 Political—the role of government

- The government's transmigration policy: the aim is to relieve overcrowding in big cities like Jakarta by clearing forests for settlements and farmland. Up to one million hectares of forest have already been destroyed.

- The military government in 1998 gave concessions to logging companies which are run by powerful people with a lot of political influence.

- Little attempt is made to stop illegal logging and enforce selective logging or replanting schemes.

2 Economic—the need to develop

- Indonesia is a major exporter of wood and wood products; its hardwoods are in big demand in the developed world and bring in a high revenue.

- Money is needed to pay off international debts and to develop economically.

- About 700,000 people work in logging in a country with high rates of unemployment, made worse by rapid population growth.

3 Social—the growing population

- More people need more food, work, and public services, putting more pressure on natural resources.

- Slash and burn farming is increasing the number of plots used in a non-sustainable way.

Impacts of deforestation

1 **On the biosphere**: there is reduced biodiversity and biomass, lower rates of net primary productivity, loss of animal habitats.

2 **On the indigenous people**: conflicts have arisen, for example, between the logging companies and Moi people, whose way of life is threatened with extinction. The government does not accept that people like the Moi have any land rights and their protests have got nowhere.

3 **On the environment**: increased soil erosion, silting of rivers, serious air pollution from forest fires (Figure 9.26). The forest fires were at their worst in the autumn of 1997; they were lit deliberately by loggers and farmers to clear land but then spread out of control due to the exceptionally dry weather. Come 2015, and not much had changed. Air pollution and poor visibility were still major issues in Indonesia and the surrounding countries every year during the forest fire season.

Forest fires in Indonesia in 1997

20 million Indonesians affected with throat and respiratory problems

5000 people a day heading for hospitals with breathing problems

**Visibility down to zero
45,000 evacuated from Rangat in Sumatra**

Indonesian brush fires spread smoke to Malaysia and Singapore

The thick smoky haze has gone from bad to worse

Industrial and automobile pollutants trapped below the smoke

Air pollution in cities reaches danger levels

FIGURE 9.26 Newspaper headlines from South-east Asia as long ago as 1997

ACTIVITIES

1 Draw a graph to show the data in Table 9.4.

2 Explain how the world learnt about deforestation in Indonesia in 1997.

3 Who or what is most to blame for deforestation in Indonesia—the government, population growth, loggers, or developed countries?

(a) Explain the part played by each of these four in causing deforestation.

(b) Choose the one that in your opinion is most to blame. Justify your choice.

Managing forests

The ways in which forests contribute to maintaining a healthy and balanced natural environment, of great value to humans, are summarized in Figure 9.27. They show us how great the need is for sustainable forest management.

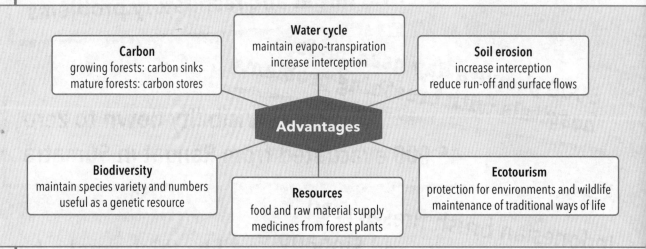

FIGURE 9.27 Why forests are of great value to people and the environment

Trees, as they grow, accumulate carbon. This is why they are referred to as **carbon sinks**. Young trees, growing quickly, accumulate carbon faster than mature trees. A mature forest acts as a **carbon store** for all the carbon it accumulated during growth. The more carbon that is stored, the less that is released into the atmosphere to contribute to the enhanced greenhouse effect, global warming, and climate change (Chapter 7).

Figure 9.28 shows how nutrient cycling works in a healthy forest. There is little leakage of either nutrients or rainwater from the cycle. There is a quick uptake of water and nutrients by the tree and plant roots to nourish the **water cycle** and limit **soil erosion**. High rates of evapo-transpiration into the atmosphere are maintained, resupplying the atmosphere with water for condensation and rainfall formation (Figure 4.3, page 105). Mineral losses from the soil by leaching (Figure 3.3, page 72) are much reduced, thereby maintaining soil fertility. Interception by forest trees and plants lowers the amount of surplus rainwater available for run-off, thereby preventing scenes like that one shown in Figure 3.27 (page 94).

Contrast this with what Figure 9.29 shows for an area cleared of forest. Without trees and the dense forest canopy, there is nothing to intercept the heavy tropical rain. One bad effect leads to another:

- more rainwater now reaches the ground surface;
- run-off increases;
- greater overland flow means rivers flood more frequently;
- more soil is carried away;
- more soil and sediment accumulate in river channels;
- both the size and frequency of river floods increase.

Could this happen next in the areas shown in Figure 9.21, and in Figure 7.4, page 201?

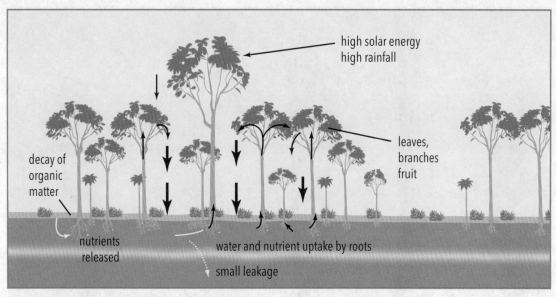

FIGURE 9.28 Nutrient cycle in tropical rainforest

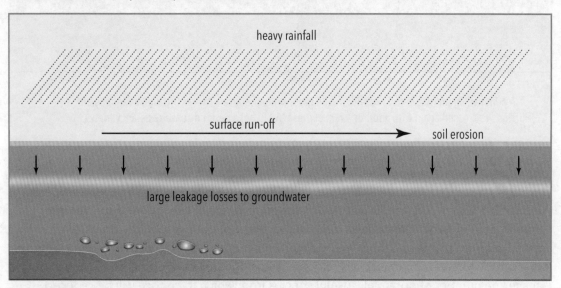

FIGURE 9.29 After rainforest deforestation: destruction of the nutrient cycle and its consequences

Biodiversity is an important **genetic resource**. Cultivation began when humans learned to plant the seeds from wild plants in a field. At first, crop yields were low; however, by learning to use seeds only from the larger and more successful crops, they improved over time. This was the beginning of **selective breeding**. Improvements in technology and in the knowledge of genetics have allowed the adoption of a more scientific approach to cross-breeding crops.

For example, one variety of maize produces a lot of grain but is not resistant to disease or drought. Another variety is resistant to disease and drought, but gives a low yield. It makes sense for scientists to try to create a hybrid variety by cross-pollination, which will give a high yield of grain and also be disease- and drought-resistant. In attempting to introduce in plants characteristics such as resistance to disease or drought, or the ability to grow in a shorter growing season, the geneticist goes back to wild varieties (Figure 9.30).

OXFORD
UNIVERSITY PRESS

A primitive strain **(I)** was crossed with a wild grass **(II)** to produce a hybrid **(III)** with a higher yield. This was crossed again with another strain of grass **(IV)** to get a better disease-resistant variety **(V)**.

FIGURE 9.30 How wheat with a much higher yield and disease resistance was bred

The Earth's genes, species, and ecosystems have evolved over 3000 million years and form the basis for human survival. However, with the current rate of extinction of species, the natural source of genetic material is diminishing. Many of our present-day drugs, like aspirin, are derived from plants and there may be many more sources yet to be discovered. At some future date, when new combinations of genes are sought for new food crops or cures for disease, the number of potentially useful species from which to choose will be reduced.

INFORMATION BOX

Plant species for food

- About 10,000 plant species have been used for food since the start of agriculture.
- Today about 150 plants make up the diets of a majority of people.
- Just four plants make up over 50% of what people eat.
- These four staple crops are rice, maize, wheat, and potatoes.

Forest resources provide both raw materials and food. For millions of people in developing countries, fuelwood remains their main source of energy for cooking and heating. Timber is widely used in the construction of buildings and for making furniture, while wood pulp is the raw material for making paper. Rubber is a tree crop of some value (Figure 9.31). Edible forest products include wild fruit, nuts, palm oil, and fungi.

Ecotourism

At its best, **ecotourism** is responsible tourism. This means that it protects the environment, respects local cultures, benefits local communities, conserves natural resources, and causes minimum pollution. Viewing birds and animals living in their natural environments is one of the big growth areas in world tourism.

FIGURE 9.31 Rubberwood tree in Malaysia. Each tree provides latex for 25–30 years. Then they can be felled and their wood sold. 80 per cent of furniture made in Malaysia comes from rubberwood.

ACTIVITIES

1 Show that you understand the difference between **(a)** carbon sinks and carbon stores, **(b)** interception and run-off, and **(c)** a food and a raw material.

2 Using Figures 9.28 and 9.29, describe how the nutrient cycle changes after rainforest deforestation.

3 **(a)** What is a hybrid?

   (b) How and why are hybrids created?

   (c) How good are the future prospects for developing new hybrids?

4 Investigate biodiversity in either Malaysia or Indonesia, or another country closer to your home area. Research the same type of information and statistics as those given for Ecuador in the Information Box (page 254).

Measuring and managing biodiversity

You can investigate and measure biodiversity in your home area—in a park, in the school grounds, in a wood, along a river bank, etc. You will want to discover

- the *variety* of different species (plants and organisms),
- the *distribution* (where each species is found),
- the *population* (total numbers of each species present).

Since it is impossible to study in detail all of the area chosen, you will need to take a **sample.** This is studying several smaller areas which are representative of the whole area.

The technique used for doing the work varies according to what is being studied. Some of the most commonly used techniques are shown and described in Figures 9.32 and 9.33.

A Catching small insects		
Pooter 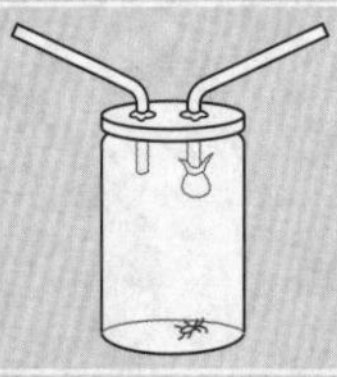		Small jar for collecting insects. It has two tubes. One is placed over the insect. The other is placed in your mouth, to suck the insect into the jar. Your tube has a fine mesh over the end to stop you swallowing the insect.
B Catching crawling insects and ground living creatures like beetles, spiders, and slugs		
Pitfall trap 		A container, such as a yoghurt carton, is buried in the ground, so that its top is level with the soil surface. It is covered with a piece of wood with a slight gap to allow insects to crawl in. The trap must be checked regularly to avoid insects escaping or feeding on one another.
C Identifying and counting plants		
Quadrat		This is a square frame. Inside, wires divide it up into smaller squares, such as 10 × 10 or 5 × 5 squares. The squares chosen for study mark off an exact area within which plants can be identified and counted.
D Identifying plants and changes in vegetation, or for small slow-moving organisms like slugs and snails		
Transect		This a straight line down a slope, or across a habitat. The line is marked by something simple such as a tape measure or rope. The types of plants and organisms can be observed and recorded at regular intervals along the transect.

FIGURE 9.32 Techniques for measuring biodiversity

The more sites that are studied, the more accurate, useful, and representative your results are likely to be. Both quadrats and transect involve choice—which square or squares to use for study (quadrat), at which points along the line should observations be taken (transect). The aim, as far as possible, is to remove human bias from the choice of study site.

In theory, **random sampling** is best. For example, number the quadrat squares from 0–9 in both directions. Then use random numbers to determine which squares are used in the study (Figure 9.33A). You can see that this unbiased approach has not led to an even coverage. There are clusters and gaps in what is learned.

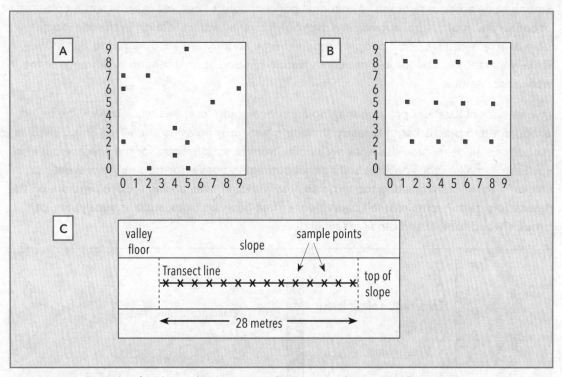

FIGURE 9.33   Examples of random and systematic sampling, using quadrats (A, B) and transect (C)

In practice, **systematic sampling** is used more (Figure 9.33B). Squares for study within the quadrat are selected at regular intervals. Likewise along a transect, sample points are placed at regular intervals along the line (Figure 9.33C). Divide the length of the line by the number of study points; this will give you the regular interval to use. In Figure 9.33C, 28 metres divided by 14 sites gives an interval of 2 metres.

ACTIVITIES

1 **(a)** Draw labelled sketches to show **(i)** a pitfall trap and **(ii)** a quadrat.

   (b) Describe when and where each one is used in biological investigations of biodiversity.

2 **(a)** State one advantage and one disadvantage of **(i)** random sampling and **(ii)** systematic sampling.

   (b) Why is sampling used in most investigations of biodiversity?

OXFORD
UNIVERSITY PRESS

Management strategies for conservation in tropical rainforest

The results of a study by a conservation group working in the African rainforests is shown in Figure 9.34. Short-term economic gains are dwarfed by the sustainable long-term value of benefits from forest products, tourism, and the absence of environmental damage.

Research, education, and training are needed to make local people and administrators aware of how forests work and why they are important. Much needs to be done to change public opinion so that more people appreciate the uses and potential of these forests. Setting aside areas of rainforest as national parks or nature reserves is an important method of conservation of natural ecosystems. Not only can they attract foreign exchange income from overseas visitors, but if people from the home country are encouraged to visit as well, it is likely that they will become more conservation-minded after first-hand experience of the wonders of nature.

Involvement of local people in managing and developing forests is crucial. Many are being encouraged to practise **agro-forestry**. Including fast-growing agricultural tree crops, such as rubber and oil palm, provides not only income from forest products for many years, but also shelter for smaller crops and the soil against damaging heavy downpours. To prevent cultivation plots from creating too large an area without cover, and to reduce pressure on the natural forests that remain, small plantations of fast-growing trees, such as eucalyptus, can provide wood for fuel and other essential uses.

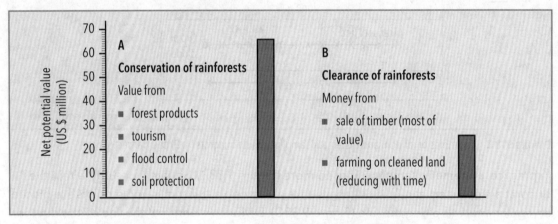

FIGURE **9.34**   Estimated net potential value from two African rainforest national parks

Any commercial logging needs to be carefully controlled. **Selective logging** of mature hardwood trees is more expensive than total logging. This is why checks on logging companies need to be frequent and ruthless. Left to itself, big business always takes the cheap option. Where large gaps in the forest already exist due to over-logging, the only management option

INFORMATION BOX

Good logging practices
- Draw up a logging plan in advance.
- Take into account the number and maturity of trees.
- Issue specific licenses for numbers and locations.
- Check cutting and harvesting of timber.
- Ensure a long gap between cuttings.

may be **reforestation** using plantation types of trees, such as acacia and eucalyptus. Although providing surface cover and income from the wood, these artificial replacement forests are nothing like the fine originals.

ACTIVITIES

1 **(a)** Describe what the graphs in Figure 9.34 show.

   (b) Explain what needs to be done to make sure that cash benefits from forest conservation are achieved.

2 Write a short paragraph for each of the following as methods for preservation of forests:

   (a) reforestation   **(b)** agro-forestry   **(c)** selective logging

   (d) forest trading without forest clearance.

3 Design a poster to promote the public's knowledge and understanding of the value of tropical rainforests.

4 Undertake an investigation of forest conservation methods in your country or region.

Sustainable harvesting of wild plant and animal species

Ever since humans have been on the Earth, people have gathered plant and animal resources for their own needs. Hundreds of millions of people in developing countries still rely upon them for a significant part of their subsistence needs. Pressure on wild plants and animals has reached non-sustainable levels due to population increases at home, and the continued growth in commercial activity for export. International trading of up to 10,000 different medicinal and aromatic wild plants has become big business.

INFORMATION BOX

Examples of what humans have collected

Food:

- Fruits, nuts, herbs, spices, gum, game (bush meat)

Raw materials

- Fibre, bark and wood for shelter, clothing, or utensils

Medical, cosmetic, or cultural

- Up to 50,000 plants are used in Chinese medicine (e.g. ginseng)

The increased realization that many varieties of wild plants and animals were being over-exploited led to activity at the international level and among conservation groups. As early as 1992 at the Earth Summit in Rio de Janeiro, 168 countries signed up to the Convention on Biological Diversity (CBD). Its main aim is preservation of world biodiversity. A new global strategy plan was agreed in 2002 specifically to address the conservation challenges for medicinal and aromatic plants. The IUCN (International Union for Conservation of Nature) has set up a group to identify species threatened by non-sustainable harvesting. CITES (Convention on International Trade in Endangered Species of Wild Fauna and Flora) tries to ensure that the international trade in wild animals and plants does not threaten their survival.

FIGURE **9.35** White rhinos, poached only for their horns, are greatly endangered. Traditionally used in Chinese medicine, the main demand for rhino horn is now in Vietnam as a status symbol of wealth.

One strategy of IUCN is to improve collection techniques. In Karnataka, India, by using a new way of collecting the resin from the White Palle tree (used in traditional medicines and incense), the bark no longer needs to be removed. The old method of collection was killing the trees. Another strategy is to encourage more cultivation of plants, especially in home gardens, or as inter-cropping in fields, to relieve pressure on the wild plants. The problem here, however, is that many customers complain that the cultivated plants are inferior (in taste and smell) to those gathered in the wild.

Environmental groups are putting more and more pressure on the large cosmetic and drug companies, based in the developed world, to take only sustainably harvested products from tropical forests, located in the developing world. They are being strongly encouraged to work with local communities, whose very survival depends on sustainable forest activities. This is a way of improving the livelihoods of the people who have the knowledge of the forest and its products. A women's cooperative in Amazonas State in Brazil is an example.

INFORMATION BOX

Extractive reserves

Definition: an area of land, generally state owned, where access and rights of use pass to local communities, including natural resource extraction

Example: Chico Mendez Reserve

- about 1m hectares in size
- set up in 1990
- main activity is rubber tapping.

Extractive reserves are a Brazilian idea. The main idea is that local communities own and control the harvesting of all forest products within the reserve. The Brazilian government was pushed into creating these after environmental and workers' groups joined forces following the murder of Chico Mendez in the late 1980s. He was a rubber tapper and community organizer, who battled to defend the rubber tappers against cattle ranchers invading and clearing the Amazon rainforest, destroying the rubber trees, and the livelihoods of people who had always lived there.

The idea is that they will limit deforestation by

- using local people to stop deforestation attempts within their reserve,

- acting as a buffer zone to keep ranching and extractive industries out of the natural forests beyond.

Whether or not they are a success is questionable. The interested parties in Amazon forest clearance in Brazil are rich and powerful. Local communities in the reserves are poor. To increase living standards, communities need other activities. The young are less enthusiastic than their parents about spending the rest of their lives making daily rounds through the forest to tap rubber trees or collect Brazil nuts. The collectors have no control over world market prices for rubber. There is more and more pressure on them to improve their incomes by forest clearance for crops and cattle farming beyond the amount allowed.

Even so, forest losses in the extractive reserves are probably lower and slower than they would have been if they had not been created.

ACTIVITIES

1 (a) Explain why an international approach to world conservation of plant and animal species is needed.

(b) Name an example of an international organization for conservation, and describe the work that is does.

2 (a) Why has harvesting of wild plants and animals always been an important human activity?

(b) Why was it not too great a problem in earlier times?

(c) State two main reasons why it has become a big issue today.

3 Give more information for these statements about extractive reserves.

(a) Extractive reserves are an example of a national strategy for conserving biodiversity.

(b) Extractive reserves depend upon local people for forest conservation.

(c) Local people living in extractive reserves are too poor to do this.

OXFORD
UNIVERSITY PRESS

National parks, wildlife reserves, and corridors

The strategy most widely used by governments for the conservation of areas is to pass laws to designate certain areas of natural protection. Many wildlife reserves cover quite small areas, often where a valuable ecosystem is surrounded by settled areas from which it is increasingly at risk. These are often equivalent to the core areas identified in biosphere reserves, where the demand for strong protection is undeniable. Management and maintenance of the reserve, supported by scientific research into matters related to conservation, are usually essential requirements for success.

In most countries interest in wildlife conservation is quite recent. Previously, whether or not areas of great biodiversity survived was a matter of chance. Many did so due to lack of economic value or because they were protected for other reasons, such as for hunting grounds or as religious and historical sites. In China, wildlife reserves were not set up until after 1980; then government policy changed and over 600 new ones have been designated since that date. The best known of these are the dozen or more reserves devoted to the conservation and protection of the giant panda. The Indian equivalent is tiger reserves.

National parks are similarly protected areas, but usually on a larger scale and can cover hundreds of square kilometres. They encompass two elements—wildlife conservation and access for visitors.

Once a national park is designated, damaging activities such as hunting, poaching, gathering, and logging should cease. However, there needs to be the threat of harsh penalties and regular patrols for these not to continue. As for coping with visitors, provision of services, such as access roads and tracks, look-out points with parking, picnic sites, and accommodation, should be planned for minimum disturbance to natural and living environments. Tourists must be issued with a code of conduct.

Without the protection afforded early on by national park status, the unique wildlife in the Galapagos Islands, 1000 km into the Pacific Ocean off the coast of Ecuador, would have already vanished. Certain bird species such as the Darwin finches and flightless cormorant are unique to these islands, as also are several species of giant tortoise, the islands' best known inhabitants. Previously, sailors passing the islands carried away giant tortoises for a future food supply. Rats escaped from their ships and on some islands they wiped out the unique ground-living species which had evolved here due to the absence of land predators.

The management strategies necessary will vary with the ecosystem. The following measures are used for coral reefs:

- training programmes for boat owners;

- boats licensed so that numbers can be controlled;

- restricted access to certain parts of the reef;

- floating buoys for mooring boats in the most popular diving sites.

OXFORD
UNIVERSITY PRESS

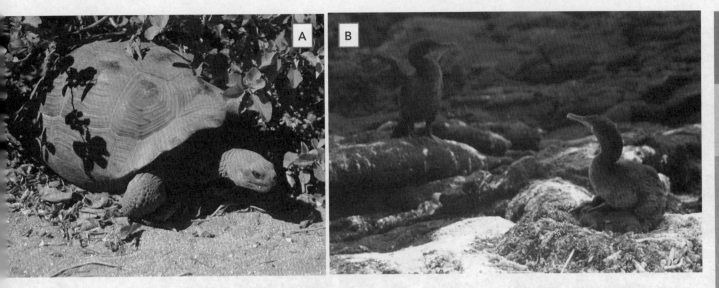

FIGURE 9.36 Galapagos Islands—giant tortoise (A) and flightless cormorant (B)

National parks and wildlife reserves are quite recent arrivals. Since population pressure on the natural ecosystems was the main reason for creating them, only a few are big enough to protect wide areas of land. More typically, natural habitats keep being interrupted by farmland, settlements, and roads. This leaves wildlife populations isolated from one another, in fragmented patches of habitat. In turn, this is not good for the maintenance of an area's biodiversity. A healthy exchange of individuals among animal populations is needed to avoid the negative effects of in-breeding. Reduced genetic biodiversity often occurs in isolated plant communities.

The creation of **wildlife corridors** is an attempt to overcome these problems. They are also called conservation corridors. These are areas of protected natural habitat, typically long relative to their width, as the title corridor suggests. They are created to make it easier for individuals to move between habitats for dispersion, or to follow seasonal migration routes. Examples include:

- 88 elephant corridors in India;

- tiger corridor between China and Russia;

- overpass over a highway for deer in Alberta, Canada;

- wolf corridor through a golf course in Jasper, Canada.

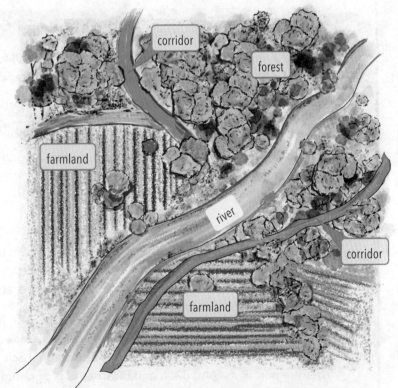

FIGURE 9.37 Woodland corridor by a river valley

OXFORD
UNIVERSITY PRESS

FIGURE 9.38 Wildlife corridors: overpasses over busy highways

Although their main aim is to maintain and increase biodiversity, they can also be used to repopulate areas badly affected by natural disasters, such as wildfires or disease. Success of these corridors is difficult to assess. Many tend to be species specific. Some are costly to construct. However, some do work well; but whether any animal in the wild is going to behave in the way that people plan for them to do is another matter.

> ## ACTIVITIES
>
> 1 With the help of examples, explain how **(a)** wildlife reserves, **(b)** national parks, and **(c)** wildlife corridors conserve natural habitats and species diversity.
>
> 2 Investigation of wildlife reserves and national parks in your country or region:
>
>   **(a)**   Draw a map to show locations and names.
>
>   **(b)**   Describe the environments and habitats under protection.

World biosphere reserves

Their origin goes back to 1968 and they are an attempt to meet one of the most challenging issues facing the world today, namely 'How can we conserve the diversity of the living biosphere and maintain healthy natural systems while, at the same time, meeting the needs and aspirations of an increasing number of people?'

Biosphere reserves are internationally recognized areas of land and coastal ecosystems supported by UNESCO (United Nations Educational Scientific and Cultural Organization). They are part of its MAB (Man and Biosphere) programme for 'people living in and caring for the biosphere'. By 2017, 686 biosphere reserves had been set up in 122 countries.

Although set up and run by national governments, they are internationally recognized, which often makes it easier for governments to attract funding, outside expertise, and support to sustain the reserve against forces for development within the country. A scientific approach to conservation is adopted, but biosphere reserves are more than just protected areas. They recognize that the conservation objective is likely to be achieved more successfully with the cooperation of local people, using their expertise of living in the environment and taking into account their needs and hopes. To this end reserves are organized into three interrelated zones known as the core area, buffer zone, and transition area (Figure 9.39).

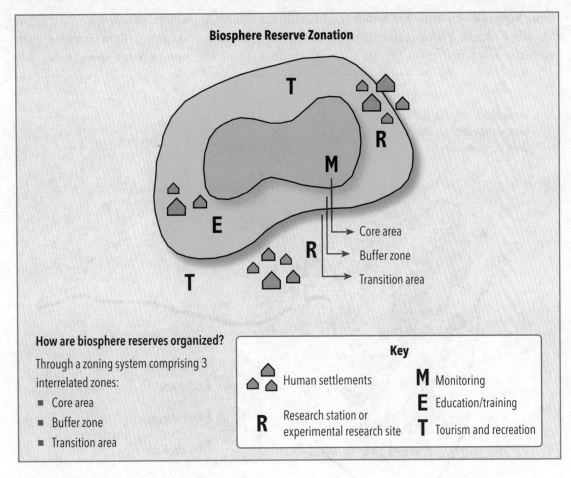

Biosphere Reserve Zonation

→ Core area
→ Buffer zone
→ Transition area

How are biosphere reserves organized?

Through a zoning system comprising 3 interrelated zones:

- Core area
- Buffer zone
- Transition area

Key

△ Human settlements

R Research station or experimental research site

M Monitoring
E Education/training
T Tourism and recreation

FIGURE 9.39 Biosphere reserve zonation

The core area contains the landscapes, ecosystems, and species that need conservation. There may be more than one core area in a reserve if there are different ecological systems to protect. Normally it is not subject to human activity except for research and monitoring. Only the core needs legal protection. Activities in the buffer zone must not hinder the conservation of the core. Favoured activities in this zone include experimental research about increasing output while preserving biodiversity and soil resources; the emphasis is upon how natural resources can be used in a sustainable manner. Education, training, tourism, and recreation facilities may be located here. The transition area can be described as an area of cooperation. It is here that local communities, conservation agencies, cultural groups, and other interested parties must agree to work together to manage and sustainably develop the area's resources for the benefit of the people who live there.

Case study of a named biosphere reserve: Guadeloupe Archipelago in the Caribbean

This biosphere reserve has two protected core areas (Figure 9.40).

1 Wet tropical forest, located in the west of Basse-Terre Island: uninhabited, the forest is home to 300 species of trees and bushes

2 The Grand Cul-de-Sac Marine Nature Reserve, located in the north.

Here, there is a rich variety of habitats, including coral reefs, mud-flats, swamps, and mangrove forests. Fish are abundant in the lagoon; there are also turtles, giant sponges, and sea urchins. The mangrove forests are rich in bird life (pelicans, herons, kingfishers).

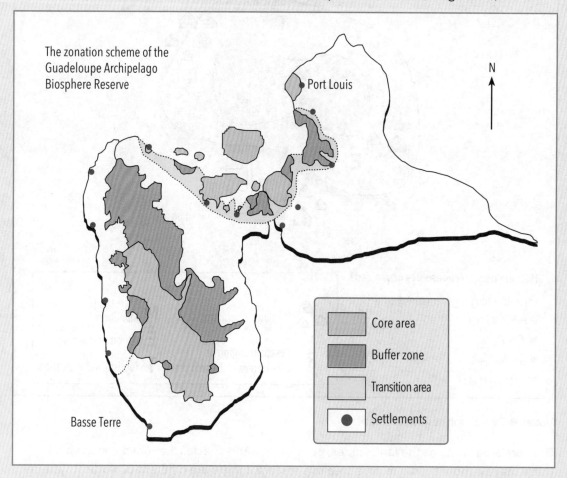

FIGURE 9.40 Zones within the Guadeloupe Archipelago Biosphere Reserve

The transition zones include numerous small towns and villages and many tourist facilities. Up to a quarter of a million people live permanently within the reserve, and there are about 25,000 visitors a year.

The main threats to the biosphere reserve are hurricanes (natural hazard), deforestation and water pollution (human factors), and boats dropping anchor on coral reefs (damage from tourism).

Summary: Who benefits from biosphere reserves?

1 Local communities

- more protection of natural resources
- better opportunities to maintain lifestyles
- less chance of outside developers encroaching on resources
- benefits from training and demonstration projects

2 Scientists

- encourage research on ecological processes and biodiversity
- provide a growing database for further experiments
- provide long-term sites for study
- more likely to attract international research funding

3 Governments

- provide them with better information on natural resources
- working example of sustainable resource use
- help them meet international obligations for conservation

4 The world community

- demonstrate practical ways to resolve land use conflicts
- show that protection and development can exist together
- raise people's awareness of sustainable development

ACTIVITIES

1 Write an account of biosphere reserves using the following headings:

   (a) purpose (b) number and location   (c) layout

   (d) benefits to local people (e) sustainable development.

2 (a) Explain why the Guadeloupe Archipelago Biosphere Reserve has two core areas.

   (b) Describe and explain the layout of this reserve.

3 Research investigation: name, locate, and give information about the biosphere reserve nearest to where you live.

Conservation of species: seed banks, zoos, and captive breeding

Sustainable harvesting of wild plants and animal species is possible, as a few groups of indigenous peoples, living in remote locations, continue to prove. However, population pressure and growth in technology mean that more ecosystems than ever are now at risk. One idea is to set up **seed banks** to preserve as wide a range of existing plants as is possible,

FIGURE 9.41 Indus River dolphin—only about 1100 remain

to guard against continued losses in the Earth's gene pool. The need could not be more urgent, with some 25,000 plant species under threat of extinction, on top of a 10 per cent loss already in the genes available for crop improvement.

By having seed banks, future scientists will have access to genes from which to develop new seeds: to increase yield, improve nutritional quality, and develop seeds with more tolerance of drought or resistance to disease. It is doing something now, before further genetic losses occur as currently endangered plant species become extinct. It is a way to preserve seeds, widely used in the past, but little used today. Most seed banks are publicly funded and available for use by research scientists.

The world's largest seed bank is in Sussex, south of London. The Millennium Seed Bank has the space to store billions of seeds, underground, in nuclear bomb-proof, multi-storey stores. The ultimate aim is to store every plant species known. The 10 per cent target was reached in 2009, the 2020 target is 25 per cent. From here seeds are sent to research centres all around the world.

Animal species conservation can be difficult. Species becoming extinct is a natural process; it is part of evolution. At one time dinosaurs ruled the world, but they suffered mass extinction about 65 million years ago. The worry today is the alarming increase in the rate of extinction as a result of human actions. Current species losses are frightening (Information Box). Destruction of wild habitats, hunting, and pollution are to blame. For the future, there are worries about the effects of climate change.

INFORMATION BOX

Report, October 2016
- Wild animal populations: down by 58% between 1970 and 2012
- African elephant numbers: down to 110,000 in 10 years
- Animals living in river and lake habitats: down by 81 per cent since 1970

The dodo in Mauritius, for example, is now an extinct species. But if zoos had existed at that time, would some have remained today? Some species have shrunk to such dangerously low numbers of individuals that they are classified as endangered. In 2016 there were just 880 mountain gorillas remaining in the wild, and only 1864 giant pandas. Although there is more than one reason for loss of species, the most important is obviously habitat loss.

Clearly there is a role for **zoos** and **captive breeding programmes** for species conservation. Fortunately, good zoos do more than simply display animals as visitor attractions. They have breeding programmes in place to maintain and increase the numbers of animals in danger of extinction in the wild. Zoos in Europe cooperate with each other and swap animals for breeding based on information kept on a computer data base. This is to prevent in-breeding and achieve as great a genetic variation as possible between the captive animal communities. They also play a vital role in educating public visitors about endangered species. Some species like the Arabian oryx and Californian condor would not exist today if it were not for zoos.

Captive breeding programmes aim to boost existing population numbers in the wild or to achieve a population size large enough for the species to be reintroduced into the wild. This has been less successful with animals bred in captivity than with those captured in the wild and later released. For example, cubs of big cats such as lions and cheetahs brought into captivity after their mother's death, and fed until they became adults, have been successfully released into the wild. Others, without the benefits of natural parental guidance, have struggled to feed themselves and lack awareness of potential predators.

FIGURE 9.42 African elephant eating on the move, as elephants do. A great hindrance to African farmers, or an economic asset in national parks, or a target for poachers and hunters? Natural savanna habitats like the one shown here are shrinking.

OXFORD
UNIVERSITY PRESS

Case study: Conservation of giant pandas

FIGURE 9.43 Giant panda

They look cuddly. They are an icon of conservation. Visitors flock to zoos to see a new panda arrival. Zoos with pandas attract more visitors than those without, which helps to fund their other conservation work.

Once they were widespread throughout the bamboo forests in south and east China. Due to population growth and economic development, more and more of the bamboo forests were cleared. For an animal whose diet is 99 per cent bamboo, and who needs to eat up to 38kg of bamboo a day, this spelt disaster. Total numbers dropped to a low of just over 1200 animals in the 1980s.

By 2015, there was a big difference. Adult numbers in the wild had climbed back up to over 1800, high enough for IUCN (International Union for the Conservation of Nature) to change the panda's status on its Red List from 'endangered' to 'vulnerable'. There are up to 1000 more in zoos in China and around the world.

Why the big change? It was mainly due to the change in attitude of the Chinese government, which recognized that there was international prestige to be gained from panda conservation. Bamboo forest clearances were stopped. More than 60 protected areas (wildlife reserves) for pandas have been set up in the wild. After panda habitats were restored, and they were given more space with increased food supply, their numbers increased.

There are active captive breeding programmes in zoos as well, although successful breeding has not been easy. Having the captive population is an insurance policy against climate change or a natural disaster badly affecting wild populations. Attempts to introduce pandas bred in captivity into the wild have not proved successful. So, although the aim of most captive breeding programmes is to let animals back into the wild eventually, in effect today there are two separate giant panda populations, one in the wild and another in zoos.

ACTIVITIES

1 (a) Give details and examples of decline in wild species over the last 50 years.

   (b) State the main reason for this decline, and explain why it is happening.

2 (a) What is a seed bank?

   (b) Why are seed banks needed?

   (c) Internet investigation: find out information about the Global Seed Bank in Svalbard.

3 (a) State (i) the advantages and (ii) the disadvantages of zoos and captive breeding programmes for animal species conservation.

   (b) Which is the stronger—advantages or disadvantages? Explain your view.

4 The only secure way to preserve the full range of genes for possible future use is to offer more protection for plants and animals in their natural environments.

   (a) Name the four types of protected areas referred to in this chapter.

   (b) Of the four, which one in your view is the most secure way to preserve genetic diversity? Justify your choice.

   (c) Do you agree with the statement at the start of the question? Explain your view.

5 (a) Name examples of endangered species of animals in your country or world region.

   (b) Describe the attempts being made to prevent extinction.

Ecotourism

This was named in Figure 9.27. It is described in the Information Box.

Many national parks charge entry fees, US$100 in the case of the Galapagos Islands. If this is used for management, instead of just being added to the pool of government income, there is a good chance of improved protection for natural environments and ecosystems. Ecotourism is being more widely promoted.

The tourist industry in Mauritius depends heavily upon its international image as an Indian Ocean paradise. The coral island, Ile aux Aigrettes, is now managed by the MWF (Mauritian Wildlife Foundation) as an ecotourism destination. A nursery financed by the World Bank grows 45,000 native plants a year for replanting, while MWF workers are trapping non-indigenous animals and uprooting foreign plants such as the acacia. All of this is part of an attempt to return the island as nearly as possible to its original state for visitors to enjoy. Elsewhere in Mauritius, laws which have existed for many years are being enforced with vigour for the first time, such as

- compulsory environmental impact surveys for planned developments,
- inclusion of waste treatment works in plans for all new resort hotels,
- bans on collection of corals and turtle shells.

Today, in Mauritius, it is recognized that tourist growth and the maintenance of environmental quality go together.

When holiday companies use the word 'ecotourism' to describe their tours, it is a powerful sales tool. However, care is needed. It may do no more than describe a tour, such as a safari holiday to Kenya to see the 'Big Five' (elephant, lion, leopard, buffalo, and rhino) in one of the country's many national parks. The safari lodge may be foreign-owned. The minibus drivers may be from the capital Nairobi. The wildlife viewing may be badly organized. Lions resting in the late afternoon heat can be surrounded by tourist vehicles (Figure 9.45).

Three quarters of Kenyan wildlife is found outside the game parks, much of it on land owned by Masai tribes. Their traditional way of life, planting crops and keeping cattle, does not fit well with encouraging wildlife. Some of the Masai have been able to benefit from ecotourism. Tented camps, owned and run by Kenyans, have been set up near Kimana on an important migration corridor for wildlife between Amboseli and Tsavo National Parks (named in Figure 9.44). The Masai are paid rent for use of their land.

INFORMATION BOX

Ecotourism

Tourism that is environmentally sound:

- natural environments and wildlife are safeguarded;
- natural resources are protected in a sustainable manner.

Tourism that is socially sound:

- local communities are not damaged;
- local people can share the benefits;
- ways of life and traditions are maintained.

Ecotourism should lead to sustainable tourism.

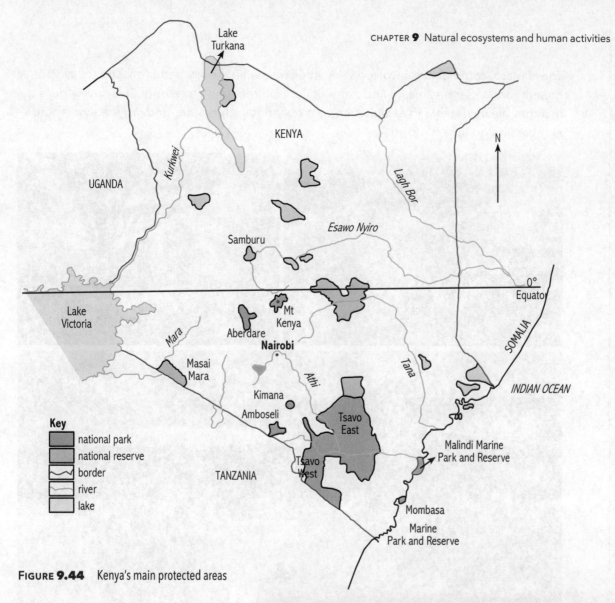

FIGURE 9.44 Kenya's main protected areas

The Kenya Tourist Board supports the growth of small-scale camps outside game reserves. Close to the entrance of the Masai Mara Park, over 150 Masai have joined their plots together. In return for not grazing their cows and chopping down wood, they rent their land out for a number of tented camps and eco-lodges. Each Masai landowner is paid a monthly rental. Some young Masai men make money as tourist guides. They are the ones with the keen eyesight and local knowledge to find the animals, thereby much enhancing the safari experience for visitors.

FIGURE 9.45 Lions in the Masai Mara. Is this ecotourism?

Those Masai communities involved in ecotourism are financially better off. The social benefits are better healthcare and more of the children going to school. The downside is that they are vulnerable to exploitation by crooked tour operators, and international tourist numbers do go up and down.

FIGURE **9.46**   Traditional way of life of the Masai; subsistence farming on the African savanna.

ACTIVITIES

1 (a) List the distinctive characteristics of ecotourism.

   (b) Make clear how it is different from ordinary mass tourism.

2 For one example of ecotourism:

   (a) gives its location and describe how it operates;

   (b) state its benefits (to the environment and people);

   (c) comment on whether or not it is sustainable.

CHAPTER 10

Techniques for investigation and examination

OBJECTIVES

In this chapter you will learn about

- investigation skills
- methods for local investigations
- examination technique
- command words

Investigation Skills

How do you begin tackling an environmental management study in your home area?

Undertaking and completing the work is a four-stage process.

Stage 1

Choosing an enquiry chapter

- Think of an **idea** for a local environmental management study.
- Do a bit of research and suggest a **title**.
- Talk it over with your teacher.
- Write down what you want to find out: these are the **aims** of your study.
- Think about the data you need to collect.
- What **methods** of data collection will you use?

Stage 2

Collecting data

- Assemble any **equipment** needed: quadrat, tape measure, marker poles etc.
- Compose and print off **questionnaires**.
- Think carefully about best **locations** for data collection.
- Decide on the best **people** for answering questionnaires.

Stage 3

Processing and presenting the data collected

- Use a **map** to show the study area's location.
- Make **tables** for any statistical data collected.
- Draw **graphs** (bar, line, and pie graphs) to show data.
- Where appropriate, illustrate your work with **photos** and **sketches**.

Stage 4

Writing about what you have discovered

- Describe what your tables and graphs show.
- Explain how they help you to meet the aims of your study.
- Write a conclusion for your study.
- Finally, attempt an evaluation of your data collection (methods and results).
- What were their strengths and weaknesses?

Methods for local investigations

Some of these, for local studies of biodiversity of plants and animals, were covered in Chapter 9. Pooters, pitfall traps, quadrats and transects were described and shown in Figure 9.32 (page 266). Examples of how to choose sites for study, whether by random or systematic sampling, were shown in Figure 9.33 (page 267).

Using **questionnaires** is another widely used method for collecting data. They are particularly useful for collecting people's opinions about local issues. The golden rule is the more questionnaires filled in, the more reliable the results. But even more important is questionnaire composition, both its lay out and the questions asked. The better the questionnaire, the greater the chance of gaining useful answers for your study aims.

Often it is worth spending time on a **pilot study** first. Do a draft questionnaire and try it out on five or six people to see if they understand the questions and how to fill in the questionnaire. You will be able to check whether the answers are likely to give the expected types of answers.

Look closely at Figure 10.1 to see what makes a good questionnaire, one that increases your chances of gaining information useful to the aims of your study.

Strengths of a good questionnaire	Weaknesses of a bad questionnaire
✓ Short introduction about you and the questionnaire	✗ No introduction; opening question which people will struggle to understand
✓ Not too many questions (perhaps 5-8)	✗ Too many questions (more than 10), many asking similar things
✓ Precise, closed questions with easy to record answers	✗ Too many questions with Yes / No as the only answers
✓ Questions which target the aims of the study	✗ Questions of no relevance to study aims, such as personal questions
✓ Well laid out; boxes or spaces for answers	✗ The question followed by an empty space or a long line left for answering

FIGURE 10.1 Good and bad questionnaires

Look at the two questionnaires in Figure 10.2. They were compiled by two college students who were investigating the likely impacts on local people of a company increasing the size of its limestone quarry. The company was seeking government permission to double the quarry size, despite local opposition.

FIGURE 10.2 Two questionnaires seeking people's views on quarry expansion

---

Questionnaire A

I am a student at _____ College. I am investigating the possible effects of the proposed quarry expansion. Please help by answering a few short questions.

1   Where do you live? _____

2   How far away from the quarry is it? Please tick one box.

under 500 metres	under 1 km	1 - 2km	more than 2km
☐	☐	☐	☐

3   How are you affected at the moment by the quarry? Please tick all the boxes which apply.

noise	dust and dirt	quarry traffic	eyesore / ugly
☐	☐	☐	☐
another problem ☐ Please name it _____			not affected ☐

4   What are the good things about the quarry at the moment? Please tick all boxes which apply.

provides work	helps the local economy	better roads	more services
☐	☐	☐	☐
another good thing ☐ Please name it _____			no good things ☐

5   On a scale of 1 - 5 (1 = only a little affected, 5 = very badly affected), how badly affected you are at the moment by the quarry? Please tick one box.

Not affected	1	2	3	4	5
☐	☐	☐	☐	☐	☐

6   Are you in favour of the government giving the quarry company permission to double the quarry size? Please tick one box.

Yes for bigger quarry	No to a bigger quarry	Undecided / don't know
☐	☐	☐

7 On a scale of 1 – 5 (1 = only a little affected, 5 = very badly affected), how badly do you think you will be affected in future if the quarry company gets permission to double the quarry size?

Not affected ☐	1 ☐	2 ☐	3 ☐	4 ☐	5 ☐

8 Please write down the main ways, good or bad, that you think you and your family will be affected if the quarry doubles in size.

_____

_____

Thank you for your help.

Questionnaire B

Quarry questionnaire

1 Are you male or female?   Male ☐   Female ☐

2 Where do you live? _____

3 Do you think the quarry is good for the area?   Yes ☐   No ☐

4 Are there any problems with the quarry? _____

5 Are there any good things about the quarry? _____

6 If the quarry increases in size, will you move?   Yes ☐   No ☐

7 Will it be good or bad if the quarry increases in size?   Good ☐   Bad ☐

8 How do you think the area will change if the quarry increases in size?

_____

9 Have you lived here for a long time? _____

10 Do any of your family work in the quarry? _____

11 Have they had any health problems? _____

Look at the two questionnaires in Figure 10.2. List all the reasons why Questionnaire A is most likely to obtain

- information for the study aims that is more useful,

- more data useful for presenting in tables and graphs,

- people's views so that meaningful conclusions about the likely impacts of quarry growth can be made.

OXFORD
UNIVERSITY PRESS

Examination technique

When Environmental Management examination questions are set, it is taken for granted that every student is able to identify and name the world's continents and oceans (Figure 10.3).

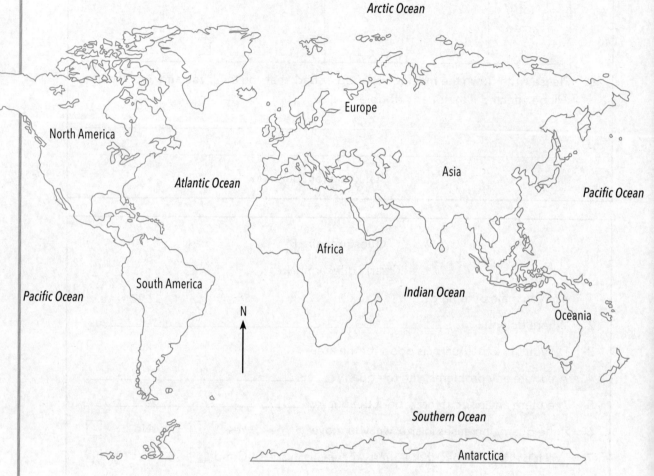

FIGURE **10.3** Continents and oceans

Every Environmental Management question consists of at least two parts.

1   **Command word or words** – what you are being asked to do.

More information about command words, for example the difference between 'Describe' and 'Explain', is given further on. This is because the command word is so important.

2   **Question theme** – what the question is all about.

Some questions also make the question theme narrower by limiting the scope of the question, and referring, for example, to just one ecosystem, or only one part of the world.

Equally important is the **number of marks** for each question, which is shown at the end of every examination question. This is the best guide to the amount of detail expected and needed for full marks.

Command words

A Simple and clear

Name   State   Give   List

All these require are short concise answers, with little or no supporting detail expected.

B Asking for definitions, usually of key terms

What is meant by ....?   Define ....   Give a definition of ......

The number of marks for the question is critical. It will guide you on how long or how detailed a definition is needed. Many of the terms asked for in these questions will be those named in the syllabus. These are the ones most likely to have been highlighted in bold in the text for Chapters 1 - 9.

C Describe

This is probably the most used command word. When a question starts with a figure, whether a map, graph, sketch, or photo, the most common first question will be:

'Describe what Figure xx shows.'

Describe instructs you to write about what is there, its appearance, or what it shows. Again, the number of marks for the question is critical for controlling how much detail you are expected to give.

For example, look at the photo in Figure 10.4. It was previously used in Figure 3.1 (page 71).

Question 'Describe what Figure 10.4 shows.'

Answers that should be given are controlled by the number of marks stated.

FIGURE 10.4   Cattle farming in Central America

If it is a 1 mark question then answer 'cattle farming', and that is enough (1/1). Full marks.

If it is a 4 mark question and you give the same answer, 'cattle farming', that is still one mark (1/4), and three marks are lost. You need to look more closely at the photo and describe more, at least three more things that can be seen—something about the grass cover, the size of the grazing area, tree cover around the edges, the cattle themselves. Better still, instead of three, look to make four points based on observation, in case one of the descriptive points you make is not included in the examiner's mark scheme. Play safe.

Note that there are no marks for 'explanation' when you are asked to 'describe'. Look at this answer to the 4 mark question based on Figure 10.4.

'It shows cattle farming. The forest has been cleared for cattle rearing because more land was wanted for farming and ranchers can make good profits exporting beef. The same has happened in Brazil. Rainforests and biodiversity are lost to cattle farming.'

Do you understand why this answer will only be given 1 mark (1/4)? As soon as the word 'because' was included, it showed that the candidate had stopped describing the photo and drifted into explanation.

D Asking for explanation

Explain why	Explain the causes of	Give reasons for
Why do…?	Why have…?	Why is it that …?

For these questions you need more than observational skills: you require knowledge and understanding. You are being asked to account for the appearance or occurrence of a natural or human feature. Again, the amount of explanation or the number of reasons that are needed, is determined by the number of marks given for the question.

Answering questions based on source materials

Source materials used in Environmental Management examinations include:

tables of data; maps; flow and spider diagrams; photographs and sketches; bar, line, and pie graphs; population pyramids; climate graphs (line graph for temperature, vertical bars for rainfall).

There is only a small chance that you will have studied any of these previously. The data will look unfamiliar. This is why the first part of a question about one of them will give you the chance to look at it and identify what it shows. That is why you are normally asked to describe what it shows in the first part of the question. Always try to home in first on the **general trend** or on what is **most important** about the information given. Then support your answer by quoting and using data, in a selective way. Do not just repeat everything that is shown in the figure.

For example, look at the line graph in Figure 10.5. It was previously used in Figure 8.2 (page 225).

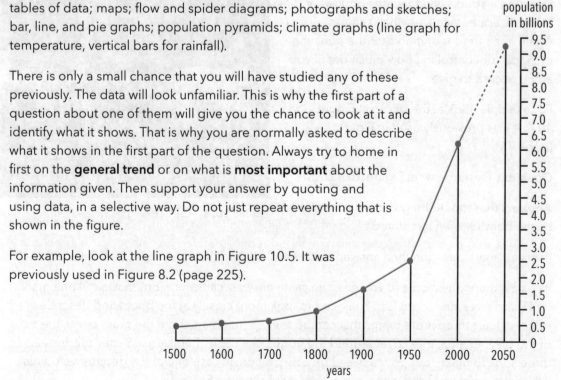

FIGURE 10.5

Question 'Describe what Figure 10.5 shows.'   (4 marks)

Guidance for answering this question:

First, look at the number of marks; 4 marks means at least four good points need to be made; play safe and look for five.

Secondly, identify and state the general trend—it shows great population growth.

Thirdly, identify and state variations or changes in this general trend—only slow increase until 1800, growth speeded up between 1800 and 1950, very fast (exponential) growth since 1950, predicted to continue growing fast up to 2050.

Lastly, quote and use data from the graph to support the general trend—you have choice for the data used; some points you could make are given below, but there are plenty of others.

- Population grew from 500,000 in 1500 to over 7.6 billion today.

- Population grew by 6.5 billion in 500 years.

- Total population increased by almost three times / tripled since 1950.

- In contrast, it took it 300 years (1500-1800) to double from half a million to one million.

Finally, before you finish, check that you have made enough different points for the number of marks.

Adopt a similar approach when describing other types of graph. For **climate graphs** and **population pyramids** it is possible to give more specific guidance about what to look for. Look at Figures 10.6 and 10.7.

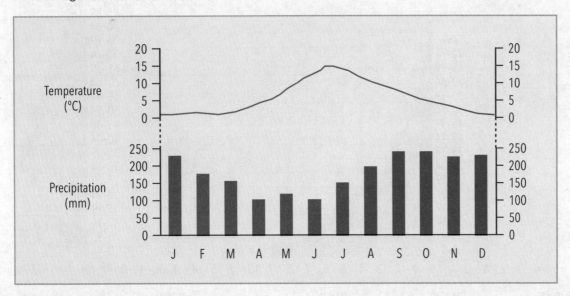

FIGURE 10.6   Climate in southern Norway

environmental management

How to interpret climate graphs and tables of climate data

Identifying the key features of temperature	Identifying the key features of precipitation (rainfall)
1 State the highest temperature and month.	1 State the highest precipitation and month.
2 State the lowest temperature and month.	2 State the lowest precipitation and month.
3 Work out the annual range of temperature (highest minus lowest).	3 Describe the distribution during the year: for example, precipitation all year, or wet and dry seasons.
	4 Calculate total annual rainfall and state whether it is high or low.

NB: Remember to quote units of measurement as well.

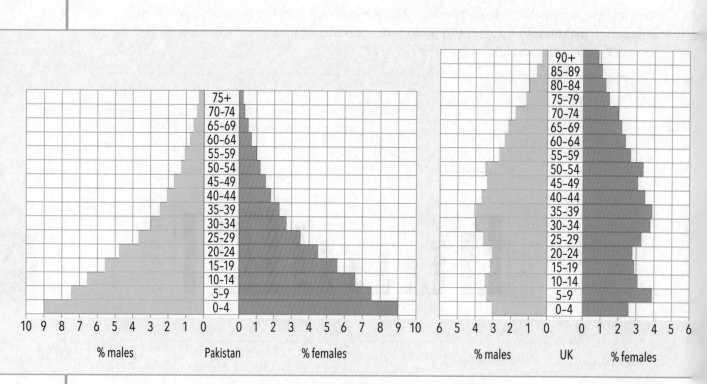

FIGURE **10.7**   Population pyramids of Pakistan and the UK

How to describe and interpret population pyramids

1 Look first at the base.

- If it is wide, there are many children, suggesting a high birth rate.
- If it is narrow, a low birth rate is suggested.

2 Look at the top.

- If it is high and wide, there are many old people, suggesting long life expectancy.
- If it is narrow and goes to a point, low life expectancy is suggested.

3 Look at the overall shape.

- If it is like a triangle, it is likely to be for a developing country.
- If it is more straight up and down, it is likely to be for a more developed country.

4 Separate out age group ranges by drawing lines across between the three groups below

- 0–14 young and part of the non-working population
- 15–64 middle-aged making up the working population
- 65+–old aged, no longer part of the working population

What are the relative percentages of the three groups?

OXFORD
UNIVERSITY PRESS

Index

OXFORD
UNIVERSITY PRESS

Book Piracy and **Plagiarism** are **Crimes.**

Buy Genuine Oxford Books

Look out for the new security label whenever you purchase an Oxford textbook or supplementary reader. Labels with the features shown below are proof of genuine Oxford books.

The image of Quaid's Mausoleum changes colour from orange to green when viewed from different angles. ❶

The labels have security cut marks to prevent them from being peeled off and reused. ❷

The word 'ORIGINAL' appears when the area under 'RUB HERE' is rubbed with a coin. ❸

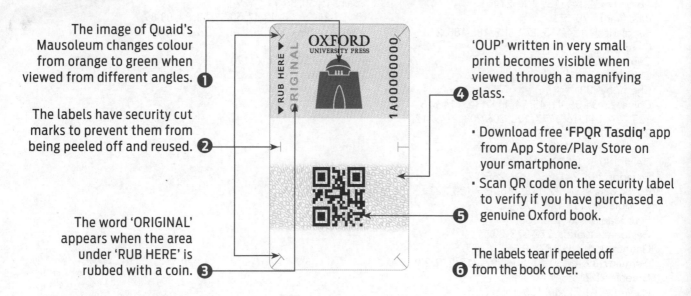

'OUP' written in very small print becomes visible when viewed through a magnifying ❹ glass.

· Download free **'FPQR Tasdiq'** app from App Store/Play Store on your smartphone.

· Scan QR code on the security label to verify if you have purchased a ❺ genuine Oxford book.

The labels tear if peeled off ❻ from the book cover.

Pirated books can be recognised by:
· inferior production quality
· low-grade paper
· variations in texture and colour
· poor print quality
· blurred text and images
· poor binding and trimming
· substandard appearance of the book

Do not accept the book if the label is missing, has been torn or tampered with, the colour on the security label does not change, or the word **'ORIGINAL'** does not appear upon rubbing the area with a coin.

If you suspect that you are being sold a pirated book without the security label, please contact:

Oxford University Press,
No. 38, Sector 15, Korangi Industrial Area, Karachi-74900, Pakistan.
Tel.: (92-21) 35071580-86 Fax: (92-21) 35055071-72
Toll-free No.: 0800-68775 (9 a.m. to 5 p.m.; Monday to Friday)
Email: central.marketing.pk@oup.com
Website: www.oup.com.pk Find us on: